Book 3: Equity

SchweserNotes™ 2019

Level II CFA®

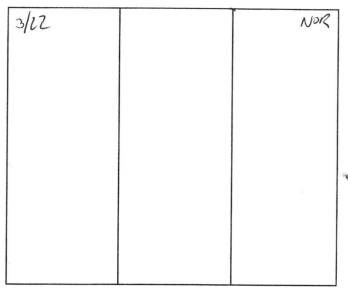

KAPLAN® SCHWESER

SCHWESERNOTES™ 2019 LEVEL II CFA® BOOK 3: EQUITY

Published in 2018 by Kaplan, Inc.

Printed in the United States of America.

978-1-4754-7971-3

CONTENTS

STUDY SESSION 11—EQUITY VALUATION (3)

LEARNING OUTCOME STATEMENTS (LOS)

STUDY SESSION 9

The topical coverage corresponds with the following CFA Institute assigned reading:
26. Equity Valuation: Applications and Processes
The candidate should be able to:
a. define valuation and intrinsic value and explain sources of perceived mispricing. (page 1)
b. explain the going concern assumption and contrast a going concern value to a liquidation value. (page 2)
c. describe definitions of value and justify which definition of value is most relevant to public company valuation. (page 2)
d. describe applications of equity valuation. (page 2)
e. describe questions that should be addressed in conducting an industry and competitive analysis. (page 4)
f. contrast absolute and relative valuation models and describe examples of each type of model. (page 5)
g. describe sum-of-the-parts valuation and conglomerate discounts. (page 6)
h. explain broad criteria for choosing an appropriate approach for valuing a given company. (page 7)

The topical coverage corresponds witfh the following CFA Institute assigned reading:
27. Return Concepts
The candidate should be able to:
a. distinguish among realized holding period return, expected holding period return, required return, return from convergence of price to intrinsic value, discount rate, and internal rate of return. (page 13)
b. calculate and interpret an equity risk premium using historical and forward-looking estimation approaches. (page 15)
c. estimate the required return on an equity investment using the capital asset pricing model, the Fama–French model, the Pastor–Stambaugh model, macroeconomic multifactor models, and the build-up method (e.g., bond yield plus risk premium). (page 19)
d. explain beta estimation for public companies, thinly traded public companies, and nonpublic companies. (page 23)
e. describe strengths and weaknesses of methods used to estimate the required return on an equity investment. (page 25)
f. explain international considerations in required return estimation. (page 25)
g. explain and calculate the weighted average cost of capital for a company. (page 26)
h. evaluate the appropriateness of using a particular rate of return as a discount rate, given a description of the cash flow to be discounted and other relevant facts. (page 27)

STUDY SESSION 10

The topical coverage corresponds with the following CFA Institute assigned reading:
28. Industry and Company Analysis
The candidate should be able to:

a. compare top-down, bottom-up, and hybrid approaches for developing inputs to equity valuation models. (page 35)

b. compare "growth relative to GDP growth" and "market growth and market share" approaches to forecasting revenue. (page 36)

c. evaluate whether economies of scale are present in an industry by analyzing operating margins and sales levels. (page 36)

d. forecast the following costs: cost of goods sold, selling general and administrative costs, financing costs, and income taxes. (page 37)

e. describe approaches to balance sheet modeling. (page 39)

f. describe the relationship between return on invested capital and competitive advantage. (page 40)

g. explain how competitive factors affect prices and costs. (page 40)

h. judge the competitive position of a company based on a Porter's Five Forces analysis. (page 40)

i. explain how to forecast industry and company sales and costs when they are subject to price inflation or deflation. (page 41)

j. evaluate the effects of technological developments on demand, selling prices, costs, and margins. (page 44)

k. explain considerations in the choice of an explicit forecast horizon. (page 45)

l. explain an analyst's choices in developing projections beyond the short-term forecast horizon. (page 45)

m. demonstrate the development of a sales-based pro forma company model. (page 46)

The topical coverage corresponds with the following CFA Institute assigned reading:
29. Discounted Dividend Valuation
The candidate should be able to:

a. compare dividends, free cash flow, and residual income as inputs to discounted cash flow models and identify investment situations for which each measure is suitable. (page 61)

b. calculate and interpret the value of a common stock using the dividend discount model (DDM) for single and multiple holding periods. (page 64)

c. calculate the value of a common stock using the Gordon growth model and explain the model's underlying assumptions. (page 67)

d. calculate and interpret the implied growth rate of dividends using the Gordon growth model and current stock price. (page 69)

e. calculate and interpret the present value of growth opportunities (PVGO) and the component of the leading price-to-earnings ratio (P/E) related to PVGO. (page 69)

f. calculate and interpret the justified leading and trailing P/Es using the Gordon growth model. (page 70)

g. calculate the value of noncallable fixed-rate perpetual preferred stock. (page 72)

h. describe strengths and limitations of the Gordon growth model and justify its selection to value a company's common shares. (page 73)

i. explain the assumptions and justify the selection of the two-stage DDM, the H-model, the three-stage DDM, or spreadsheet modeling to value a company's common shares. (page 74)

j. explain the growth phase, transition phase, and maturity phase of a business. (page 77)

k. describe terminal value and explain alternative approaches to determining the terminal value in a DDM. (page 78)

l. calculate and interpret the value of common shares using the two-stage DDM, the H-model, and the three-stage DDM. (page 79)

m. estimate a required return based on any DDM, including the Gordon growth model and the H-model. (page 84)

n. explain the use of spreadsheet modeling to forecast dividends and to value common shares. (page 86)

o. calculate and interpret the sustainable growth rate of a company and demonstrate the use of DuPont analysis to estimate a company's sustainable growth rate. (page 87)

p. evaluate whether a stock is overvalued, fairly valued, or undervalued by the market based on a DDM estimate of value. (page 89)

STUDY SESSION 11

The topical coverage corresponds with the following CFA Institute assigned reading:
30. Free Cash Flow Valuation
The candidate should be able to:

a. compare the free cash flow to the firm (FCFF) and free cash flow to equity (FCFE) approaches to valuation. (page 107)

b. explain the ownership perspective implicit in the FCFE approach. (page 109)

c. explain the appropriate adjustments to net income, earnings before interest and taxes (EBIT), earnings before interest, taxes, depreciation, and amortization (EBITDA), and cash flow from operations (CFO) to calculate FCFF and FCFE. (page 110)

d. calculate FCFF and FCFE. (page 118)

e. describe approaches for forecasting FCFF and FCFE. (page 122)

f. compare the FCFE model and dividend discount models. (page 122)

g. explain how dividends, share repurchases, share issues, and changes in leverage may affect future FCFF and FCFE. (page 123)

h. evaluate the use of net income and EBITDA as proxies for cash flow in valuation. (page 123)

i. explain the single-stage (stable-growth), two-stage, and three-stage FCFF and FCFE models and select and justify the appropriate model given a company's characteristics. (page 124)

j. estimate a company's value using the appropriate free cash flow model(s). (page 127)

k. explain the use of sensitivity analysis in FCFF and FCFE valuations. (page 133)

l. describe approaches for calculating the terminal value in a multistage valuation model. (page 134)
m. evaluate whether a stock is overvalued, fairly valued, or undervalued based on a free cash flow valuation model. (page 134)

The topical coverage corresponds with the following CFA Institute assigned reading:

31. Market-Based Valuation: Price and Enterprise Value Multiples

The candidate should be able to:

a. distinguish between the method of comparables and the method based on forecasted fundamentals as approaches to using price multiples in valuation, and explain economic rationales for each approach. (page 149)
b. calculate and interpret a justified price multiple. (page 151)
c. describe rationales for and possible drawbacks to using alternative price multiples and dividend yield in valuation. (page 151)
d. calculate and interpret alternative price multiples and dividend yield. (page 151)
e. calculate and interpret underlying earnings, explain methods of normalizing earnings per share (EPS), and calculate normalized EPS. (page 163)
f. explain and justify the use of earnings yield (E/P). (page 165)
g. describe fundamental factors that influence alternative price multiples and dividend yield. (page 165)
h. calculate and interpret the justified price-to-earnings ratio (P/E), price-to-book ratio (P/B), and price-to-sales ratio (P/S) for a stock, based on forecasted fundamentals. (page 165)
i. calculate and interpret a predicted P/E, given a cross-sectional regression on fundamentals, and explain limitations to the cross-sectional regression methodology. (page 169)
j. evaluate a stock by the method of comparables and explain the importance of fundamentals in using the method of comparables. (page 171)
k. calculate and interpret the P/E-to-growth ratio (PEG) and explain its use in relative valuation. (page 173)
l. calculate and explain the use of price multiples in determining terminal value in a multistage discounted cash flow (DCF) model. (page 174)
m. explain alternative definitions of cash flow used in price and enterprise value (EV) multiples and describe limitations of each definition. (page 175)
n. calculate and interpret EV multiples and evaluate the use of EV/EBITDA. (page 177)
o. explain sources of differences in cross-border valuation comparisons. (page 178)
p. describe momentum indicators and their use in valuation. (page 179)
q. explain the use of the arithmetic mean, the harmonic mean, the weighted harmonic mean, and the median to describe the central tendency of a group of multiples. (page 179)
r. evaluate whether a stock is overvalued, fairly valued, or undervalued based on comparisons of multiples. (page 171)

The topical coverage corresponds with the following CFA Institute assigned reading:

32. Residual Income Valuation

a. calculate and interpret residual income, economic value added, and market value added. (page 193)
b. describe the uses of residual income models. (page 196)

c. calculate the intrinsic value of a common stock using the residual income model and compare value recognition in residual income and other present value models. (page 196)

d. explain fundamental determinants of residual income. (page 199)

e. explain the relation between residual income valuation and the justified price-to-book ratio based on forecasted fundamentals. (page 200)

f. calculate and interpret the intrinsic value of a common stock using single-stage (constant-growth) and multistage residual income models. (page 201)

g. calculate the implied growth rate in residual income, given the market price-to-book ratio and an estimate of the required rate of return on equity. (page 202)

h. explain continuing residual income and justify an estimate of continuing residual income at the forecast horizon, given company and industry prospects. (page 203)

i. compare residual income models to dividend discount and free cash flow models. (page 209)

j. explain strengths and weaknesses of residual income models and justify the selection of a residual income model to value a company's common stock. (page 209)

k. describe accounting issues in applying residual income models. (page 210)

l. evaluate whether a stock is overvalued, fairly valued, or undervalued based on a residual income model. (page 212)

The topical coverage corresponds with the following cFa Institute assigned reading:

33. Private Company Valuation

The candidate should be able to:

a. compare public and private company valuation. (page 223)

b. describe uses of private business valuation and explain applications of greatest concern to financial analysts. (page 225)

c. explain various definitions of value and demonstrate how different definitions can lead to different estimates of value. (page 226)

d. explain the income, market, and asset-based approaches to private company valuation and factors relevant to the selection of each approach. (page 228)

e. explain cash flow estimation issues related to private companies and adjustments required to estimate normalized earnings. (page 229)

f. calculate the value of a private company using free cash flow, capitalized cash flow, and/or excess earnings methods. (page 234)

g. explain factors that require adjustment when estimating the discount rate for private companies. (page 237)

h. compare models used to estimate the required rate of return to private company equity (for example, the CAPM, the expanded CAPM, and the build-up approach). (page 238)

i. calculate the value of a private company based on market approach methods and describe advantages and disadvantages of each method. (page 243)

j. describe the asset-based approach to private company valuation. (page 247)

k. explain and evaluate the effects on private company valuations of discounts and premiums based on control and marketability. (page 248)

l. describe the role of valuation standards in valuing private companies. (page 252)

READING 26

Equity Valuation: Applications and Processes

EXAM FOCUS

This review is simply an introduction to the process of equity valuation and its application. Many of the concepts and techniques introduced are developed more fully in subsequent topic reviews. Candidates should be familiar with the concepts introduced here, including intrinsic value, analyst perception of mispricing, going concern versus liquidation value, and the difference between absolute and relative valuation techniques.

MODULE 26.1: EQUITY VALUATION: APPLICATIONS AND PROCESSES

Video covering this content is available online.

LOS 26.a: Define valuation and intrinsic value and explain sources of perceived mispricing.

CFA® Program Curriculum: Volume 4, page 6

Valuation is the process of determining the value of an asset. There are many approaches and estimating the inputs for a valuation model can be quite challenging. Investment success, however, can depend crucially on the analyst's ability to determine the values of securities.

When we use the term **intrinsic value** (IV), we are referring to the valuation of an asset or security by someone who has complete understanding of the characteristics of the asset or issuing firm. To the extent that stock prices are not perfectly (informationally) efficient, they may diverge from the intrinsic values.

Analysts seeking to produce positive risk-adjusted returns do so by trying to identify securities for which their estimate of intrinsic value differs from current market price. One framework divides mispricing perceived by the analyst into two sources: the difference between market price and the intrinsic value (actual mispricing) and the difference between the analyst's estimate of intrinsic value and actual intrinsic value (valuation error). We can represent this relation as follows:

$$IV_{analyst} - price = (IV_{actual} - price) + (IV_{analyst} - IV_{actual})$$

LOS 26.b: Explain the going concern assumption and contrast a going concern value to a liquidation value.

CFA® Program Curriculum: Volume 4, page 8

The **going concern assumption** is simply the assumption that a company will continue to operate as a business, as opposed to going out of business. The valuation models we will cover are all based on the going concern assumption. An alternative, when it cannot be assumed that the company will continue to operate (survive) as a business, is a firm's **liquidation value**. The liquidation value is the estimate of what the assets of the firm would bring if sold separately, net of the company's liabilities.

LOS 26.c: Describe definitions of value and justify which definition of value is most relevant to public company valuation.

CFA® Program Curriculum: Volume 4, page 8

As stated earlier, intrinsic value is the most relevant metric for an analyst valuing public equities. However, other definitions of value may be relevant in other contexts. **Fair market value** is the price at which a hypothetical willing, informed, and able seller would trade an asset to a willing, informed, and able buyer. This definition is similar to the concept of fair value used for financial reporting purposes. A company's market price should reflect its fair market value over time if the market has confidence that the company's management is acting in the interest of equity investors.

Investment value is the value of a stock to a particular buyer. Investment value may depend on the buyer's specific needs and expectations, as well as perceived synergies with existing buyer assets.

When valuing a company, an analyst should be aware of the purpose of valuation. For most investment decisions, intrinsic value is the relevant concept of value. For acquisitions, investment value may be more appropriate.

LOS 26.d: Describe applications of equity valuation.

CFA® Program Curriculum: Volume 4, page 9

PROFESSOR'S NOTE

This is simply a list of the possible scenarios that may form the basis of an equity valuation question. No matter what the scenario is, the tools you will use are the same.

Valuation is the process of estimating the value of an asset by (1) using a model based on the variables the analyst believes influence the fundamental value of the asset or (2) comparing it to the observable market value of "similar" assets. Equity valuation models are used by analysts in a number of ways. Rather than an end unto itself, valuation is a tool that is used in the pursuit of other objectives like those listed in the following paragraphs.

The general steps in the equity valuation process are:

1. Understand the business.
2. Forecast company performance.
3. Select the appropriate valuation model.
4. Convert the forecasts into a valuation.
5. Apply the valuation conclusions.

Stock selection. The most direct use of equity valuation is to guide the purchase, holding, or sale of stocks. Valuation is based on both a comparison of the intrinsic value of the stock with its market price and a comparison of its price with that of comparable stocks.

Reading the market. Current market prices implicitly contain investors' expectations about the future value of the variables that influence the stock's price (e.g., earnings growth and expected return). Analysts can estimate these expectations by comparing market prices with a stock's intrinsic value.

Projecting the value of corporate actions. Many market professionals use valuation techniques to determine the value of proposed corporate mergers, acquisitions, divestitures, management buyouts (MBOs), and recapitalization efforts.

Fairness opinions. Analysts use equity valuation to support professional opinions about the fairness of a price to be received by minority shareholders in a merger or acquisition.

Planning and consulting. Many firms engage analysts to evaluate the effects of proposed corporate strategies on the firm's stock price, pursuing only those that have the greatest value to shareholders.

Communication with analysts and investors. The valuation approach provides management, investors, and analysts with a common basis upon which to discuss and evaluate the company's performance, current state, and future plans.

Valuation of private business. Analysts use valuation techniques to determine the value of firms or holdings in firms that are not publicly traded. Investors in nonpublic firms rely on these valuations to determine the value of their positions or proposed positions.

Portfolio management. While equity valuation can be considered a stand-alone function in which the value of a single equity position is estimated, it can be more valuable when used in a portfolio management context to determine the value and risk of a portfolio of investments. The investment process is usually considered to have three parts: planning, execution, and evaluation of results. Equity valuation is a primary concern in the first two of these steps.

■ *Planning.* The first step of the investment process includes defining investment objectives and constraints and articulating an investment strategy for selecting securities based on valuation parameters or techniques. Sometimes investors may not select individual equity positions, but the valuation techniques are implied in the selection of an index or other preset basket of securities. Active investment managers may use benchmarks as indicators of market expectations and then purposely deviate in composition or weighting to take advantage of their differing expectations.

■ *Executing the investment plan.* The valuation of potential investments guides the implementation of an investment plan. The results of the specified valuation methods determine which investments will be made and which will be avoided.

LOS 26.e: Describe questions that should be addressed in conducting an industry and competitive analysis.

CFA® Program Curriculum: Volume 4, page 12

The five **elements of industry structure** as developed by Professor Michael Porter are:

1. Threat of new entrants in the industry.
2. Threat of substitutes.
3. Bargaining power of buyers.
4. Bargaining power of suppliers.
5. Rivalry among existing competitors.

The attractiveness (long-term profitability) of any industry is determined by the interaction of these five competitive forces (Porter's five forces).

There are three generic strategies a company may employ in order to compete and generate profits:

1. *Cost leadership:* Being the lowest-cost producer of the good.
2. *Product differentiation:* Addition of product features or services that increase the attractiveness of the firm's product so that it will command a premium price in the market.
3. *Focus:* Employing one of the previous strategies within a particular segment of the industry in order to gain a competitive advantage.

Once the analyst has identified a company's strategy, she can evaluate the performance of the business over time in terms of how well it executes its strategy and how successful it is.

The basic building blocks of equity valuation come from accounting information contained in the firm's reports and releases. In order for the analyst to successfully estimate the value of the firm, the financial factors must be disclosed in sufficient detail and accuracy. Investigating the issues associated with the accuracy and detail of a firm's disclosures is often referred to as a **quality of financial statement**

information. This analysis requires examination of the firm's income statement, balance sheet, and the notes to the financial statements. Studies have shown that the quality of earnings issue is reflected in a firm's stock price, with firms with more transparent earnings having higher market values.

An analyst can often only discern important results of management discretion through a detailed examination of the footnotes accompanying the financial reports. Quality of earnings issues can be broken down into several categories and may be addressed only in the footnotes and disclosures to the financial statements.

Accelerating or premature recognition of income. Firms have used a variety of techniques to justify the recognition of income before it traditionally would have been recognized. These include recording sales and billing customers before products are shipped or accepted and bill and hold schemes in which items are billed in advance and held for future delivery. These schemes have been used to obscure declines in operating performance and boost reported revenue and income.

Reclassifying gains and nonoperating income. Firms occasionally have gains or income from sources that are peripheral to their operations. The reclassification of these items as operating income will distort the results of the firm's continuing operations, often hiding underperformance or a decline in sales.

Expense recognition and losses. Delaying the recognition of expenses, capitalizing expenses, and classifying operating expenses as nonoperating expenses is an opposite approach that has the same effect as reclassifying gains from peripheral sources, increasing operating income. Management also has discretion in creating and estimating reserves that reflect expected future liabilities, such as a bad debt reserve or a provision for expected litigation losses.

Amortization, depreciation, and discount rates. Management has a great deal of discretion in the selection of amortization and depreciation methods, as well as the choice of discount rates in determination of pension plan obligations. These decisions can reduce the current recognition of expenses, in effect deferring recognition to later periods.

Off-balance-sheet issues. The firm's balance sheet may not fully reflect the assets and liabilities of the firm. Special purpose entities (SPEs) can be used by the firm to increase sales (by recording sales to the SPE) or to obscure the nature and value of assets or liabilities. Leases can be structured as operating, rather than finance, leases in order to reduce the total liabilities reported on the balance sheet.

LOS 26.f: Contrast absolute and relative valuation models and describe examples of each type of model.

CFA® Program Curriculum: Volume 4, page 23

Absolute valuation models. An absolute valuation model is one that estimates an asset's intrinsic value, which is its value arising from its investment characteristics without regard to the value of other firms. One absolute valuation approach is to determine the value of a firm today as the *discounted* or *present value* of all the cash flows expected in the future. *Dividend discount models* estimate the value of a share based on the present value of all expected dividends discounted at the opportunity cost of capital. Many analysts realize that equity holders are entitled to more than just the dividends and so expand the measure of cash flow to include all expected cash flow to the firm that is not payable to senior claims (bondholders, taxing authorities, and senior stockholders). These models include the free cash flow approach and the residual income approach.

Another absolute approach to valuation is represented by *asset-based* models. This approach estimates a firm's value as the sum of the market value of the assets it owns or controls. This approach is commonly used to value firms that own or control natural resources, such as oil fields, coal deposits, and other mineral claims.

Relative valuation models. Another very common approach to valuation is to determine the value of an asset in relation to the values of other assets. This is the approach underlying relative valuation models. The most common models use market price as a multiple of an individual financial factor of the firm, such as earnings per share. The resulting ratio, price-to-earnings (P/E), is easily compared to that of other firms. If the P/E is higher than that of comparable firms, it is said to be *relatively* overvalued, that is, overvalued relative to the other firms (not necessarily overvalued on an intrinsic value basis). The converse is also true: if the P/E is lower than that of comparable firms, the firm is said to be relatively undervalued.

LOS 26.g: Describe sum-of-the-parts valuation and conglomerate discounts.

CFA® Program Curriculum: Volume 4, page 26

Rather than valuing a company as a single entity, an analyst can value individual parts of the firm and add them up to determine the value for the company as a whole. The value obtained is called the *sum-of-the-parts value,* or sometimes *breakup value* or *private market value*. This process is especially useful when the company operates multiple divisions (or product lines) with different business models and risk characteristics (i.e., a conglomerate).

Conglomerate discount is based on the idea that investors apply a markdown to the value of a company that operates in multiple unrelated industries, compared to the value a company that has a single industry focus. Conglomerate discount is thus the amount by which market value under-represents sum-of-the-parts value.

Three explanations for conglomerate discounts are:

1. Internal capital inefficiency: The company's allocation of capital to different divisions may not have been based on sound decisions.

2. Endogenous (internal) factors: For example, the company may have pursued unrelated business acquisitions to hide poor operating performance.

3. Research measurement errors: Some hypothesize that conglomerate discounts do not exist, but rather are a result of incorrect measurement.

LOS 26.h: Explain broad criteria for choosing an appropriate approach for valuing a given company.

CFA® Program Curriculum: Volume 4, page 29

When selecting an approach for valuing a given company, an analyst should consider whether the model:

- Fits the characteristics of the company (e.g., Does it pay dividends? Is earnings growth estimable? Does it have significant intangible assets?).
- Is appropriate based on the quality and availability of input data.
- Is suitable given the purpose of the analysis.

The purpose of the analysis may be, for example, valuation for making a purchase offer for a controlling interest in the company. In this case, a model based on cash flow may be more appropriate than one based on dividends because a controlling interest would allow the purchaser to set dividend policy.

One thing to remember with respect to choice of a valuation model is that the analyst does not have to consider only one. Using multiple models and examining differences in estimated values can reveal how a model's assumptions and the perspective of the analysis are affecting the estimated values.

 MODULE QUIZ 26.1

To best evaluate your performance, enter your quiz answers online.

1. Susan Weiber, CFA, has noted that even her best estimates of a stock's intrinsic value can differ significantly from the current market price. The *least likely* explanation is:
    A. differences between her estimate and the actual intrinsic value.
    B. differences between the actual intrinsic value and the market price.
    C. differences between the intrinsic value and the going concern value.

2. An appropriate valuation approach for a company that is going out of business would be to calculate its:
    A. residual income value.
    B. dividend discount model value.
    C. liquidation value.

3. Davy Jarvis, CFA, is performing an equity valuation as part of the planning and execution phase of the portfolio management process. His results will also be useful for:
    A. communication with analysts and investors.
    B. technical analysis.
    C. benchmarking.

4. The five elements of industry structure, as outlined by Michael Porter, include:
    A. the threat of substitutes.
    B. product differentiation.
    C. cost leadership.

5. Tom Walder has been instructed to use absolute valuation models, and not relative valuation models, in his analysis. Which of the following is *least likely* to be an example of an absolute valuation model? The:
   A. dividend discount model.
   B. price-to-earnings market multiple model.
   C. residual income model.

6. Davy Jarvis, CFA, is performing an equity valuation and reviews his notes for key points he wanted to cover when planning the valuation. He finds the following questions:
   ■ Does the company pay dividends?
   ■ Is earnings growth estimable?
   ■ Does the company have significant intangible assets?

   Which of the following general questions is Jarvis trying to answer when planning this phase of the valuation?
   A. Does the model fit the characteristics of the investment?
   B. Is the model appropriate based on the availability of input data?
   C. Can the model be improved to make it more suitable, given the purpose of the analysis?

Use the following information to answer Questions 7 and 8.

Sun Pharma is a large pharmaceutical company based in Sri Lanka that manufactures prescription drugs under license from large multinational pharmaceutical companies. Delenga Mahamurthy, CEO of Sun Pharma, is evaluating a potential acquisition of Island Cookware, a small manufacturing company that produces cooking utensils.

Mahamurthy feels that Sun Pharma's excellent distribution network could add value to Island Cookware. Sun Pharma plans to acquire Island Cookware for cash. Several days later, Sun Pharma announces that they have acquired Island Cookware at market price.

7. Sun Pharma's *most appropriate* valuation for Island Cookware is its:
   A. sum-of-the-parts value.
   B. investment value.
   C. liquidation value.

8. Upon announcement of the merger, the market price of Sun Pharma drops. This is *most likely* a result of the:
   A. unrelated business effect.
   B. tax effect.
   C. conglomerate discount.

KEY CONCEPTS

LOS 26.a

Intrinsic value is the value of an asset or security estimated by someone who has complete understanding of the characteristics of the asset or issuing firm. To the extent that market prices are not perfectly (informationally) efficient, they may diverge from intrinsic value. The difference between the analyst's estimate of intrinsic value and the current price is made up of two components: the difference between the actual intrinsic value and the market price, and the difference between the actual intrinsic value and the analyst's estimate of intrinsic value:

$$IV_{analyst} - price = (IV_{actual} - price) + (IV_{analyst} - IV_{actual})$$

LOS 26.b

The going concern assumption is simply the assumption that a company will continue to operate as a business as opposed to going out of business. The liquidation value is the estimate of what the assets of the firm would bring if sold separately, net of the company's liabilities.

LOS 26.c

Fair market value is the price at which a hypothetical willing, informed, and able seller would trade an asset to a willing, informed and able buyer. Investment value is the value to a specific buyer after including any additional value attributable to synergies. Investment value is an appropriate measure for strategic buyers pursuing acquisitions.

LOS 26.d

Equity valuation is the process of estimating the value of an asset by (1) using a model based on the variables the analyst believes influence the fundamental value of the asset or (2) comparing it to the observable market value of "similar" assets. Equity valuation models are used by analysts in a number of ways. Examples include stock selection, reading the market, projecting the value of corporate actions, fairness opinions, planning and consulting, communication with analysts and investors, valuation of private business, and portfolio management.

LOS 26.e

The five elements of industry structure as developed by Professor Michael Porter are:

1. Threat of new entrants in the industry.
2. Threat of substitutes.
3. Bargaining power of buyers.
4. Bargaining power of suppliers.
5. Rivalry among existing competitors.

Quality of earnings issues can be broken down into several categories and may be addressed only in the footnotes and disclosures to the financial statements:

■ Accelerating or premature recognition of income.

■ Reclassifying gains and nonoperating income.

■ Expense recognition and losses.

■ Amortization, depreciation, and discount rates.

■ Off-balance-sheet issues.

LOS 26.f

An absolute valuation model is one that estimates an asset's intrinsic value (e.g., the discounted dividend approach). Relative valuation models estimate an asset's investment characteristics compared to the value of other firms (e.g., comparing P/E ratios to those of other firms in the industry).

LOS 26.g

Sum-of-the-parts valuation is the process of valuing the individual components of a company and then adding these values together to obtain the value of the whole company. Conglomerate discount refers to the amount by which market price is lower than the sum-of-the-parts value. Conglomerate discount is an apparent price reduction applied by the markets to firms that operate in multiple industries.

LOS 26.h

When selecting an approach for valuing a given company, an analyst should consider whether the model fits the characteristics of the company, is appropriate based on the quality and availability of input data, and is suitable, given the purpose of the analysis.

ANSWER KEY FOR MODULE QUIZZES

Module Quiz 26.1

1. **C** The difference between the analyst's estimate of intrinsic value and the current price is made up of two components:

$$IV_{analyst} - price = (IV_{actual} - price) + (IV_{analyst} - IV_{actual})$$

   (LOS 26.a)

2. **C** The liquidation value is the estimate of what the assets of the firm will bring when sold separately, net of the company's liabilities. It is most appropriate because the firm is not a going concern and will not pay dividends. The residual income model is based on the going concern assumption and is not appropriate for valuing a firm that is expected to go out of business. (LOS 26.b)

3. **A** Communication with analysts and investors is one of the common uses of an equity valuation. Technical analysis and benchmarking do not require equity valuation. (LOS 26.d)

4. **A** The five elements of industry structure as developed by Professor Michael Porter are:

   1. Threat of new entrants in the industry.

   2. Threat of substitutes.

   3. Bargaining power of buyers.

   4. Bargaining power of suppliers.

   5. Rivalry among existing competitors.

   (LOS 26.e)

5. **B** Absolute valuation models estimate value as some function of the present value of future cash flows (e.g., dividend discount and free cash flow models) or economic profit (e.g., residual income models). Relative valuation models estimate an asset's value relative to the value of other similar assets. The price-to-earnings market multiple model is an example of a relative valuation model. (LOS 26.f)

6. **A** Jarvis is most likely trying to be sure the selected model fits the characteristics of the investment. Model selection will depend heavily on the answers to these questions. (LOS 26.f)

7. **B** The appropriate valuation for Sun Pharma's acquisition is the investment value, which incorporates the value of any synergies present in the acquisition. Sum-of-the-parts value is not applicable, as the valuation does not require separate valuation of different divisions of Island Cookware. Liquidation value is also not relevant, as Sun Pharma does not intend to liquidate the assets of Island Cookware. (LOS 26.c)

8. **C** Upon announcement of the acquisition, the market price of Sun Pharma should not change if the acquisition was at fair value. However, the market is valuing the whole company at a value less than the value of its parts: this is a conglomerate discount. We are not given any information about tax consequences of the merger and hence a tax effect is unlikely to be the cause of the market price drop. The acquisition of an unrelated business may result in a conglomerate discount, but there is no defined 'unrelated business effect.' (LOS 26.c)

The following is a review of the Equity Valuation (1) principles designed to address the learning outcome statements set forth by CFA Institute. Cross-Reference to CFA Institute Assigned Reading #27.

READING
27

Return Concepts

EXAM FOCUS

Much of this material builds on concepts covered elsewhere in the Level II curriculum. Be able to distinguish among return concepts such as holding period return, realized return, expected return, required return, and discount rate. Understand the concept of convergence of price to intrinsic value. Be able to explain the equity risk premium, the various methods and models used to calculate the equity risk premium, and the strengths and weaknesses of those methods. The review also covers the weighted average cost of capital (WACC). You must be able to explain and calculate the WACC and be able to select the most appropriate discount rate for a given cash flow stream.

MODULE 27.1: RETURN CONCEPTS

LOS 27.a: Distinguish among realized holding period return, expected holding period return, required return, return from convergence of price to intrinsic value, discount rate, and internal rate of return.

Video covering this content is available online.

CFA® Program Curriculum: Volume 4, page 53

Holding Period Return

Holding period return is the increase in price of an asset plus any cash flow received from that asset, divided by the initial price of the asset. The measurement or *holding period* can be a day, a month, a year, and so on. In most cases, we assume the cash flow is received at the end of the holding period, and the equation for calculating holding period return is:

$$\text{holding period return} = r = \frac{P_1 - P_0 + CF_1}{P_0} = \frac{P_1 + CF_1}{P_0} - 1$$

The subscript 1 simply denotes one period from today. *P* stands for price and *CF* stands for cash flow. For a share of common stock, we might think of this in terms of

$$r = \frac{CF_1}{P_0} + \frac{P_1 - P_0}{P_0}$$

where:

$\frac{CF_1}{P_0} = $ the cash flow yield

$\frac{P_1 - P_0}{P_0} = $ the return from price appreciation

If the cash flow is received before the end of the period, then CF_1 would equal the cash flow received during the period plus any interest earned on the reinvestment of the cash flow from the time it was received until the end of the measurement period.

In most cases, holding period returns are annualized. For example, if the return for one month is 1% (0.01), then the analyst might report an annualized holding period return of $(1 + 0.01)^{12} - 1 = 0.1268$ or 12.68%. Annualized holding period returns should be scrutinized to make sure that the return for the actual holding period truly represents what could be earned for an entire year.

Realized and Expected Holding Period Return

A **realized return** is a historical return based on past observed prices and cash flows. An **expected return** is based on forecasts of future prices and cash flows. Such expected returns can be derived from elaborate models or subjective opinions.

Required Return

An asset's **required return** is the minimum return an investor requires given the asset's risk. A more risky asset will have a higher required return. Required return is also called the *opportunity cost* for investing in the asset. If expected return is greater (less) than required return, the asset is undervalued (overvalued).

Price Convergence

If the *expected return* is not equal to required return, there can be a "return from convergence of price to intrinsic value." Letting V_0 denote the true intrinsic value, and given that price does not equal that value (i.e., $V_0 \neq P_0$), then the return from convergence of price to intrinsic value is $(V_0 - P_0) / P_0$. If an analyst expects the price of the asset to converge to its intrinsic value by the end of the horizon, then

$(V_0 - P_0) / P_0$ is also the difference between the expected return on an asset and its required return:

$$\text{expected return} = \text{required return} + \frac{(V_0 - P_0)}{P_0}$$

It is possible that there are chronic inefficiencies that impede price convergence. Therefore, even if an analyst feels that $V_0 \neq P_0$ for a given asset, the convergence yield may not be realized.

Discount Rate

The **discount rate** is the rate used to find the present value of an investment. While it is possible to estimate a discount rate subjectively, a much sounder approach is to use a market determined rate.

Internal Rate of Return

For publicly traded securities, the **internal rate of return** (IRR) is a market-determined rate. It is the rate that equates the value of the discounted cash flows to the current price of the security. If markets are efficient, then the IRR represents the required return.

LOS 27.b: Calculate and interpret an equity risk premium using historical and forward-looking estimation approaches.

CFA® Program Curriculum: Volume 4, page 58

The **equity risk premium** is the return in excess of the risk-free rate that investors require for holding equity securities. It is usually defined as the difference between the required return on a broad equity market index and the risk-free rate:

equity risk premium = required return on equity index − risk-free rate

An estimate of a future equity risk premium, based on historical information, requires the following preliminary steps:

- Select an equity index.
- Select a time period.
- Calculate the mean return on the index.
- Select a proxy for the risk-free rate.

The risk-free return should correspond to the time horizon for the investment (e.g., T-bills for shorter-term and T-bonds for longer-term horizons).

PROFESSOR'S NOTE

While the curriculum recommends using the risk-free rate that matches the investor's investment horizon for CAPM, the GGM (presented later) uses a long-term rate for the risk-free rate in computing ERP, while other models (also presented later) use a short-term risk-free rate.

The broad market equity risk premium can be used to determine the required return for individual stocks using beta:

required return for stock j = risk-free return + β_j × (equity risk premium)

where:

β_j = the "beta" of stock j and serves as the adjustment for the level of systematic risk inherent in the stock.

If the systematic risk of stock j equals that of the market, then $\beta_j = 1$. If systematic risk is greater (less) than that of the market, then $\beta_j > 1$ (< 1). A more general representation is:

required return for stock j = risk-free return + (equity risk premium) + other risk premia/discounts appropriate for j

The general model is used in the build-up method (discussed later) and is typically used for valuation of private businesses. It does not account for systematic risk.

Note that an equity risk premium is an estimated value and may not be realized. Also keep in mind that these estimates can be derived in several ways. An analyst reading a report that discusses a "risk premium" should take note to see how the author of the report has arrived at the estimated value.

PROFESSOR'S NOTE

As you work through this topic review, keep in mind that the risk premiums, including the equity risk premium, are differences in rates—typically a market rate minus the risk-free rate.

ESTIMATES OF THE EQUITY RISK PREMIUM: STRENGTHS AND WEAKNESSES

There are two types of estimates of the equity risk premium: historical estimates and forward-looking estimates.

HISTORICAL ESTIMATES

A **historical estimate** of the equity risk premium consists of the difference between the historical mean return for a broad-based equity-market index and a risk-free rate over a given time period. Its strength is its objectivity and simplicity. Also, if investors are rational, then historical estimates will be unbiased.

A weakness of the approach is the assumption that the mean and variance of the returns are constant over time (i.e., that they are stationary). This does not seem to be the case. In fact, the premium actually appears to be countercyclical—it is low during good times and high during bad times. Thus, an analyst using this method to estimate the current equity premium must choose the sample period carefully. The historical estimate can also be upward biased if only firms that have survived during the period of measurement (called **survivorship bias**) are included in the sample.

Other considerations include the method for calculating the mean and which risk-free rate is most relevant to the analysis. Because a geometric mean is less than or equal to the corresponding arithmetic mean, the risk premium will always be lower when the geometric mean is used instead of the arithmetic mean. If the yield curve is upward sloping, the use of longer-term bonds rather than shorter-term bonds to estimate the risk-free rate will cause the estimated risk premium to be smaller.

FORWARD-LOOKING ESTIMATES

Forward-looking or **ex ante estimates** use current information and expectations concerning economic and financial variables. The strength of this method is that it does not rely on an assumption of stationarity and is less subject to problems like survivorship bias. There are three main categories of forward-looking estimates: those based on the Gordon growth model, supply-side models, and estimates from surveys.

Gordon Growth Model

The **constant growth model** (a.k.a. the **Gordon growth model**) is a popular method to generate forward-looking estimates. The assumptions of the model are reasonable when applied to developed economies and markets, wherein there are typically ample sources of reliable forecasts for data such as dividend payments and growth rates. This method estimates the risk premium as the expected dividend yield plus the expected growth rate minus the current long-term government bond yield.

$$\begin{array}{c} \text{GGM equity} \\ \text{risk premium} \end{array} = \begin{array}{c} \text{(1-year forecasted} \\ \text{dividend yield on} \\ \text{market index)} \end{array} + \begin{array}{c} \text{(consensus long-term} \\ \text{earnings growth rate)} \end{array} - \begin{array}{c} \text{(long-term} \\ \text{government bond} \\ \text{yield)} \end{array}$$

Denoting each component by (D_1 / P), $\hat{g}$, and $r_{LT,0}$, respectively, the forward-looking equity risk premium estimate is:

$$(D_1 / P) + \hat{g} - r_{LT,0}$$

A weakness of the approach is that the forward-looking estimates will change through time and need to be updated. During a typical economic boom, dividend yields are low and growth expectations are high, while the opposite is generally true when the economy is less robust. For example, suppose that during an economic boom (bust) dividend yields are 2% (4%), growth expectations are 6% (3%), and long-term bond yields are 6% (3%). The equity risk premia during these two different periods would be 2% during the boom and 4% during the bust. And, of course, there is no assurance that the capital appreciation realized will be equal to the earnings growth rate during the forecast period.

Another weakness is the assumption of a stable growth rate, which is often not appropriate in rapidly growing economies. Such economies might have three or more stages of growth: rapid growth, transition, and mature growth. In this case, another forward-looking estimate would use the required return on equity derived from the IRR from the following equation:

$$\text{equity index price} = PV_{rapid}(r) + PV_{transition}(r) + PV_{mature}(r)$$

where:
PV_{rapid} = present value of projected cash flows during the rapid growth stage
$PV_{transition}$ = present value of projected cash flows during the transitional growth stage
PV_{mature} = present value of projected cash flows during the mature growth stage

The forward-looking estimate of the equity premium would be the *r* from this equality minus the corresponding government bond yield.

Supply-Side Estimates (Macroeconomic Models)

Macroeconomic model estimates of the equity risk premium are based on the relationships between macroeconomic variables and financial variables. A strength of this approach is the use of proven models and current information. A weakness is that the estimates are only appropriate for developed countries where public equities represent a relatively large share of the economy, implying that it is reasonable to believe there should be some relationship between macroeconomic variables and asset prices.

One common model [Ibbotson-Chen (2003)] for a supply-side estimate of the risk premium is:

$$\text{equity risk premium} = \left[1 + \hat{\imath}\right] \times \left[1 + \widehat{rEg}\right] \times \left[1 + \widehat{PEg}\right] - 1 + \hat{Y} - \widehat{RF}$$

where:
$\hat{\imath}$ = expected inflation
$\widehat{rEg}$ = expected real growth in EPS
$\widehat{PEg}$ = expected changes in the P/E ratio
$\hat{Y}$ = the expected yield on the index
$\widehat{RF}$ = the expected risk-free rate

The analyst must determine appropriate techniques with which to compute values for these inputs. For example, a market-based estimate of expected inflation can be derived from the differences in the yields for T-bonds and Treasury Inflation Protected Securities (TIPS) having comparable maturities:

$$\hat{\imath} = [(1 + \text{YTM of 20-year T-bonds}) \div (1 + \text{YTM of 20-year TIPS})] - 1$$

PROFESSOR'S NOTE

TIPS are inflation-indexed bonds issued by the U.S. Treasury. TIPS pay interest every six months and principal at maturity. The coupon and principal are automatically increased by the consumer price index (CPI).

Expected real growth in EPS should be approximately equal to the real GDP growth rate. Growth in GDP can be estimated as the sum of labor productivity growth and growth in the labor supply:

$$\widehat{rEg} = \text{real GDP growth}$$

$$\widehat{rEg} = \text{labor productivity growth rate} + \text{labor supply growth rate}$$

The $\widehat{PEg}$ would depend upon whether the analyst thought the market was over or undervalued. If the market is believed to be overvalued, P/E ratios would be expected to decrease $\left(\widehat{PEg} < 0\right)$ and the opposite would be true if the market were believed to be undervalued $\left(\widehat{PEg} > 0\right)$. If the market is correctly priced, $\widehat{PEg} = 0$. The $\hat{Y}$ can be estimated using estimated dividends on the index (including reinvestment return).

Survey Estimates

Survey estimates of the equity risk premium use the consensus of the opinions from a sample of people. If the sample is restricted to people who are experts in the area of equity valuation, the results are likely to be more reliable. The strength is that survey results are relatively easy to obtain. The weakness is that, even when the survey is restricted to experts in the area, there can be a wide disparity between the consensuses obtained from different groups.

LOS 27.c: Estimate the required return on an equity investment using the capital asset pricing model, the Fama–French model, the Pastor–Stambaugh model, macroeconomic multifactor models, and the build-up method (e.g., bond yield plus risk premium).

CFA® Program Curriculum: Volume 4, page 71

Capital Asset Pricing Model

The **capital asset pricing model** (CAPM) estimates the required return on equity using the following formula:

required return on stock j = risk-free rate + (equity risk premium × beta of j)

> **EXAMPLE: Using the CAPM to calculate the required return on equity**
>
> The current expected risk-free rate is 4%, the equity risk premium is 3.9%, and the beta is 0.8. Calculate the required return on equity.
>
> **Answer:**
>
> 7.12% = 4% + (3.9% × 0.8)

Multifactor Models

Multifactor models can have greater explanatory power than the CAPM, which is a single-factor model. The general form of an n-factor multifactor model is:

$$\text{required return} = RF + (\text{risk premium})_1 + (\text{risk premium})_2 + \ldots + (\text{risk premium})_n$$

$$(\text{risk premium})_i = (\text{factor sensitivity})_i \times (\text{factor risk premium})_i$$

The factor sensitivity is also called the *factor beta*, and it is the asset's sensitivity to a particular factor, all else being equal. The factor risk premium is the expected return above the risk-free rate from a unit sensitivity to the factor and zero sensitivity to all other factors.

Fama-French Model

The **Fama-French model** is a multifactor model that attempts to account for the higher returns generally associated with small-cap stocks. The model is:

$$\text{required return of stock } j = RF + \beta_{mkt,j} \times (R_{mkt} - RF) + \beta_{SMB,j} \times (R_{small} - R_{big})$$
$$+ \beta_{HML,j} \times (R_{HBM} - R_{LBM})$$

where:

$(R_{mkt} - RF)$	= return on a value-weighted market index minus the risk-free rate
$(R_{small} - R_{big})$	= a small-cap return premium equal to the average return on small-cap portfolios minus the average return on large-cap portfolios
$(R_{HBM} - R_{LBM})$	= a value return premium equal to the average return on high book-to-market portfolios minus the average return on low book-to-market portfolios

The baseline value (i.e., the expected value for the variable) for $\beta_{mkt,j}$ is one, and the baseline values for $\beta_{SMB,j}$ and $\beta_{HML,j}$ are zero.

The latter two of these factors corresponds to the return of a zero-net investment in the corresponding assets [e.g., $(R_{small} - R_{big})$ represents the return on a portfolio that shorts large-cap stocks and invests in small-cap stocks]. The goal is to capture the effect of other underlying risk factors. Many developed economies and markets have sufficient data for estimating the model.

> **EXAMPLE: Applying the CAPM and the Fama-French Model**
>
> Suppose we derive the following factor values from market data:
>
> | | |
> |---|---|
> | $(R_{mkt} - RF)$ | = 4.8% |
> | $(R_{small} - R_{big})$ | = 2.4% |
> | $(R_{HBM} - R_{LBM})$ | = 1.6% |
> | risk-free rate | = 3.4% |

We estimate that stock j has a CAPM beta equal to 1.3. Stock j is a small-cap growth stock that has traded at a low book to market in recent years. Using the Fama-French model, we estimate the following betas for stock j:

$$\beta_{mkt,j} = 1.2$$
$$\beta_{SMB,j} = 0.4$$
$$\beta_{HML,j} = -0.2$$

Calculate the required return on equity using the CAPM and the Fama-French models:

Answer:

CAPM estimate: required return $= 3.4\% + (1.3 \times 4.8\%) = 9.64\%$

Fama-French model estimate: required return $= 3.4\% + (1.2 \times 4.8\%) + (0.4 \times 2.4\%) + (-0.2 \times 1.6\%) = 9.8\%$

Pastor-Stambaugh Model

The **Pastor-Stambaugh model** adds a liquidity factor to the Fama-French model. The baseline value for the liquidity factor beta is zero. Less liquid assets should have a positive beta, while more liquid assets should have a negative beta.

EXAMPLE: Applying the Pastor-Stambaugh model

Assume a liquidity premium of 4%, the same factor risk premiums as before, and the following sensitivities for stock k:

$$\beta_{mkt,k} = 0.9$$
$$\beta_{SMB,k} = -0.2$$
$$\beta_{HML,k} = 0.2$$
$$\beta_{liquidity,k} = -0.1$$

Calculate the cost of capital using the Pastor-Stambaugh model.

Answer:

cost of capital $= 3.4\% + (0.9 \times 4.8\%) + (-0.2 \times 2.4\%) + (0.2 \times 1.6\%) + (-0.1 \times 4\%) = 7.16\%$

Macroeconomic Multifactor Models

Macroeconomic multifactor models use factors associated with economic variables that can be reasonably believed to affect cash flows and/or appropriate discount rates. The Burmeister, Roll, and Ross model incorporates the following five factors:

1. *Confidence risk*: unexpected change in the difference between the return of risky corporate bonds and government bonds.

2. *Time horizon risk*: unexpected change in the difference between the return of long-term government bonds and Treasury bills.

3. *Inflation risk*: unexpected change in the inflation rate.

4. *Business cycle risk*: unexpected change in the level of real business activity.

5. *Market timing risk*: the equity market return that is not explained by the other four factors.

As with the other models, to compute the required return on equity for a given stock, the factor values are multiplied by a sensitivity coefficient (i.e., beta) for that stock; the products are summed and added to the risk-free rate.

EXAMPLE: Applying a multifactor model

Imagine that we are given the following values for the factors:

confidence risk	= 2.0%
time horizon risk	= 3.0%
inflation risk	= 4.0%
business cycle risk	= 1.6%
market timing risk	= 3.4%

Suppose that we are also given the following sensitivities for stock j: 0.3, –0.2, 1.1, 0.3, 0.5, respectively. Using the risk-free rate of 3.4%, calculate the required return using a multifactor approach.

Answer:

required return = 3.4% + (0.3 × 2%) + (–0.2 × 3%) + (1.1 × 4%) + (0.3 × 1.6%) + (0.5 × 3.4%) = 9.98%

Build-Up Method

The **build-up method** is similar to the risk premium approach. It is usually applied to closely held companies where betas are not readily obtainable. One popular representation is:

required return = RF + equity risk premium + size premium + specific-company premium

The size premium would be scaled up or down based on the size of the company. Smaller companies would have a larger premium.

As before, computing the required return would be a matter of simply adding up the values in the formula. Some representations use an estimated beta to scale the size of the company-specific equity risk premium but typically not for the other factors.

The formula could have a factor for the level of controlling versus minority interests and a factor for marketability of the equity; however, these latter two factors are usually used to adjust the value of the company directly rather than through the required return.

Bond-Yield Plus Risk Premium Method

The **bond-yield plus risk premium method** is a build-up method that is appropriate if the company has publicly traded debt. The method simply adds a risk premium to the yield to maturity (YTM) of the company's *long-term* debt. The logic here is that the yield to maturity of the company's bonds includes the effects of inflation, leverage, and the firm's sensitivity to the business cycle. Because the various risk factors are already taken into account in the YTM, the analyst can simply add a premium for the added risk arising from holding the firm's equity. That value is usually estimated at 3–5%, with the specific estimate based upon some model or simply from experience.

> **EXAMPLE: Applying the bond-yield plus risk premium approach**
>
> Company LMN has bonds with 15 years to maturity. They have a coupon of 8.2% and a price equal to 101.70. An analyst estimates that the additional risk assumed from holding the firm's equity justifies a risk premium of 3.8%. Given the coupon and maturity, the YTM is 8%. Calculate the cost of equity using the bond-yield plus risk premium approach.
>
> **Answer:**
>
> cost of equity = 8% + 3.8% = 11.8%

PROFESSOR'S NOTE

Although most of our examples in this section have focused on the calculation of the return using various approaches, don't lose sight of what information the components of each equation might convey. The betas tell us about the characteristics of the asset being evaluated, and the risk premia tell us how those characteristics are priced in the market. If you encounter a situation on the exam where you are asked to evaluate style and/or the overall impact of a component on return, separate out each factor and its beta—paying careful attention to whether there is a positive or negative sign attached to the component—and work through it logically.

LOS 27.d: Explain beta estimation for public companies, thinly traded public companies, and nonpublic companies.

CFA® Program Curriculum: Volume 4, page 73

Beta Estimates for Public Companies

Up to this point, we have concerned ourselves with methods for estimating the equity risk premium. Now we turn our attention to the estimation of beta, the measure of the level of systematic risk assumed from holding the security. For a public company, an analyst can compute beta by regressing the returns of the company's stock on the returns of the overall market. To do so, the analyst must determine which index to use in the regression and the length and frequency of the sample data.

Popular choices for the index include the S&P 500 and the NYSE Composite. The most common length and frequency are five years of monthly data. A popular alternative (and the default setting on Bloomberg terminals) is two years of weekly data, which may be more appropriate for fast-growing markets.

Adjusted Beta for Public Companies

When making forecasts of the equity risk premium, some analysts recommend adjusting the beta for **beta drift**. Beta drift refers to the observed tendency of an estimated beta to revert to a value of 1.0 over time. To compensate, the **Blume** method can be used to adjust the beta estimate:

adjusted beta = (2/3 × regression beta) + (1/3 × 1.0)

> **EXAMPLE: Calculating adjusted beta**
>
> Suppose that an analyst estimates a beta of 0.8 using regression and historical data and adjusts the beta as described previously. Calculate the adjusted beta and use it to estimate a forward-looking required return.
>
> **Answer:**
>
> adjusted beta = (2/3 × regression beta) + (1/3 × 1.0)
> = (2/3 × 0.8) + (1/3 × 1.0) = 0.867
>
> Note that this adjusted beta is closer to one than the regression beta.
>
> If the risk-free rate is 4% and the equity risk premium is 3.9%, then the required return would be:
>
> required return on stock = risk-free rate + (equity risk premium × beta of stock) = 4% + (3.9% × 0.867) = 7.38%
>
> Note that the required return is higher than the 7.12% derived using the unadjusted beta. Naturally, there are other methods for adjusting beta to compensate for beta drift. Statistical services selling financial information often report both unadjusted and adjusted beta values.

PROFESSOR'S NOTE

Note that some statistical services use reversion to a peer mean rather than reversion to one.

Beta Estimates for Thinly Traded Stocks and Nonpublic Companies

Beta estimation for thinly traded stocks and nonpublic companies involves a 4-step procedure. If ABC is the nonpublic company the steps are:

Step 1: Identify a benchmark company, which is publicly traded and similar to ABC in its operations.

Step 2: Estimate the beta of that benchmark company, which we will denote XYZ. This can be done with a regression analysis.

Step 3: Unlever the beta estimate for XYZ with the formula:

$$\text{unlevered beta for X} = (\text{beta of XYZ}) \times \frac{1}{\left[1 + \frac{\text{debt of XYZ}}{\text{equity of XYZ}}\right]}$$

Step 4: Lever up the unlevered beta for XYZ using the debt and equity measures of ABC to get an estimate of ABC's beta for computing the required return on ABC's equity:

$$\text{estimate of beta for ABC} = (\text{unlevered beta of XYZ}) \times \left[1 + \frac{\text{debt of ABC}}{\text{equity of ABC}}\right]$$

PROFESSOR'S NOTE

This formula is slightly different than the one you may remember from Level I. Please use this one for Level II.

The procedure is the same if ABC is a thinly traded company. With the beta estimate for ABC in hand, the analyst would then use that value in the CAPM.

LOS 27.e: Describe strengths and weaknesses of methods used to estimate the required return on an equity investment.

CFA® Program Curriculum: Volume 4, page 72

The CAPM has the advantage of being very simple in that it uses only one factor. The weakness is choosing the appropriate factor. If a stock trades in more than one market, for example, there can be more than one market index, and this can lead to more than one estimate of required return. Another weakness is low explanatory power in some cases.

A strength of multifactor models is that they usually have higher explanatory power, but this is not assured. Multifactor models have the weakness of being more complex and expensive.

A strength of build-up models is that they are simple and can apply to closely held companies. The weakness is that they typically use historical values as estimates that may or may not be relevant to current market conditions.

LOS 27.f: Explain international considerations in required return estimation.

CFA® Program Curriculum: Volume 4, page 89

Additional considerations when investing internationally include exchange rate risk and data issues. The availability of good data may be severely limited in some markets. Note that these issues are of particular concern in emerging markets.

International investment, if not hedged, exposes the investor to exchange rate risk. To compensate for anticipated changes in exchange rates, an analyst should compute the required return in the home currency and then adjust it using forecasts for changes in the relevant exchange rate. Two methods for building risk premia into the required return are discussed in the following.

Country Spread Model

One method for adjusting data from emerging markets is to use a corresponding developed market as a benchmark and add a premium for the emerging market. One premium to use is the difference between the yield on bonds in the emerging market minus the yield on corresponding bonds in the developed market.

Country Risk Rating Model

A second method is the country risk rating model. This model estimates a regression equation using the equity risk premium for developed countries as the dependent variable and risk ratings (published by *Institutional Investor*) for those countries as the independent variable. Once the regression model is fitted (i.e., we estimate the regression coefficients), the model is then used for predicting the equity risk premium (i.e., dependent variable) for emerging markets using the emerging markets risk-ratings (i.e., independent variable).

LOS 27.g: **Explain and calculate the weighted average cost of capital for a company.**

CFA® Program Curriculum: Volume 4, page 90

The **cost of capital** is the overall required rate of return for those who supply a company with capital. The *suppliers* of capital are equity investors and those who lend money to the company. An often-used measure is the weighted average cost of capital (WACC):

WACC =

$$\frac{\text{market value of debt}}{\text{market value of debt and equity}} \times r_d \times (1 - \text{tax rate}) + \frac{\text{market value of equity}}{\text{market value of debt and equity}} \times r_e$$

In this representation, r_d and r_e are the required return on debt and equity, respectively. In many markets, corporations can take a deduction for interest expense. The inclusion of the term $(1 - \text{tax rate})$ adjusts the cost of the debt so it is on an after-tax basis. Since the measure should be forward-looking, the tax rate should be the marginal tax rate, which better reflects the future cost of raising funds. For markets where interest expense is not deductible, the relevant tax rate would be zero, and the pre- and after-tax cost of debt would be equal.

WACC is appropriate for valuing a total firm. To obtain the value of equity, first use WACC to calculate the value of a firm and then subtract the market value of long-term debt. We typically assume that the market value weights of debt and equity are equal to their target weights. When this is not the case, the WACC calculation should use the target weights for debt and equity.

LOS 27.h: Evaluate the appropriateness of using a particular rate of return as a discount rate, given a description of the cash flow to be discounted and other relevant facts.

CFA® Program Curriculum: Volume 4, page 92

The discount rate should correspond to the type of cash flow being discounted. Cash flows to the entire firm should be discounted with the WACC. Alternatively, cash flows in excess of what is required for debt service should be treated as cash flows to equity and discounted at the required return to equity.

An analyst may wish to measure the present value of real cash flows, and a real discount rate (i.e., one that has been adjusted for expected inflation) should be used in that case. In most cases, however, analysts discount nominal cash flows with nominal discount rates.

MODULE QUIZ 27.1

To best evaluate your performance, enter your quiz answers online.

1. A positive return from return from convergence of price to intrinsic value would *most likely* occur if:
   A. expected return is greater than required return.
   B. required return is greater than expected return.
   C. required return equals expected return.

2. For a particular stock, the required return can be determined by:
   A. multiplying the equity risk premium times the risk-free rate.
   B. multiplying an appropriate beta times the equity risk premium and adding a risk-free rate.
   C. multiplying an appropriate beta times the equity risk premium and subtracting the risk-free rate.

3. Which of the following is *most appropriate* to use as an estimate of the market risk premium in the capital asset pricing model (CAPM)?
   A. Geometric mean of historical returns on a market index.
   B. Long-term government bond yield plus 1-year forecasted market index dividend yield minus long-term earnings growth forecast.
   C. 1-year forecasted market index dividend yield plus long-term earnings growth forecast minus long-term government bond yield.

4. In computing a historical estimate of the equity risk premium, with respect to possible biases, choosing an arithmetic average of equity returns and Treasury bill rates would *most likely*:
   A. have an indeterminate effect because using the arithmetic average would tend to increase the estimate, and using the Treasury bill rate would tend to decrease the estimate.
   B. have an indeterminate effect because using the arithmetic average would tend to decrease the estimate, and using the Treasury bill rate would tend to increase the estimate.
   C. bias the estimate upwards because using the arithmetic average would tend to increase the estimate, and using the Treasury bill rate would tend to increase the estimate.

5. Which of the following is included in the Pastor-Stambaugh model but not the Fama-French model?
   A. A liquidity premium.
   B. A book-to-market premium.
   C. A market capitalization premium.

6. An analyst wishes to estimate a beta for a public company and use it to compute a forward-looking required return. The analyst would *most likely*:
   A. delever the market beta and relever that value for the company.
   B. regress the returns of the company on returns on an equity market index and adjust the estimated beta for leverage.
   C. regress the returns of the company on returns on an equity market index and adjust the estimated beta for beta drift.

7. Consider the following statements with respect to international considerations in determining the cost of capital.

   Statement 1: Exchange rates are an issue.

   Statement 2: The country risk rating model uses a corresponding developed market as a benchmark and adds a premium for the emerging market.

   Are the statements correct?
   A. Yes.
   B. No, because exchange rates are not an issue.
   C. No, because the country risk rating model estimates an equation for the equity risk premium for developed countries and then uses the equation and inputs associated with the emerging market to estimate the required return for emerging markets.

8. An analyst wishes to calculate the WACC for a company. The company's debt is twice that of the equity. The required returns on the company's debt and equity are 8% and 10%, respectively. The company's marginal tax rate is 30%. The WACC is *closest* to:
   A. 6.07%.
   B. 7.07%.
   C. 8.67%.

KEY CONCEPTS

LOS 27.a

Return concepts:

- Holding period return is the increase in price of an asset plus any cash flow received from that asset, divided by the initial price of the asset. The holding period can be any length. Usually, it is assumed the cash flow comes at the end of the period:

$$\text{holding period return} = r = \frac{P_1 - P_0 + CF_1}{P_0} = \frac{P_1 + CF_1}{P_0} - 1$$

- An asset's required return is the minimum expected return an investor requires given the asset's characteristics.

- If expected return is greater (less) than required return, the asset is undervalued (overvalued). The mispricing can lead to a return from convergence of price to intrinsic value.

- The discount rate is a rate used to find the present value of an investment.

- The internal rate of return (IRR) is the rate that equates the discounted cash flows to the current price. If markets are efficient, then the IRR represents the required return.

LOS 27.b

The equity risk premium is the return over the risk-free rate that investors require for holding equity securities. It can be used to determine the required return for specific stocks:

required return for stock j = risk-free return + β_j × equity risk premium

where:
β_j = the "beta" of stock j and serves as the adjustment for the level of systematic risk

A more general representation is:

required return for stock j = risk-free return + equity risk premium + other adjustments for j

A historical estimate of the equity risk premium consists of the difference between the mean return on a broad-based, equity-market index and the mean return on U.S. Treasury bills over a given time period.

Forward-looking or ex ante estimates use current information and expectations concerning economic and financial variables. The strength of this method is that it does not rely on an assumption of stationarity and is less subject to problems like survivorship bias.

There are three types of forward-looking estimates of the equity risk premium:

- Gordon growth model.

- Macroeconomic models, which use current information, but are only appropriate for developed countries where public equities represent a relatively large share of the economy.

- Survey estimates, which are easy to obtain, but can have a wide disparity between opinions.

The Gordon growth model can be used to estimate the equity risk premium based on expectational data:

> GGM equity risk premium = 1-year forecasted dividend yield on market index + consensus long-term earnings growth rate − long-term government bond yield

LOS 27.c

Models used to estimate the required return on equity:

- CAPM:

$$\text{required return on stock j} = \text{current risk-free return} + (\text{equity risk premium} \times \text{beta of j})$$

- Multifactor model:

$$\text{required return} = RF + (\text{risk premium})_1 + \ldots + (\text{risk premium})_n$$

- Fama-French model:

$$\text{required return of stock j} = RF + \beta_{mkt,j} \times (R_{mkt} - RF) + \beta_{SMB,j} \times (R_{small} - R_{big}) + \beta_{HML,j} \times (R_{HBM} - R_{LBM})$$

  where:
  $(R_{mkt} - RF)$ = market risk premium
  $(R_{small} - R_{big})$ = a small-cap risk premium
  $(R_{HBM} - R_{LBM})$ = a value risk premium

- The Pastor-Stambaugh model adds a liquidity factor to the Fama-French model.

- Macroeconomic multifactor models use factors associated with economic variables that would affect the cash flows and/or discount rate of companies.

- The build-up method is similar to the risk premium approach. One difference is that this approach does not use betas to adjust for the exposure to a factor. The bond yield plus risk premium method is a type of build-up method.

LOS 27.d

Beta estimation:

- A regression of the returns of a publicly traded company's stock returns on the returns of an index provides an estimate of beta. For forecasting required returns using the CAPM, an analyst may wish to adjust for beta drift using an equation such as:

adjusted beta = (2/3 × regression beta) + (1/3 × 1.0)

■ For thinly traded stocks and non-publicly traded companies, an analyst can estimate beta using a 4-step process: (1) identify publicly traded benchmark company, (2) estimate the beta of the benchmark company, (3) unlever the benchmark company's beta, and (4) relever the beta using the capital structure of the thinly traded/nonpublic company.

LOS 27.e

Each of the various methods of estimating the required return on an equity investment has strengths and weaknesses.

■ The CAPM is simple but may have low explanatory power.

■ Multifactor models have more explanatory power but are more complex and costly.

■ Build-up models are simple and can apply to closely held companies, but they typically use historical values as estimates that may or may not be relevant to the current situation.

LOS 27.f

In making estimates of required return in the international setting, an analyst should adjust the required return to reflect expectations for changes in exchange rates.

When dealing with emerging markets, a premium should be added to reflect the greater level of risk present. Two methods for estimating the size of the risk premium:

■ The country spread model uses a corresponding developed market as a benchmark and adds a premium for the emerging market risk. The premium can be estimated by taking the difference between the yield on bonds in the emerging market minus the yield of corresponding bonds in the developed market.

■ The country risk rating model estimates an equation for the equity risk premium for developed countries and then uses the equation and inputs associated with the emerging market to estimate the required return for the emerging market.

LOS 27.g

The weighted average cost of capital (WACC) is the required return averaged across all suppliers of capital (i.e., the debt and equity holders). The formula for WACC is:

WACC =

$$\frac{\text{market value of debt}}{\text{market value of debt and equity}} \times r_d \times (1 - \text{tax rate}) + \frac{\text{market value of equity}}{\text{market value of debt and equity}} \times r_e$$

where:
r_d and r_e = the required return on debt and equity, respectively

The term $(1 - \text{tax rate})$ is an adjustment to reflect the fact that, in most countries, corporations can take a tax deduction for interest payments. The tax rate should be the marginal rate.

LOS 27.h

The discount rate should correspond to the type of cash flow being discounted: cash flows to the entire firm at the WACC and those to equity at the required return on equity.

An analyst may wish to measure the present value of real cash flows, and a real discount rate should be used in that case. In most cases, however, analysts discount nominal cash flows with nominal discount rates.

ANSWER KEY FOR MODULE QUIZZES

Module Quiz 27.1

1. **A** In this case, the asset is underpriced. If market participants recognize the mispricing, the correction in price will generate additional return. (LOS 27.a)

2. **B** Required return for stock j = risk-free return + (β_j × equity risk premium). (LOS 27.b)

3. **C** The Gordon growth model equity risk premium (choice C) is appropriate for estimating the market risk premium. The geometric or arithmetic mean of the *excess* market returns (NOT the actual returns on the market itself, as in choice A) is also appropriate. (LOS 27.b)

4. **C** When using the historical method, the other choices are using the geometric average and a long-term bond rate. The geometric mean is less than the arithmetic average, which results in a lower risk premium. The long-term bond rate is usually greater than the Treasury bill rate, which also results in a lower risk premium. So, using the arithmetic average and the shorter-term Treasury bill rate would likely bias the equity risk premium estimate upwards. (LOS 27.b)

5. **A** The Pastor-Stambaugh model adds a liquidity factor to the Fama-French model. The average liquidity premium for equity should be zero. Less liquid assets should have a positive liquidity beta, and more liquid assets should have a negative beta. (LOS 27.c)

6. **C** For a public company, an analyst can usually compute beta by regressing the returns of the company's stock on the returns of an appropriate market index. This requires a choice of the index to use in the regression and the length and frequency of the sample. When making forecasts of the equity risk premium, some analysts recommend adjusting the beta for beta drift. Beta drift refers to the observed tendency of a computed beta to revert to a value of 1.0 over time. (LOS 27.d)

7. **C** Statement 1 is correct; exchange rates are an issue. Statement 2 is incorrect because it explains the country spread model. (LOS 27.f)

8. **B** The first step is to determine the percentage debt and equity in the capital structure. With a debt-to-equity ratio of 2 to 1, there is 2/3 = 66.7% debt and 1/3 = 33.3% equity. Then,

$$\text{WACC} = (w_e \times r_e) + [w_d \times r_d \times (1 - \text{tax rate})]$$
$$= (0.333 \times 10\%) + [0.667 \times 8\% \times (1 - 30\%)]$$
$$= 7.07\% \text{ (LOS 27.g)}$$

READING 28

Industry and Company Analysis

EXAM FOCUS

This topic review discusses estimation of inputs for the price multiples and DCF valuation models discussed in subsequent topic reviews. Be able to forecast income statement and balance sheet items given specific assumptions. Understand the different approaches to developing inputs, the influence of Porter's five forces on forecasts, and the concepts of inflection points and cannibalization factor.

MODULE 28.1: FORECASTING FINANCIAL STATEMENTS

Video covering this content is available online.

LOS 28.a: Compare top-down, bottom-up, and hybrid approaches for developing inputs to equity valuation models.

CFA® Program Curriculum: Volume 4, page 111

Bottom-up analysis starts with analysis of an individual company or its reportable segments. Revenue projections based on historical revenue growth or a company's new product introductions over the forecast horizon are considered bottom-up approaches.

Top-down analysis begins with expectations about a macroeconomic variable, often the expected growth rate of nominal GDP. Revenue projections that are derived from an estimate of GDP growth and an expected relationship between GDP growth and company sales are an example of a top-down approach.

A **hybrid** analysis incorporates elements of both top-down and bottom-up analysis. By using elements of both methods, a hybrid analysis can highlight any inconsistencies in assumptions between the top-down and bottom-up approaches. A hybrid analysis is the most common type.

LOS 28.b: Compare "growth relative to GDP growth" and "market growth and market share" approaches to forecasting revenue.

CFA® Program Curriculum: Volume 4, page 111

When forecasting revenue with a "**growth relative to GDP growth**" approach, the relationship between GDP and company sales could be modeled as "GDP growth plus x%" or "to increase at the growth rate of GDP times 1 + x%." For example, if we forecast that GDP will grow at 5% and we believe that our company's revenue will grow at a 20% faster rate, then our forecast of increase in company revenue would be 5% × (1 + 0.20) = 6%.

An alternative approach, the "**market growth and market share**" approach, begins with an estimate of industry sales (market growth), and then company revenue is estimated as a percentage of industry sales (market share). Market share times estimated industry sales provides the estimate of company revenues. Note that different business or geographic segments may have significantly different relationships between GDP growth and revenue growth. For example, a company's Chinese division may be forecast to grow at a lower rate than the Chinese GDP growth rate while the Japanese division may be forecast to grow at a rate higher than the Japanese GDP growth rate.

LOS 28.c: Evaluate whether economies of scale are present in an industry by analyzing operating margins and sales levels.

CFA® Program Curriculum: Volume 4, page 115

If the average cost of production decreases as industry sales increase, we say that the industry exhibits **economies of scale**. A company with economies of scale will have higher operating margins (because of lower average cost) as production volume increases, and sales volume and margins will tend to be positively correlated.

Economies of scale are observed when larger companies (i.e., companies with higher sales) in an industry have larger margins. One way to evaluate if economies of scale are present is to look at common-size income statements. Economies of scale in COGS are evidenced by lower COGS as a proportion of sales for larger companies. Similarly, lower SG&A as a proportion of sales for larger companies is evidence of economies of scale in SG&A.

©2018 Kaplan, Inc.

LOS 28.d: Forecast the following costs: cost of goods sold, selling general and administrative costs, financing costs, and income taxes.

CFA® Program Curriculum: Volume 4, page 118

Cost of Goods Sold (COGS)

Because cost of goods sold is closely related to revenue, future COGS is usually estimated as a percentage of future revenue:

forecast COGS = (historical COGS / revenue) × (estimate of future revenue)

or

forecast COGS = (1 − gross margin)(estimate of future revenue)

If a company's gross margin shows an increasing or decreasing trend (reflecting changes in business or market conditions), an analyst forecasting future gross margins should consider the probability that this trend might continue.

It can be worthwhile to examine the gross margins of a firm's competitors in the market as a check of the reasonableness of future gross margin estimates. In some cases, differences between firms' business models may be the underlying reason for differences in gross margins. However, when differences in firms' business models are accounted for, any remaining difference should be investigated.

A closer examination of the volume and price of a firm's inputs may improve the quality of a forecast of COGS, especially in the short run. For example, fuel costs can be volatile, and will have a significant impact on an airline's COGS, gross margins, and net margins. Firms with commodity-type inputs that cannot easily pass on higher input costs to their customers often hedge their future input costs by using forward contracts or other derivative securities. An analyst must be aware of the proportion of future input costs hedged in this way or, at a minimum, whether the firm has historically hedged these costs and over what horizon. It's important to note that a hedge works both ways: a hedge that protects the firm's gross margins from declining when input prices rise will also "protect" the firm's gross margins from increasing when input prices fall.

Estimates of a firm's COGS may also be improved by forecasting COGS for the firm's various product categories and business segments separately.

Selling General and Administrative Costs (SG&A)

Compared to COGS, SG&A operating expenses are less sensitive to changes in sales volume; SG&A's fixed cost component is generally greater than its variable cost component. Research and development (R&D) expenditures may be set by management, especially over a near-term horizon, and may be uncorrelated with revenues. Expenses for corporate headquarters, management salaries, and IT operations are other examples of costs that are more fixed than variable in nature. These costs tend to grow gradually as the firm grows rather than being driven by changes in firm sales in the current period.

Selling and distribution costs, on the other hand, may be more directly related to sales volumes, because it is likely that more salespeople will be hired to support higher firm sales. If a firm's financial statements break out the components of SG&A separately, the different components can be considered separately to improve the overall forecast of SG&A expenses. If segment information for SG&A is provided and different segments have significant differences in SG&A as a percentage of revenue, SG&A for each segment can be forecasted to produce better estimates of segment operating margins going forward.

Financing Cost

The financial structure of a company includes both debt and equity financing. The primary determinants of **gross interest expense** are the level of (gross) debt and market interest rates.

Companies may also have interest income from investments. This is especially true for banks and other financial companies, and less so for nonfinancial companies such as manufacturers. **Net debt** is *gross debt* minus cash, cash equivalents, and short-term securities. **Net interest expense** is gross interest expense minus interest income on cash and short-term debt securities.

Given these definitions, we can calculate the interest rates on both gross and net debt, as the following example illustrates.

EXAMPLE: Calculating gross and net interest rates

Atwood Inc., a small manufacturer of knobs and switches, provided the following information:

$ (000s)	20X1	20X2	Average*
Gross debt	3,200	3,600	3,400
Cash + ST securities	800	700	750
Net debt	2,400	2,900	2,650
Gross interest expense for 20X2		220	
Interest income for 20X2		8	
Net interest expense 20X2		212	

*Average values = (beginning value + ending value) / 2

Calculate Atwood's 20X2 interest expense on average gross and average net debt and the yield on average cash balances.

Answer:

Gross interest expense rate is 220 / 3,400 = 6.47%. Net interest expense rate is 212 / 2,650 = 8.00%. Yield on average cash balance is 8 / 750 = 1.07%.

Analysts should also use any planned debt issuance or retirement and the maturity structure of existing debt (disclosed in footnotes to financial statements) to improve the forecasts of future financing costs.

Income Tax Expense

There are three primary tax rates used in analysis:

1. The **statutory rate** is the percentage tax charged in the country where the firm is domiciled.

2. The **effective tax rate** is income tax expense as a percentage of pretax income on the income statement.

3. The **cash tax rate** is cash taxes paid as a percentage of pretax income.

Changes in deferred tax items account for the difference between income tax expense and cash taxes due. Recall that income tax expense is cash tax due plus changes in deferred tax liabilities minus changes in deferred tax assets.

Differences between the statutory and effective tax rates can arise for a variety of reasons. A reconciliation of these two rates is contained in the footnotes to financial statements and can provide information about one-time events as well as tax rates for the various tax jurisdictions in which the firm operates. The statutory and effective tax rates may differ because there are expenses recognized in the income statement that are not deductible for tax purposes (a permanent difference). The effective tax rate for a corporation that has taxable income in several countries will be a weighted average of the effective tax rates in each country (where the weights equal the proportion of taxable income from each country). Note that if a company has relatively higher (lower) earnings growth in a high tax country, its effective tax rate will increase (decrease).

An analyst should pay special attention to estimates of tax rates for companies that consistently report an effective tax rate that is less than the statutory rate (or consistently less than that of comparable peer companies).

LOS 28.e: Describe approaches to balance sheet modeling.

CFA® Program Curriculum: Volume 4, page 132

When building a forecast model, many balance sheet items flow from the forecasted income statement items. Net income less dividends declared will flow through to retained earnings. Working capital items can be forecast based on their historical relationship with income statement items.

One of the measures of inventory management is inventory turnover. The forecasted annual COGS divided by the inventory turnover ratio can be used to forecast an inventory value for the balance sheet that is consistent with income statement projections of COGS.

"Days sales outstanding," a measure of accounts receivable management, can be used to forecast accounts receivable for the balance sheet:

projected accounts receivable = (days sales outstanding) × (forecasted sales/365)

Estimates derived in this way will preserve working capital items' relationship with income statement items, and absent any complicating factors, working capital items will increase at the same rate as revenues.

Property, plant, and equipment (PP&E) on the balance sheet is determined by depreciation and capital expenditures (capex). One approach to estimating PP&E is to assume it will be equal to its historical average proportion of sales so that PP&E will grow at the same rate as revenue. However, by having an understanding of the company's operations and future plans and incorporating this information into her model, an analyst can make more accurate projections of a company's future capital needs. Forecasts may also be improved by analyzing **capital expenditures for maintenance** separately from **capital expenditures for growth**. Historical depreciation should be increased by the inflation rate when estimating capital expenditure for maintenance because replacement cost can be expected to increase with inflation.

Once the forecasted financial statements are constructed, an analyst should perform sensitivity analysis for individual assumptions, or perform analyses with alternative assumptions (scenario analysis), to examine the sensitivity of net income to changes in assumptions.

Video covering this content is available online.

MODULE 28.2: COMPETITIVE ANALYSIS AND GROWTH RATE

LOS 28.f: Describe the relationship between return on invested capital and competitive advantage.

CFA® Program Curriculum: Volume 4, page 133

Once financial projections are completed, the **return on invested capital (ROIC)** can be calculated. While analysts use varying definitions of ROIC, it can be thought of as net operating profit adjusted for taxes (NOPLAT) divided by invested capital (operating assets minus operating liabilities). ROIC is a return to both equity and debt and is preferable to return on equity (ROE) in some contexts because it allows comparisons across firms with different capital structures. Firms with higher ROIC (relative to their peers) are likely exploiting some **competitive advantage** in the production and/or sale of their products.

A related measure, **return on capital employed**, is similar to ROIC but uses pretax operating earnings in the numerator to facilitate comparison between companies that face different tax rates.

LOS 28.g: Explain how competitive factors affect prices and costs.

LOS 28.h: Judge the competitive position of a company based on a Porter's five forces analysis.

CFA® Program Curriculum: Volume 4, page 136

The competitive environment that a firm operates in and how successful it is in that environment are very important determinants of the firm's future financial results. There are no formulas for, or clear rules about, how a firm's competitive environment affects its future revenue and costs, but a firm's future competitive success is possibly the most important factor in determining future revenue and profitability. Recall from a previous topic review the analysis of industry competition based on **Porter's five forces.** Let's review how these five industry characteristics may affect future financial results and, therefore, financial forecasts.

1. Companies have less (more) pricing power when the **threat of substitute products** is high (low) and switching costs are low (high).

2. Companies have less (more) pricing power when the **intensity of industry rivalry** is high (low). Pricing power is low when industry concentration is less, when fixed costs and exit barriers are high, when industry growth is slow or negative, and when products are not differentiated to a significant degree.

3. Company prospects for earnings growth are lower when the **bargaining power of suppliers** is high. If suppliers are few, they may be able to extract a larger portion of any value added.

4. Companies have less pricing power when the **bargaining power of customers** is higher, especially in a circumstance where a small number of customers are responsible for a large proportion of a firm's sales and also when switching costs are low.

5. Companies have more pricing power and better prospects for earnings growth when the **threat of new entrants** is low. Significant barriers to entry into an industry make it possible for existing companies to maintain high returns on invested capital.

LOS 28.i: Explain how to forecast industry and company sales and costs when they are subject to price inflation or deflation.

CFA® Program Curriculum: Volume 4, page 145

Input costs can be significant in many industries. The cost of jet fuel in the airline industry, the cost of grains to cereal and baking companies, and the cost of coffee beans to coffee shops are all variable. Changes in these costs can significantly affect earnings.

Companies with commodity-type inputs can hedge their exposure to changes in input prices through derivatives or, more simply, fixed-price contracts for future delivery. Such hedging will reduce the effect of short-term changes in input prices and increase the time until longer-term price changes affect costs and earnings. Companies that are vertically integrated (and are in effect their own suppliers) will be less subject to the effects of variations in input prices.

For a company that neither hedges input price exposure nor is vertically integrated, the issue for the analyst is to determine how rapidly, and to what extent, the increase in costs can be passed on to customers, as well as the expected effect of price increases on sales volume and sales revenue.

An analyst should monitor a company's production costs by product category and geographic location with a focus on the significant factors that affect input prices, such as weather, governmental regulation and taxation, tariffs, and the characteristics of input markets. It may be the case that a firm can reduce the impact of an increase in an input price by switching to a substitute input; for example, rising oil prices may lead power generation firms to switch from oil to natural gas.

When estimating the effects of an increase in input prices, an analyst must make assumptions about the company's pricing strategy and the effects of price increases on unit sales. When increases in input costs are thought to be temporary, a company may cut other costs (e.g., advertising expense) in order to preserve operating margins. This strategy is, however, not appropriate for long-term increases in input costs.

The effects of increasing a product's price depend on the product's elasticity of demand. For most firms, product demand is relatively elastic. With elastic demand, the percentage reduction in unit sales is greater than the percentage increase in price, and a price increase will decrease total sales revenue. If the dollar amount of the increase in cost per unit is added to product price and unit sales do not decrease (this is unlikely), the amount of operating profit is unchanged but gross margins, operating margins, and net margins will fall.

EXAMPLE: Effect of price inflation on gross profits, gross margins, and operating margins

Alfredo, Inc., sells a specialized network component. The firm's income statement for the past year is given below.

Alfredo, Inc., Income Statement for the Year Ended 20X1

Revenues	1,000 @ $100	$ 100,000
COGS	1,000 @ $40	$ 40,000
Gross profit		$ 60,000
SG&A		$ 30,000
Operating profit		$ 30,000

For 20X2, the input costs (COGS) will increase by $5 per unit.

1. Calculate the gross margin and operating margin for Alfredo, Inc., for 20X1.

2. Calculate the 20X2 gross margin and operating margin assuming that the:

   a. Entire increase in input cost is passed on to the customers through an equal increase in selling price. The number of units sold is not affected.

   b. Selling price is increased by 5% and the number of units sold decreases by 5%.

   c. Selling price is increased by 5% and the number of units sold decreases by 10%.

Answer:

1. gross margin = gross profit / sales = $60,000 / $100,000 = 60%

   operating margin = operating profit / sales = $30,000 / $100,000 = 30%

2.

a. 20X2, given an increase in unit price by $5 and no change in units sold:

Revenues	1,000 units @ $105	$	105,000
COGS	1,000 units @ $45	$	45,000
Gross profit		$	60,000
SG&A		$	30,000
Operating profit		$	30,000
Gross margin		57%	
Operating margin		29%	

gross margin = gross profit / sales = $60,000 / $105,000 = 57%

operating margin = operating profit / sales = $30,000 / $105,000 = 29%

b. 20X2, given an increase in unit price by $5 and a decrease of 50 in units sold:

Revenues	950 units @ $105	$	99,750
COGS	950 units @ $45	$	42,750
Gross profit		$	57,000
SG&A		$	30,000
Operating profit		$	27,000
Gross margin		57%	
Operating margin		27%	

gross margin = gross profit / sales = $57,000 / $99,750 = 57%

operating margin = operating profit / sales = $27,000 / $99,750 = 27%

c. 20X2, given an increase in unit price by $5 and a decrease of 100 in units sold:

Revenues	900 units @ $105	$	94,500
COGS	900 units @ $45	$	40,500
Gross profit		$	54,000
SG&A		$	30,000
Operating profit		$	24,000
Gross margin		57%	
Operating margin		25%	

gross margin = gross profit / sales = $54,000 / $94,500 = 57%

operating margin = operating profit / sales = $24,000 / $94,500 = 25%

The elasticity of demand is most affected by the availability of substitute products. In a competitive industry, the pricing decisions of other firms in the industry can affect the market shares of all firms in an industry. A company that is the first to increase prices in response to increased costs will experience a greater decrease in unit sales than a company that increases prices after other firms have already done so. A firm may decide to delay increasing prices in order to gain market share when other firms increase prices in response to increased costs. Firms that are too quick to increase prices will experience declining sales volumes, though firms that are slow to increase prices will experience declining gross margins.

An analyst must also understand a company's hedging activities and vertical integration, if any, to guide assumptions about a subject company's response to increasing costs and the effect of price increase on sales volume, total revenue, and profit margins. As always, different business and geographic segments should be considered separately when appropriate, and scenario and/or sensitivity analysis should be conducted.

LOS 28.j: Evaluate the effects of technological developments on demand, selling prices, costs, and margins.

CFA® Program Curriculum: Volume 4, page 153

Some advances in technology decrease costs of production, which will increase profit margins (at least for early adopters), and, over time, increase industry supply and unit sales as well.

Other advances in technology will result in either improved substitutes or wholly new products. The introduction of tablets created a substitute for desktop and laptop computers that did not previously exist. Some technological advances can disrupt not only markets but entire industries, as digital photography has done in the camera and film industries.

One way for an analyst to model the introduction of new substitutes for a company's products is to estimate a *cannibalization factor*, which is the percentage of new product sales that will replace existing product sales.

$$\text{cannibalization rate} = \frac{\text{new product sales that } \textit{replace} \text{ existing product sales}}{\text{total new product sales}}$$

This cannibalization factor can be different for different sales channels and is likely to be lower for business customers than for direct purchases by consumers.

As always, scenario or sensitivity analysis using a variety of scenarios encompassing new product introductions can be informative.

> **EXAMPLE: Cannibalization**
>
> Alpha, Inc., manufactures LED lightbulbs for sale to businesses as well as to households. Seventy-five percent of Alpha's unit sales are to business customers. Technological advances have enabled bulb manufacturers to produce a new bulb that is more energy efficient, and Alpha is planning to introduce a bulb next year that uses this new technology. Projected sales for the new bulb are shown below:
>
> | Market | Units |
> |---|---|
> | Businesses | 87,000 |
> | Households | 11,000 |
> | **Total units** | **98,000** |

Calculate the lost unit sales of current product due to cannibalization, assuming a cannibalization factor of 50% for businesses and 20% for households.

Answer:

Cannibalization in business market segment = 87,000 × 0.50 = 43,500 units.
Cannibalization in household market segment = 11,000 × 0.20 = 2,200 units.
Total lost unit sales = 45,700 units.

LOS 28.k: Explain considerations in the choice of an explicit forecast horizon.

CFA® Program Curriculum: Volume 4, page 163

For a buy-side analyst, the appropriate forecast horizon may simply be the expected holding period for a stock. For example, for a portfolio with a 25% annual turnover, the average holding period of a stock is 4 years, so 4 years may be the most appropriate forecast horizon. Hence, the forecast horizon should be considered in conjunction with the investment strategy for which the stock is being considered.

Highly cyclical companies present difficulties when choosing a forecast horizon. The horizon should be long enough that the effects of the current phase of the economic cycle are not driving above-trend or below-trend earnings effects. The forecast horizon should be long enough to include the middle of a business cycle so the analyst's forecast includes mid-cycle level of sales and profits. **Normalized earnings** are expected mid-cycle earnings or, alternatively, expected earnings when the current (temporary) effects of events or cyclicality are no longer affecting earnings.

When there are recent impactful events, such as acquisitions, mergers, or restructurings, these events should be considered temporary, and the forecast horizon should be long enough that the perceived benefits of such events can be realized (or not).

It may also be the case that the forecast horizon is dictated by the analyst's manager.

LOS 28.l: Explain an analyst's choices in developing projections beyond the short-term forecast horizon.

CFA® Program Curriculum: Volume 4, page 163

For earnings projections beyond the short term, one method of forecasting future financial results is to assume that a trend growth rate of revenue over the previous cycle will continue. Pro forma financial results can be estimated based on the projection of each future period's revenue.

An analyst will typically value a stock using the earnings or some measure of cash flow over a forecast period, along with the stock's *terminal value* at the end of the forecast horizon. This terminal value is usually estimated using either a relative valuation (i.e., price multiple) approach or a discounted cash flow approach.

When using a multiples approach, an analyst must ensure that the multiple used is consistent with the estimate of the company's growth rate and required rate of return. Using the average P/E ratio for the company over the last 10 years, for example, presupposes that the growth in earnings and required rate of return of the stock will be, on average, the same in the future as over the previous 10 years.

When using a discounted cash flow approach to estimate the terminal value, two key inputs are a cash flow or earnings measure and an expected future growth rate. The expected earnings or cash flow should be normalized to a mid-cycle value that is not affected by temporary initiatives and events. Because the terminal value is calculated as the present value of a perpetuity, small changes in the estimated (perpetual) growth rate of future earnings or cash flows can have large effects on estimated terminal values and, hence, the current stock value. Assuming that the growth in future profitability will be the same as average profitability growth in the past may not be justified. A difficult part of an analyst's job is recognizing **inflection points**—those instances when the future will not be like the past, due to change in a company's or an industry's competitive environment or to changes in the overall economy.

Inflection points occur due to changes in:

■ Overall economic environment.

■ Business cycle stage.

■ Government regulations.

■ Technology.

LOS 28.m: Demonstrate the development of a sales-based pro forma company model.

CFA® Program Curriculum: Volume 4, page 170

Sales-based pro forma financial statements are the end result of all of the assumptions and estimates developed using the techniques we have covered so far. Rather than repeat all of those points here, we present the steps in producing pro forma statements, leaving aside the choice of estimation method and the complexities of estimating the important financial statement items.

Do not forget the usual caveats. Use segment information and create segment forecasts when the subject company has business or geographical segments that differ from each other in important respects. Use sensitivity analysis or scenario analysis to estimate a range of possible outcomes and their probabilities when appropriate.

Steps in developing a sales-based pro forma model:

1. Estimate revenue growth and future expected revenue (using market growth plus market share, trend growth rate, or growth relative to GDP growth).

2. Estimate COGS (based on a percentage of sales, or on a more detailed method based on business strategy or competitive environment).

3. Estimate SG&A (as either fixed, growing with revenue, or using some other estimation technique).

4. Estimate financing costs (using interest rates, debt levels, and the effects of any large anticipated increases or decreases in capital expenditures or anticipated changes in financial structure).

5. Estimate income tax expense and cash taxes (using historical effective rates and trends, segment information for different tax jurisdictions, and anticipated growth in high- and low-tax segments).

6. Estimate cash taxes, taking into account changes in deferred tax items.

7. Model the balance sheet based on items that flow from the income statement [working capital accounts (i.e., accounts receivable, accounts payable, and inventory)].

8. Use depreciation and capital expenditures (for maintenance and for growth) to estimate capital expenditures and net PP&E for the balance sheet.

9. Use the completed pro forma income statement and balance sheet to construct a pro forma cash flow statement.

Clearly, estimation methods can be simple (as when we modeled COGS as a constant percentage of sales) or more complex (as when we forecast the prices of significant productive inputs based on the competitive environment of input markets). An analyst must always decide when additional or more complex analysis is warranted and when additional complexity in the estimation method provides real benefits in terms of improved forecasts and value estimates.

MODULE QUIZ 28.1, 28.2
Use the following information to answer Questions 1 through 6.

Jane Larsted, CFA, works as an equity analyst for Rivington Capital where she heads up a team of three analysts covering the retail sector. Larsted is currently reviewing forecasts made by her team for two home improvement retailers in the United States.

The first company, Retail, Inc., has a dominant market share. The second, Midsize, Inc., has a significantly smaller share of the market. Financial results for the most recent three years for Retail, Inc., and Midsize, Inc., are shown in Exhibit 2.

Larsted believes in allowing her team to reach a group conclusion, and she always starts by letting each member of the team choose their own method of forecasting. The results are then discussed in a team meeting where the team arrives at a common approach.

Larsted asked the team to state the assumptions used to forecast revenues. The responses are shown in Exhibit 1.

Exhibit 1: Assumptions Used for Modeling Revenue

E. Meyers

"I have assumed that the U.S. economy will expand sufficiently to post output growth in nominal terms of 2% for the coming year. Retail, Inc., is positioned in the home improvement sector, which is currently enjoying an upswing due to the recent strength of the housing sector. My model assumes that Retail, Inc., will see revenue growth that is 10% faster than U.S. output growth."

J. Conway

"My model used to forecast the revenue of Retail, Inc., assumes that the company will be able to increase its market share for next year from the current level of 35% to 38%. This is a realistic assumption given the number of new Retail, Inc., stores coming online and the demise of a significant competitor. However, I have assumed that housing growth will falter, and that the size of the home improvement retail sector will decrease from a total revenue figure of $40 billion this year to $38 billion for the forecast period."

E. Dominguez

"Revenue growth includes the following assumptions:
- U.S. GDP will grow at a long-term real rate of 1% per year into the foreseeable future.

- Retail Inc. has seen an average revenue growth rate of 4% per year for the last five years. I expect this growth rate to decline linearly over the next five years until it is equal to the long-term U.S. GDP growth rate.

- Long-term inflation is expected to be 2%."

Exhibit 2: Financial Results for Retail, Inc., and Midsize, Inc.

Retail, Inc.

	2017 ($ million)	2018 ($ million)	2019 ($ million)
Revenue	14,020	14,585	15,091
Cost of goods sold	9,255	9,635	9,966
Selling, general, administrative	3,433	3,559	3,645
Operating income	1,332	1,391	1,480

Midsize, Inc.

	2017 ($ million)	2018 ($ million)	2019 ($ million)
Revenue	8,040	8,281	8,488
Cost of goods sold	5,548	5,715	5,857
Selling, general, administrative	1,932	1,986	2,033
Operating income	560	580	598

Larsted is concerned that the U.S. tax code may change in the near future. She has asked her team to prepare for the meeting by analyzing potential effects of a change in tax rules. Larsted provides selected information for Retail, Inc., as shown in Exhibit 3.

Exhibit 3: Tax Rate for Retail, Inc.

Retail, Inc.

	2019 ($ million)
Profit before tax	1,480
Effective tax rate	28%

Larsted wants to know the likely effect on the cash tax rate next year if, in the current period, the tax authorities in the United States increase the allowance for depreciation expense. Larsted has asked the team to assume the following:

1. The result would be a 25% reduction in the amount of taxes charged in the current period and an increase by the same amount in the following period. This would be repeated each year in the future.

2. The profit before tax increases by 10% next year.

Larsted also intends to forecast the amount of debt that would be shown on Retail, Inc.'s, balance sheet for the next three years. For this task, she makes the assumptions shown in Exhibit 4.

Exhibit 4: Balance Sheet Debt Assumptions

■ Retail, Inc., will continue to maintain a constant debt-to-equity ratio.

■ Due to excess cash balances, the company has announced a policy of paying out 100% of net income for the year as dividends for each of the next five years. There will be no share repurchases.

■ The company expects to see no gains or losses in other comprehensive income for the next three years.

■ Profits are expected to be positive and to increase by 5% per year for the next five years.

1. Which of the following statements regarding the three team members' assumptions shown in Exhibit 1 is *most accurate*?
   A. Myers and Conway are using a top-down approach, while Dominguez is using a bottom-up approach.
   B. Conway is using a top-down approach, and Myers is using a bottom-up approach.
   C. No member of the team is using a strictly bottom-up approach.

2. Which of the following statements regarding the three analyst's models in Exhibit 1 is *most accurate*?
   A. The analyst using the "growth relative to GDP growth" approach is predicting a higher growth rate in Retail, Inc.'s, revenue than the analyst using the "market growth and market share" approach.
   B. The analyst using the "growth relative to GDP growth" approach is predicting a lower growth rate in Retail, Inc.'s, revenue than the analyst using the "market growth and market share" approach.
   C. The analyst using the "growth relative to GDP growth" approach is predicting a growth rate in Retail, Inc.'s, revenue that is more than 5% higher than the analyst using the "market growth and market share" approach.

3. Using the financial results for 2019 shown in Exhibit 2, it would be *most appropriate* for Larsted to conclude that economies of scale for firms in the home improvements retail sector:
   A. do not exist.
   B. exist and are realized in cost of goods sold only.
   C. exist and are realized in both cost of goods sold and SG&A.

4. Using the information in Exhibit 3 and Larsted's two assumptions, the cash tax rate should be *closest* to:
   A. 21% in 2019 and 27% in 2020.
   B. 21% in 2019 and subsequent years.
   C. 26% in 2019 and 27% in subsequent years.

5. Under the assumptions given in Exhibit 4, Retail, Inc.'s, level of debt on the balance sheet is *most likely* to:
   A. increase over the next three years.
   B. remain constant over the next three years.
   C. decrease over the next three years.

6. Which of the following statements regarding return on invested capital is *most accurate*?
   A. A company will gain a competitive advantage if it maintains high levels of invested capital by investing in intangible assets.
   B. The ownership of a patent on a successful product will often lead to high and persistent levels of return on invested capital.
   C. High and persistent levels of return on invested capital are usually an indication that a company has a high percentage of very new assets on its balance sheet.

Use the following information to answer Questions 7 through 13.

Jorge Stanza, CFA, is a sell-side equity analyst who covers Entertaining Kids, Inc., (ENK), a large retailer of children's toys based in the United States. Stanza is reviewing the ENK annual report that has just been released. At the moment, Stanza has a buy recommendation on the company, but the impressive performance of some of ENK's competitors and a recent product recall have led him to revisit his recommendation in depth.

The product recall involved an inflatable swimming pool that ENK manufactures and sells for children 4 years and over. Unfortunately, a number of ENK customers have recently reported that an electrical problem in the pump caused injury to their children. After several such incidents in the industry in the past months, it is expected that the government will step in to impose strict regulation covering the manufacturing of all children's toys in that category.

Stanza wants to build this possibility into his five forces competitive analysis model by adding government involvement as a sixth force.

Stanza's current analysis using the five forces model is shown in Exhibit 1.

Exhibit 1: ENK Five Forces Analysis

Force	Threat to Profitability	Factors
Threat of substitutes	Medium	ENK sells a wide range of toys from sporting goods to electronics. There has been a growing trend for customers to prefer traditional hand-crafted toys made and sold by independent retailers.
Rivalry	Low	ENK has a 55% share of the market and enjoys economies of scale that give it significant cost advantages over competitors.
Bargaining power of suppliers	Low	Inputs into the vast majority of products are widely available. Suppliers of game consoles are also reliant on ENK to distribute their product.
Bargaining power of buyers	Low	ENK sells directly to consumers who represent a highly fragmented group.
Threat of new entrants	High	ENK has established a large distribution network, and the large costs of replicating such a network means the barriers to entry are high.

Another significant concern is the near term threat of increased inflation. Stanza fears that if ENK's input costs rise due to a general rise in prices, ENK will not be able to pass on the full increase in input costs to customers. Extreme weather events have already had an adverse effect on food prices, leaving families with less discretionary income to spend on children's toys.

Exhibit 2 shows ENK's current gross margin and two possible scenarios if inflation of 5% is realized next year.

Exhibit 2: Gross Margin

Entertaining Kids, Inc.	2019 ($ million)
Revenue	13,201
Cost of goods sold	8,755
Gross profit	4,446
Gross margin	33.7%

Scenarios	Scenario 1	Scenario 2
Price increase for revenues	3%	5%
Volume growth	2%	0%
Input cost increase	5%	5%

Stanza is also concerned about a new game console that was released in the final quarter of this year. Although ENK has an exclusive agreement with the maker of the new console, the XTF 2500, Stanza is concerned that the sale of the new console will reduce sales of other consoles that ENK currently sells. A significant segment of ENK's revenue is currently generated by sales of consoles to both individual customers and also to assisted living facilities (ALFs) that use the consoles as part of their rehabilitation program.

Exhibit 3: Current Year Sales Figures

	2019 ($ million)
Existing console	
Individuals	2,640
ALFs	400
Total	3,040
XTF 2500	
Individuals	45
ALFs	0
Total	45

Exhibit 4: Forecasting Assumptions

1. Individual sales of the XTF 2500 will increase by 375% next year, but the new console will not be adopted by ALFs.
2. Sales of existing consoles to ALFs will remain static.
3. Sales of existing consoles to individuals will shrink by 25% as a result of the XTF 2500.

The new console is being billed as a game changer, coming in at a price point not much higher than existing consoles but with significantly more features. Stanza has analyzed this year's sales of existing and new console using the data shown in Exhibit 3 and intends to forecast next year's sales using the assumptions listed in Exhibit 4.

Stanza based his forecasts on information obtained from a colleague, Jon Hoombert, who covers Vau Soft, the maker of the XTF 2500. Hoombert is convinced that the introduction of the XTF 2500 to the market represents an inflection point in the home console industry. As a result, he is not using his usual approach of using historic price multiples to predict the terminal value of companies in the sector. Hoombert states that he has seen three factors in recent times that have led to inflection points:
1. The addition of internet capabilities to consoles is causing a rapid shift away from PC gaming.
2. Increased competition in the sector has led to a gradual reduction in the price of gaming consoles.
3. With the introduction of the XTF 2500, which offers advanced computing capabilities at a relatively low price, analyst estimates suggests that Vau Soft's market share will double.

7. Stanza's intended treatment of government intervention in his competitive analysis model is:
   A. consistent with Porter's five forces approach.
   B. inconsistent with Porter's five forces approach, as government involvement should always be considered a reduction in the threat of new entrants.
   C. inconsistent with Porter's five forces approach, as Stanza should analyze how government involvement affects all of the five forces.

8. Stanza is *most likely* wrong regarding the threat to profitability resulting from the:
   A. bargaining power of customers, because a highly fragmented group (i.e., a large number of low-volume customers) complicates pricing strategy, which implies a high threat to profitability.
   B. threat of new entrants, as the high costs of setting up a distribution network and new stores means there is a low threat to profitability.
   C. bargaining power of suppliers, as the reliance of console suppliers on ENK gives ENK a high level of bargaining power.

9. Which of the following statements regarding the inflation scenarios in Exhibit 2 is *most accurate*?
   A. Scenario 1 would lead to an increase in gross profit but a decrease in gross margin.
   B. Both scenarios would lead to an unchanged gross margin.
   C. Only scenario 2 would leave gross profit unchanged.

10. Using the information in Exhibit 3 and 4, total estimated revenue from consoles next year should be *closest* to:
    A. $2,494 million.
    B. $2,548 million.
    C. $2,594 million.

11. Regarding the choice of forecast horizon for a discounted cash flow model, which of the following statements is *least accurate*? The forecast horizon:
    A. for a highly cyclical company should be long enough to allow the company to reach a mid-cycle level of sales and profitability.
    B. should be independent of the investment strategy for which the stock is being considered.
    C. should be long enough to allow the full benefits from an acquisition to be reflected in the financial statements.

12. Which of the three reasons suggested by Hoombert is *least likely* to be the cause of an inflection point?
    A. Reason 1.
    B. Reason 2.
    C. Reason 3.

13. Which of the following statements about building a model using pro forma financial statements is *least accurate*?
    A. The cash flow forecast can be automatically generated using the forecasted balance sheet and income statement.
    B. Depreciation is typically forecasted as a decreasing percentage of sales to reflect the ageing assets.
    C. Working capital is often forecasted as a constant percentage of sales.

KEY CONCEPTS

LOS 28.a

Bottom-up analysis starts with analysis of an individual company or reportable segments of a company. Top-down analysis begins with expectations about a macroeconomic variable, often the expected growth rate of nominal GDP. A hybrid analysis incorporates elements of both top-down and bottom-up analysis.

LOS 28.b

When forecasting revenue with a "growth relative to GDP growth" approach, the relationship between GDP and company sales is estimated, and then company sales growth is forecast based on an estimate for future GDP growth.

The "market growth and market share" approach begins with an estimate of industry sales (market growth), and then company sales are estimated as a percentage (market share) of industry sales. Forecast revenue then equals the forecasted market size multiplied by the forecasted market share.

LOS 28.c

A company with economies of scale will have lower costs and higher operating margins as production volume increases, and should exhibit positive correlation between sales volume and margins.

LOS 28.d

COGS is primarily a variable cost and is often modeled as a percentage of estimated future revenue. Expectations of changes in input prices can be used to improve COGS estimates.

The R&D and corporate overhead components of SG&A are likely to be stable over the short term, while selling and distribution costs will tend to increase with increases in sales.

The primary determinants of **gross interest expense** are the amount of debt outstanding (gross debt) and interest rates. **Net debt** is gross debt minus cash, cash equivalents, and short-term securities. **Net interest expense** is gross interest expense minus interest income on cash and short-term debt securities owned.

The expected effective tax rate times the forecasted pretax income provides a forecast of income tax expense. Any expected change in the future effective tax rate should be included in the analysis.

LOS 28.e

Some items on a pro forma balance sheet, such as retained earnings, flow from forecasted income statement items. Net income less dividends declared will flow through to retained earnings. Working capital items can be forecast based on turnover ratios. In a simple case, items such as inventory, receivables, and payables will all increase proportionately to revenues.

Property, plant and equipment (PP&E) on the balance sheet is determined by depreciation and capital expenditures (capex) and may be improved by analyzing **capital expenditures for maintenance** separately from **capital expenditures for growth**. Historical depreciation should be increased by the inflation rate when estimating capital expenditure for maintenance because replacement costs can be expected to increase.

LOS 28.f

While analysts use varying definitions of ROIC, it can be thought of as net operating earnings adjusted for taxes (NOPLAT), divided by invested capital (operating assets minus operating liabilities), and is a return to both equity and debt. Firms with ROIC consistently higher than those of peer companies are likely exploiting some **competitive advantage** in the production and sale of their products.

LOS 28.g

There are no formulas or clear rules on how a firm's competitive environment affects its future revenue and costs, but expectations of a firm's future competitive success are important factors in forecasting future revenue and financial statements.

LOS 28.h

1. Companies have less (more) pricing power when the **threat of substitute products** is high (low) and switching costs are low (high).

2. Companies have less (more) pricing power when the **intensity of industry rivalry** is high (low).

3. Company prospects for earnings growth are lower when the **bargaining power of suppliers** is high. If suppliers are few, these suppliers may be able to extract a larger portion of any increase in profits.

4. Companies have less pricing power when the **bargaining power of customers** is high, especially in a circumstance where a small number of customers are responsible for a large proportion of a firm's sales and when switching costs are low.

5. Companies have more pricing power and better prospects for earnings growth when the **threat of new entrants** is low. Significant barriers to entry into an industry make it possible for existing companies to maintain high returns on invested capital.

LOS 28.i

Increases in input costs will increase COGS unless the company has hedged the risk of input price increases with derivatives or contracts for future delivery. Vertically integrated companies are likely to be less affected by increasing input costs. The effect on sales of increasing product prices to reflect higher COGS will depend on the elasticity of demand for the products, and on the timing and amount of competitors' price increases.

LOS 28.j

Some advances in technology decrease costs of production, which will increase profit margins, at least for early adopters.

Other advances in technology will result in either improved substitutes or wholly new products. One way for an analyst to model the introduction of new substitutes for a company's products is to estimate a cannibalization factor, the percentage of a new product's sales that are stolen from an existing product's sales.

LOS 28.k

For a buy-side analyst, the appropriate forecast horizon to use may simply be the expected holding period for a stock.

For highly cyclical companies, the forecast horizon should include the middle of a cycle so that the analyst can forecast **normalized earnings** (i.e., expected mid-cycle earnings).

When there have been recent impactful events, such as acquisitions, mergers, or restructurings, these events should be considered temporary, and the forecast horizon should be long enough that the perceived benefits of such events can be realized.

It may be the case that the forecast horizon to use is dictated by the analyst's manager.

LOS 28.l

Earnings projections over a forecast period beyond the short term are often based on the historical average growth rate of revenue over the previous economic cycle.

An analyst will typically estimate a terminal value for a stock at the end of the forecast horizon, using either a price multiple or a discounted cash flow approach. Using a P/E multiple approach, the estimated earnings in the final forecast period are multiplied by a company's historical average P/E (possibly adjusted for the phase of the business cycle).

Because the terminal value using the discounted cash flow approach is calculated as the present value of a perpetuity, small changes in the estimated (perpetual) growth rate of future profits or cash flows can have large effects on the estimates of the terminal value and thus the current stock value.

LOS 28.m

The development of sales-based pro forma financial statements includes the following steps:

1. Estimate revenue growth and future expected revenue.
2. Estimate COGS.
3. Estimate SG&A.
4. Estimate financing costs.
5. Estimate income tax expense and cash taxes, taking into account changes in deferred tax items.

6. Model the balance sheet based on items that flow from the income statement and estimates for important working capital accounts.

7. Use historical depreciation and capital expenditures to estimate future capital expenditures and net PP&E for the balance sheet.

8. Use the completed pro forma income statement and balance sheet to construct a pro forma cash flow statement.

ANSWER KEY FOR MODULE QUIZZES

Module Quiz 28.1, 28.2

1. **C** Myers is using a "growth relative to GDP growth" approach, which is top-down. Conway is using a market growth and market share approach, which is also top-down. Dominguez is using both a "growth relative to GDP" and historic data for Retail Inc., which is a hybrid approach. (Module 28.1, LOS 28.b)

2. **B** Myers is using the "growth relative to GDP growth" approach.

   Growth rate predicted:

GDP growth	2%
Revenue growth	2% × 1.10 = **2.2%**

   Conway is using the "market growth and market share" approach.

   Growth rate predicted:

Revenue this year	40bn × 35% =14bn
Revenue next year	38bn × 38% = 14.44bn
Growth rate	0.44 / 14 = **3.1%**

   (Module 28.1, LOS 28.b)

3. **B**

Retail, Inc., operating margin 2019	1,480/15,091	= 9.8%
Midsize, Inc., operating margin 2019	598/8,488	= 7.0%

   Retail, Inc., is a bigger firm and has a larger operating margin, suggesting that economies of scale are more likely to exist.

Retail COGS as a % of Revenue 2019	9,966/15,091	= 66%
Midsize COGS as a % of Revenue 2019	5,857/8,488	= 69%

Retail SG&A as a % of Revenue 2019	3,645/15,091	= 24%
Midsize SG&A as a % of Revenue 2019	2,033/8,488	= 24%

   Analysis of the expense ratios shows that the economies of scale are realized in COGS rather than in SG&A. (Module 28.2, LOS 28.c)

4. **A** Retail, Inc.

	2019 ($ million)	2020 ($ million)
Profit before tax	1,480	1,628
Tax (@ 28%)	414.4	455.8
Tax reduction (25%)	(103.6)	(113.95)
Postponed tax		103.6
Total tax	310.8	445.45
Cash tax rate	21%	27.4%

(Module 28.1, LOS 28.d)

5. **B** Given a constant debt-to-equity ratio, the level of debt will remain constant if the level of equity remains constant. Given that Retail, Inc., intends to pay out all net income as dividends over the period, and there are no share repurchases or gains and losses in other comprehensive income, Retail, Inc.'s, equity will remain constant. (Module 28.1, LOS 28.e)

6. **B** Owning a successful patent will give a company a competitive advantage, which, in turn, is likely to lead to a high and persistent ROIC. High levels of capital invested will not necessarily result in higher returns. A high level of new assets will increase invested capital but may not generate returns in the short term and, hence, may actually decrease ROIC. (Module 28.2, LOS 28.f)

7. **C** Government involvement is best analyzed by considering the impact on all five of Porter's forces. (Module 28.2, LOS 28.h)

8. **B** High barriers to entry result in a low threat to profitability. (Module 28.2, LOS 28.g)

9. **A**

Entertaining Kids, Inc.	2019 ($ million)	Scenario 1 ($ million)	Explanation
Revenue	13,201	13,869	13,201 × 1.03 × 1.02
Cost of goods sold	8,755	9,377	8,755 × 1.05 × 1.02
Gross profit	4,446	4,492	
Gross margin	33.7%	32.4%	

Entertaining Kids, Inc.	2019 ($ million)	Scenario 2 ($ million)	Explanation
Revenue	13,201	13,861	13,201 × 1.05
Cost of goods sold	8,755	9,193	8,755 × 1.05
Gross profit	4,446	4,668	
Gross margin	33.7%	33.7%	

(Module 28.2, LOS 28.i)

10. **C**

	2019 ($ million)	2020 Forecast ($ million)	
Existing console			
Individual sales	2,640	1,980	$2,640 \times 0.75$
ALFs	400	400	
Total existing	3,040	2,380	
XTF 2500			
Individual sales	45	214	45×4.75
ALFs	0	0	
Total XTF 2500	45	214	
Total consoles	3,085	2,594	

Note: To forecast new sales after a 100% increase in sales, we would multiply old sales by (100% + 100%) = 2. Similarly, an increase of 375% means that old sales needs to be multiplied by (100% + 375%) = 4.75 (not 3.75) to forecast new sales. (Module 28.2, LOS 28.j)

11. **B** The forecast horizon should be influenced by the investment strategy for which the stock is being considered. (Module 28.2, LOS 28.k)

12. **B** A gradual reduction in prices can be incorporated into a long-term growth rate and so does not represent an inflection point. (Module 28.2, LOS 28.l)

13. **B** Depreciation is typically forecasted as a constant percentage of sales—or, if the company has an expanding asset base, as an increasing percentage of sales. (Module 28.2, LOS 28.m)

The following is a review of the Equity Valuation (2) principles designed to address the learning outcome statements set forth by CFA Institute. Cross-Reference to CFA Institute Assigned Reading #29.

READING 29

Discounted Dividend Valuation

EXAM FOCUS

This topic review presents the use of dividend discount models, one of the classes of models using the present value of future cash flows to determine the value of a stock. Dividend discount models use forecasted dividends as the estimate of cash flow to the shareholder. This material has several important topics that will require careful study. You should be able to choose the appropriate model for the firm to be valued (based on the pattern of expected dividend growth), forecast the future dividends to be discounted, and determine the appropriate discount rate to apply. You should also understand the concept of sustainable growth and be able to estimate a firm's sustainable growth rate.

MODULE 29.1: DDM BASICS

LOS 29.a: Compare dividends, free cash flow, and residual income as inputs to discounted cash flow models and identify investment situations for which each measure is suitable.

Video covering this content is available online.

CFA® Program Curriculum: Volume 4, page 201

In stock valuation models, there are three predominant definitions of future cash flows: dividends, free cash flow, and residual income.

Dividends. Dividend discount models (DDMs) define cash flow as the dividends to be received by the shareholders. The *primary advantage* of using dividends as the definition of cash flow is that it is theoretically justified. The shareholder's investment today is worth the present value of the future cash flows he expects to receive, and ultimately he will be repaid for his investment in the form of dividends. Even if the investor sells the stock at any time prior to the liquidation of the company, before all the dividends are paid, he will receive from the buyer of the shares the present value of the expected future dividends.

An *additional advantage* of dividends as a measure of cash flow is that dividends are less volatile than other measures (earnings or free cash flow), and therefore the value estimates derived from dividend discount models are less volatile and reflect the long-term earning potential of the company.

The *primary disadvantage* of dividends as a cash flow measure is that it is difficult to implement for firms that don't currently pay dividends. It is *possible* to estimate expected future dividends by forecasting the point in the future when the firm is expected to begin paying dividends. The problem with this approach in practice is the uncertainty associated with forecasting the fundamental variables that influence stock price (earnings, dividend payout rate, growth rate, and required return) so far into the future.

A *second disadvantage* of measuring cash flow with dividends is that it takes the perspective of an investor who owns a minority stake in the firm and cannot control the dividend policy. If the dividend policy dictated by the controlling interests bears a meaningful relationship to the firm's underlying profitability, then dividends are appropriate. However, if the dividend policy is *not* related to the firm's ability to create value, then dividends are not an appropriate measure of expected future cash flow to shareholders.

Dividends are appropriate as a measure of cash flow in the following cases:

- The company has a *history of dividend payments*.
- The dividend policy is clear and *related to the earnings of the firm*.
- The *perspective* is that of a *minority shareholder*.

Firms in the mature stage of the industry life cycle are most likely to meet the first two criteria.

EXAMPLE: Identifying the appropriate valuation model

Based on the financial information on Eastern Consolidated, Inc. provided in the following table, determine whether or not a dividend discount model is the appropriate model to value Eastern Consolidated common stock.

Earnings and Dividend Data for Eastern Consolidated

	2015	2014	2013	2012	2011
Earnings per share	$7.50	$6.25	$5.85	$5.40	$5.00
Dividends per share	$1.25	$1.25	$1.25	$1.25	$1.25

Answer:

Earnings have grown at a compound rate of $(\$7.50 \div \$5.00)^{1/4} - 1 = 0.107 = 10.7\%$ over the four years while dividends have been constant, resulting in a decrease in the dividend payout ratio. A dividend discount model is not appropriate in this case because the firm's dividend policy is not consistent with its profitability trend.

Free cash flow. *Free cash flow to the firm (FCFF)* is defined as the cash flow generated by the firm's operations that is in excess of the capital investment required to sustain the firm's current productive capacity. *Free cash flow to equity (FCFE)* is the cash available to stockholders after funding capital requirements and expenses associated with debt financing.

One advantage of free cash flow models is that they can be applied to many firms, regardless of dividend policies or capital structures. The ability to influence the distribution and application of a firm's free cash flow makes these models more pertinent to a firm's controlling shareholders. Free cash flow is also useful to minority shareholders because the firm may be acquired for a market price equal to the value to the controlling party.

However, there are cases in which the application of a free cash flow model may be very difficult. Firms that have significant capital requirements may have negative free cash flow for many years into the future. This can be caused by a technological revolution in an industry that requires greater investment to remain competitive or by rapid expansion into untapped markets. This negative free cash flow complicates the cash flow forecast and makes the estimates less reliable.

Free cash flow models are most appropriate:

■ For firms that do not have a dividend payment history or have a dividend payment history that is not clearly and appropriately related to earnings.

■ For firms with free cash flow that corresponds with their profitability.

■ When the valuation perspective is that of a controlling shareholder.

 PROFESSOR'S NOTE

See the next topic review for details on free cash flow models.

Residual income. Residual income is the amount of earnings during the period that exceeds the investors' required return. The theoretical basis for this approach is that the required return is the opportunity cost to the suppliers of capital, and the residual income is the amount that the firm is able to generate in excess of this return. The residual income approach can be applied to firms with negative free cash flow and to dividend- and non-dividend-paying firms.

Residual income models can be more difficult to apply, however, because they require in-depth analysis of the firm's accounting accruals. Management discretion in establishing accruals for both income and expense may obscure the true results for a period. If the accounting is not transparent or if the quality of the firm's reporting is poor, the accurate estimation of residual income is likely to be difficult.

The residual income approach is most appropriate for:

■ Firms that do not have dividend histories.

■ Firms that have negative free cash flow for the foreseeable future (usually due to capital demands).

■ Firms with transparent financial reporting and high quality earnings.

> **PROFESSOR'S NOTE**
>
> Residual income models are addressed in the Equity Valuation portion of the curriculum.

LOS 29.b: Calculate and interpret the value of a common stock using the dividend discount model (DDM) for single and multiple holding periods.

CFA® Program Curriculum: Volume 4, page 207

One-Period DDM

We can rearrange the holding period formula to solve for the value today of the stock given the expected dividend, the expected price in one year, and the required return:

$$V_0 = \frac{D_1 + P_1}{1 + r}$$

where:
V_0 = fundamental value
D_1 = dividends expected to be received at end of Year 1
P_1 = price expected upon sale at end of Year 1
r = required return on equity

> **EXAMPLE: Calculating value for a one-period DDM**
>
> BuyBest shares are expected to pay a dividend at the end of the year of €1.25. The analyst estimates the required return to be 8% and the expected price at the end of the year to be €28.00. The current price is €26.00. Calculate the value of the shares today, and determine whether BuyBest is overvalued, undervalued, or properly valued.
>
> **Answer:**
>
> The current value of the shares according to the DDM is equal to:
>
> $$V_0 = \frac{€1.25 + €28.00}{1.08} = €27.08$$
>
> BuyBest is undervalued. The current market price of €26.00 is less than the fundamental value of €27.08.

Two-Period DDM

The value of a share of stock using the two-period DDM is the present value of the dividends in years 1 and 2, plus the present value of the expected price in Year 2:

$$V_0 = \frac{D_1}{(1 + r)^1} + \frac{D_2 + P_2}{(1 + r)^2}$$

where:
V_0 = fundamental value
D_1 = dividends expected to be received at end of Year 1
D_2 = dividends expected to be received at end of Year 2
P_2 = price expected upon sale at end of Year 2
r = required return on equity

> **EXAMPLE: Calculating value for a two-period DDM**
>
> Machines Unlimited shares are expected to pay dividends of 1.55 Canadian dollars (C\$) and C\$1.72 at the end of each of the next two years, respectively. The investor expects the price of the shares at the end of this 2-year holding period to be C\$42.00. The investor's required rate of return is 14%. Calculate the current value of Machines Unlimited shares.
>
> **Answer:**
>
> The value of Machines Unlimited shares can be determined with a two-period DDM as:
>
> $$\frac{C\$1.55}{1.14^1} + \frac{C\$1.72 + C\$42.00}{1.14^2} = C\$35.00$$

Multi-Period DDM

The DDM can easily be adapted to any number of holding periods by adjusting the discount factor to match the time to receipt of each expected return. With this, the present value becomes the sum of the properly discounted values of all expected cash flows (dividends and terminal value):

$$V_0 = \frac{D_1}{(1 + r)^1} + \frac{D_2}{(1 + r)^2} + \ldots + \frac{D_n + P_n}{(1 + r)^n}$$

where:
V_0 = fundamental value
D_i = dividends expected to be received at end of year i, i = 1 to n
P_n = price expected upon sale at end of year n
r = required return on equity
n = length of holding period

For example, if we extend the holding period to three years, we simply extend the formula.

> **EXAMPLE: Calculating value for a three-period DDM**
>
> Reliable Motors shares are expected to pay dividends of \$1.50, \$1.60, and \$1.75 at the end of each of the next three years, respectively. The investor expects the price of the shares at the end of this 3-year holding period to be \$54.00. The investor's required rate of return is 15%. Calculate the current value of Reliable's shares.

Answer:

The value of Reliable Motors shares can be determined with a multi-period DDM as:

$$\frac{\$1.50}{1.15^1} + \frac{\$1.60}{1.15^2} + \frac{\$1.75 + \$54.00}{1.15^3} = \$39.17$$

When we have to calculate the total of three or more discounted cash flows, we can generally save a considerable amount of time (and improve accuracy) by using our financial calculators as shown in the following table:

Calculating the PV of Multiple Cash Flows With the TI BA II Plus®

Key Strokes	Explanation	Display
[CF] → [2nd] → [CLR WORK]	Clear memory registers	$CF_0 = 0$
[ENTER]	Initial cash outlay	$CF_0 = 0$
[↓]→1.50→ [ENTER]	Year 1 cash flow	$C01 = 1.50$
[↓]	Frequency of cash flow 1	$F01 = 1$
[↓]→1.60→ [ENTER]	Year 2 cash flow	$C02 = 1.60$
[↓]	Frequency of cash flow 2	$F02 = 1$
[↓]→55.75→ [ENTER]	Year 3 cash flow	$C03 = 55.75$
[↓]	Frequency of cash flow 3	$F03 = 1$
[↓][NPV] →15→[ENTER]	15% discount rate	$I = 15$
[↓]→ [CPT]	Calculate NPV of all CFs	$NPV = 39.17$

WARM-UP: THE GENERAL DIVIDEND DISCOUNT MODEL

If we extend the holding period indefinitely, the value simply becomes the present value of an infinite stream of dividends, represented by John Burr Williams's (1938) original DDM formula:

$$V_0 = \sum_{t=1}^{\infty} \frac{D_t}{(1+r)^t}$$

While the DDM is theoretically correct, applying it in practice requires the analyst to accurately forecast dividends for many periods, a task for which we rarely can expect to have sufficient information. We can use one of several growth models, including the:

- Gordon *constant* growth model.
- *Two-stage* growth model.
- *H*-model.
- *Three-stage* growth model.

With the appropriate model, we can forecast dividends up to the end of the investment horizon where we no longer have confidence in the forecasts and then forecast a terminal value based on some other method, such as a multiple of book value or earnings. Choosing the appropriate growth model is essential to accurate forecasts.

MODULE QUIZ 29.1

To best evaluate your performance, enter your quiz answers online.

1. Restoration Software is a growth stock that has never paid a dividend. Free cash flow is forecasted to be negative for the next five years because of Restoration's aggressive expansion plans. Restoration has always received an unqualified opinion from its auditors and is generally considered to have high-quality earnings. Which of the following models is *most appropriate* to value Restoration?
    A.   Free cash flow to the firm model.
    B.   Free cash flow to equity model.
    C.   Residual income model.

2. EBEE is expected to grow at a rate of 30% for the next five years. After that, competition is expected to lower EBEE's growth to a constant 7% indefinitely. The market risk premium is 6%, and the risk-free rate is 5%. EBEE's beta is 1.2, and the company just paid a dividend of $2.50. The current stock value of EBEE is *closest* to:
    A. $127.28.
    B. $154.57.
    C. $191.00.

MODULE 29.2: GORDON GROWTH MODEL

Video covering this content is available online.

LOS 29.c: Calculate the value of a common stock using the Gordon growth model and explain the model's underlying assumptions.

CFA® Program Curriculum: Volume 4, page 210

The **Gordon growth model** (GGM) assumes that *dividends increase at a constant rate indefinitely*. The simplifying factor of the constant growth assumption is that the rate of growth can be expressed per period in the same way that the required return is expressed, allowing the expression to be condensed into a simple formula:

$$V_0 = \frac{D_0 \times (1+g)^1}{(1+r)^1} + \frac{D_0 \times (1+g)^2}{(1+r)^2} + \frac{D_0 \times (1+g)^3}{(1+r)^3} + \ldots + \frac{D_0 \times (1+g)^n}{(1+r)^n}$$

which condenses to:

$$V_0 = \frac{D_0 \times (1 + g)}{r - g} = \frac{D_1}{r - g}$$

where:
V_0 = fundamental value
D_0 = dividend just paid
D_1 = dividends expected to be received at end of Year 1
r = required return on equity
g = dividend growth rate

The model assumes that:

■ The firm expects to pay a dividend, D_1, in one year.

■ Dividends grow indefinitely at a constant rate, g (which may be less than zero).

■ The growth rate, g, is less than the required return, r.

A firm's growth rate projections can be compared to the growth rate of the economy to determine if it can continue indefinitely. It is unrealistic to assume that any firm can continue to grow indefinitely at a rate higher than the long-term growth rate in real gross domestic product (GDP) plus the long-term inflation rate. In general, a perpetual dividend growth rate forecast above 5% is suspect.

> **EXAMPLE: Calculating value with the Gordon growth model**
>
> DownUnder Financial recently paid a dividend of 1.80 Australian dollars (A$). An analyst has examined the financial statements and historical dividend policy of DownUnder and expects that the firm's dividend rate will grow at a constant rate of 3.5% indefinitely. The analyst also determines DownUnder's beta is 1.5, the risk-free rate is 4%, and the expected return on the market portfolio is 8%. Calculate the current value of DownUnder's shares.
>
> **Answer:**
>
> First use the capital asset pricing model (CAPM) to estimate DownUnder's required return:
>
> $$r = 4\% + [1.5 \times (8\% - 4\%)] = 10\%$$
>
> Then use the Gordon growth model to estimate share value:
>
> $$V_0 = \frac{A\$1.80 \times 1.035}{0.10 - 0.035} = \frac{A\$1.863}{0.10 - 0.035} = A\$28.66$$

PROFESSOR'S NOTE

The dividend to be discounted is the next period dividend, D_1, not the dividend from the previous period, D_0. Use either $D_0 \times (1 + g)$ or D_1 in the numerator, depending on whether you're given the most recent dividend paid (D_0) or the expected dividend in one year (D_1).

LOS 29.d: Calculate and interpret the implied growth rate of dividends using the Gordon growth model and current stock price.

CFA® Program Curriculum: Volume 4, page 219

The Gordon growth model includes four variables, so if we know any three of them, we can solve for the fourth. In practice, we can typically observe the price and current dividend for a publicly traded stock. Consequently, we are usually interested in either backing out the implied required return, using an assumed growth rate, or the implied growth rate, using an assumed required return. In this example, we calculate the implied growth rate using an estimated return.

> **EXAMPLE: Calculating the implied growth rate using the Gordon growth model**
>
> Suppose that the current price and most recent annual dividend for Aurora Mining (AM) are $24.25 and $1.10, respectively. If the required return on Aurora is 8.5%, what is the implied growth rate?
>
> **Answer:**
>
> We can set up the Gordon growth model in its standard form using the information we know:
>
> $$P_0 = \frac{D_0(1+g)}{r-g} = \frac{1.10(1+g)}{(0.085-g)} = \$24.25$$
>
> Rearranging the terms gives us:
>
> $1.10 + 1.10g = 2.06125 - 24.25g$
> $25.35g = 0.96125$
> $g = 0.0379$
>
> So, assuming that our estimated required return is on target, the implied growth rate for Aurora Mining's dividends is 3.8%.

PROFESSOR'S NOTE

Also be prepared to solve for the implied required return given the other variables in the model.

LOS 29.e: Calculate and interpret the present value of growth opportunities (PVGO) and the component of the leading price-to-earnings ratio (P/E) related to PVGO.

CFA® Program Curriculum: Volume 4, page 220

A firm that has additional opportunities to earn returns in excess of the required rate of return would benefit from retaining earnings and investing in those growth opportunities rather than paying out dividends. The fundamental value then represents not only the present value of the future dividends (on a non-growth basis) but also the present value of the growth opportunities (PVGO):

$$V_0 = \frac{E_1}{r} + PVGO$$

where:
E_1 = earnings at t = 1
r = required return on equity

This means the value of a firm's equity has two components:

■ The value of its assets in place (E_1/r), which is the present value of a perpetual cash flow of E_1.

■ The present value of its future investment opportunities (PVGO).

A substantial portion of the value of growth companies is in their PVGO. In contrast, companies in slow-growth industries (e.g., utilities) have low PVGO, and most of their value comes from their assets in place.

> **EXAMPLE: Calculating PVGO**
>
> Reliable, Inc.'s shares trade at 60.00 Swiss francs (Sf) with expected earnings of Sf 5.00 per share and a required return of 10%. Suppose that the shares are properly pri.e., so price is equal to fundamental value. Calculate the PVGO and the portion of the leading P/E related to PVGO.
>
> **Answer:**
>
> $$V_0 = \frac{E_1}{r} + PVGO$$
>
> $$Sf60 = \frac{Sf5.00}{0.10} + PVGO \Rightarrow PVGO = Sf10.00$$
>
> P/E firm = Sf60/5 = 12x
>
> P/E PVGO = Sf10/5 = 2x
>
> 2/12 or 16.7% of the firm's leading P/E ratio is attributable to PVGO.

LOS 29.f: Calculate and interpret the justified leading and trailing P/Es using the Gordon growth model.

CFA® Program Curriculum: Volume 4, page 222

The price-to-earnings (P/E) ratio is the most commonly used relative valuation indicator. An analyst derives a **justified P/E** based on the firm's fundamentals. The two most common forms are the **leading P/E**, which is based on the earnings forecast for the next period, and the **trailing P/E**, which is based on the earnings for the previous period. Both of these can be derived from the DDM:

$$\text{justified leading P/E} = \frac{P_0}{E_1} = \frac{D_1/E_1}{r-g} = \frac{1-b}{r-g}$$

$$\text{justified trailing P/E} = \frac{P_0}{E_0} = \frac{D_0 \times (1+g)/E_0}{r-g} = \frac{(1-b) \times (1+g)}{r-g}$$

where:
P_0 = fundamental value
D_0 = dividends just paid
D_1 = dividends expected to be received in one year
E_0 = current earnings
E_1 = earnings expected in one year
b = retention ratio
(1 − b) = dividend payout ratio
g = dividend growth rate

PROFESSOR'S NOTE

The notation is tricky here. Because these are justified P/E ratios, the "price" in the numerator is actually the fundamental value of the stock derived from the Gordon growth model. It would be more accurate to label these ratios V_0 / E_0 and V_0 / E_1, but the common convention is to call them "justified P/Es."

EXAMPLE: Calculating justified leading and trailing P/E

Alliance, Inc., is currently selling for $16.00 on current earnings of $3.00 and a current dividend of $1.50. Dividends are expected to grow at 3.5% per year indefinitely. The risk-free rate is 4%, the market equity risk premium is 6%, and Alliance's beta is estimated to be 1.1. Calculate the justified leading and trailing P/E ratios of Alliance, Inc.

Answer:

required return = 4.0% + (1.1 × 6.0%) = 10.6%

$$\text{retention ratio} = b = \frac{\text{earnings} - \text{dividends}}{\text{earnings}} = \frac{\$3.00 - \$1.50}{\$3.00} = 0.5$$

$$\text{payout ratio} = (1-b) = \frac{\text{dividends}}{\text{earnings}} = \frac{\$1.50}{\$3.00} = 0.5$$

$$\text{justified leading P/E} = \frac{1-b}{r-g} = \frac{0.5}{0.106 - 0.035} = 7.04$$

$$\text{justified trailing P/E} = \frac{(1-b) \times (1+g)}{r-g} = \frac{0.5 \times 1.035}{0.106 - 0.035} = 7.29$$

or

justified trailing P/E = 7.04 × (1.035) = 7.29

PROFESSOR'S NOTE

Remember that if earnings are expected to grow, E_1 will be greater than E_0, and the justified leading P/E (P_0 / E_1) will be smaller than the justified trailing P/E (P_0 / E_0) because you're dividing by a larger number when you are calculating leading P/E. In fact, trailing P/E will be larger than leading P/E by a factor of $(1 + g)$: justified trailing P/E = justified leading P/E × $(1 + g)$.

LOS 29.g: Calculate the value of noncallable fixed-rate perpetual preferred stock.

CFA® Program Curriculum: Volume 4, page 216

A firm that has no additional opportunities to earn returns in excess of the required rate of return should distribute all of its earnings to shareholders in the form of dividends. Under this assumption the growth rate would be zero, and the current value of the firm would be equal to the current dividend divided by the required rate of return. This is exactly the same approach used to determine the value of fixed-rate perpetual preferred shares.

$$\text{value of perpetual preferred shares} = \frac{D_p}{r_p}$$

where:

D_p = preferred dividend (which is assumed not to grow)

r_p = cost of preferred equity

EXAMPLE: Calculating the value of fixed-rate perpetual preferred stock

United Publishing has a fixed-rate perpetual preferred stock outstanding with a dividend of 6% (based on an issue at par of £100). If the investors' required rate of return for holding these shares is 9.5%, calculate the current value of these shares.

Answer:

Dividends are not growing because the preferred dividend is based on a fixed rate of 6.0% on a stated par value of £100, so this is comparable to DDM with a fixed dividend in perpetuity.

$$D = 0.06 \times £100.00 = £6.00$$

$$\text{value of preferred shares} = \frac{£6.00}{0.095} = £63.16$$

LOS 29.h: Describe strengths and limitations of the Gordon growth model and justify its selection to value a company's common shares.

CFA® Program Curriculum: Volume 4, page 225

The Gordon growth model (GGM) has a number of characteristics that make it useful and appropriate for many applications. The model:

- Is applicable to stable, mature, dividend-paying firms.

- Is appropriate for valuing market indices.

- Is easily communicated and explained because of its straightforward approach.

- Can be used to determine price-implied growth rates, required rates of return, and value of growth opportunities.

- Can be used to supplement other, more complex valuation methods.

There are also some characteristics that limit the applications of the GGM:

- Valuations are very sensitive to estimates of growth rates and required rates of return, both of which are difficult to estimate with precision.

- The model cannot be easily applied to non-dividend-paying stocks.

- Unpredictable growth patterns of some firms would make using the model difficult and the resulting valuations unreliable.

Next we discuss multistage growth models, which accommodate more realistic growth rate assumptions.

MODULE QUIZ 29.2

To best evaluate your performance, enter your quiz answers online.

1. JCI Incorporated pays an annual dividend of 5.00 Canadian dollars (C$). The company is expected to continue paying this dividend with no future growth in dividends. Investors require a 9% rate of return on this investment. The current risk-free rate is 4%. The current stock value of JCI Incorporated is *closest* to:
   A. C$55.56.
   B. C$100.00.
   C. C$125.00.

2. The current stock price of MCD is $89.00. The current dividend for MCD is $2.50, and dividends are expected to grow at a constant rate of 8%. The implied required return for MCD is *closest* to:
   A. 3%.
   B. 8%.
   C. 11%.

3. CFCRegs, Inc., just paid a dividend of $2.00 per share. The required return is 13%, and the stock is currently trading at $30.28 per share. The growth rate implied by the Gordon growth model is *closest* to:
   A. 4%.
   B. 6%.
   C. 8%.

4. Video Discs Forever, Inc., manufactures and distributes a line of DVD players. The company has fallen on hard times and although it will pay a $4 dividend in the next period, it expects dividends to decline by 3% per year thereafter. If the discount rate for the company is 9%, the current value of one share of VDF's common stock is *closest* to:
    A. $33.33.
    B. $44.44.
    C. $66.67.

5. Titan Industries is not expected to pay a dividend until ten years from now, at which time it is expected to pay a dividend of $1.25 and increase the dividend at a rate of 4% thereafter. If the required rate of return is 12%, the current value of Titan is *closest* to:
    A. $5.64.
    B. $12.78.
    C. $15.63.

6. Viking Insurance forecasts earnings next year of $4.50 per share. Viking has a dividend payout ratio of 40%. The required return is 15%. Return on equity is 8.33%. The present value of growth opportunities and the value of the stock based on the Gordon growth model are *closest* to:

	PVGO	Share value
A.	$ 4.00	$34.00
B.	–$21.00	$ 9.00
C.	–$12.00	$18.00

MODULE 29.3: MULTIPERIOD MODELS

Video covering this content is available online.

LOS 29.i: Explain the assumptions and justify the selection of the two-stage DDM, the H-model, the three-stage DDM, or spreadsheet modeling to value a company's common shares.

CFA® Program Curriculum: Volume 4, page 226

For most companies, the Gordon growth model assumption of constant dividend growth that continues into perpetuity is unrealistic. For example, many companies experience growth rates in excess of the required rate of return for short periods of time as a result of a competitive advantage they have developed. We need more realistic multistage growth models to estimate value for companies with several stages of future growth. The appropriate model is the one that most closely matches the firm's expected pattern of growth. However, whichever multistage model we use, there are two important points to keep in mind:

■ We're still just forecasting dividends into the future and discounting them back to today to find intrinsic value.

■ Over the long term, growth rates tend to revert to a long-run rate approximately equal to the long-term growth rate in real gross domestic product (GDP) plus the long-term inflation rate. Historically, that number has been between 2% and 5%. Anything higher than 5% as a long-run perpetual growth rate is difficult to justify.

PROFESSOR'S NOTE

The required rate of return applicable to each stage might also be different. For instance, a firm with a supernormal growth rate is probably more risky (should have a higher required return) than a stable, mature firm with a slower growth rate. In most cases on the exam, however, a single required return is applied to all of the stages.

Two-Stage DDM: The most basic multistage model is a two-stage DDM in which we assume the company grows at a high rate for a relatively short period of time (the first stage) and then reverts to a long-run perpetual growth rate (the second stage). The length of the high-growth phase is a function of the visibility of the company's operations; in other words, it tells how far into the future the analyst can predict growth rates with a certain degree of confidence. An example in which the two-stage model would apply is a situation in which a company has a patent that will expire. For example, suppose a firm is expected to grow at 15% until patents expire in four years, then immediately revert to a long-run growth rate of 3% in perpetuity. This stock should be modeled by a two-stage model, with dividends growing at 15% before the patent expires and 3% thereafter (see Figure 29.1).

Figure 29.1: Example of a Two-Stage DDM

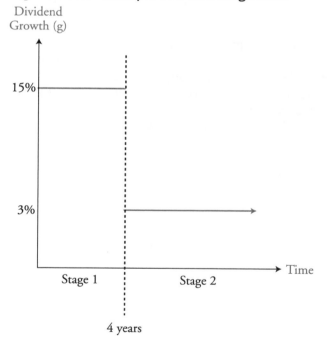

H-Model: The problem with the basic two-stage DDM is that it is usually unrealistic to assume that a stock will experience high growth for a short period, then *immediately* fall back to a long-run level. The H-model utilizes a more realistic assumption: the growth rate starts out high and then declines linearly over the high-growth stage until it reaches the long-run average growth rate. For example, consider a firm that generates high profit margins, faces little competition from within its industry, and is currently growing at 15%. We might forecast that the firm's growth rate will decline by 3% per year as competitors enter the market until it reaches 3% at the end of the fourth year, when the industry matures and growth rates stabilize (see Figure 29.2).

Figure 29.2: Example of an H-Model

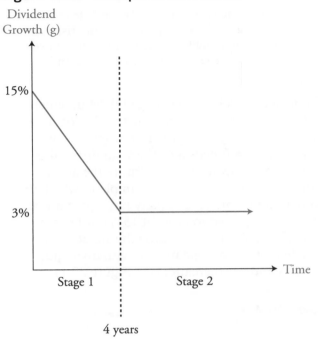

Three-stage DDM: Three-stage models are appropriate for firms that are expected to have three distinct stages of earnings growth. A three-stage model is a slightly more complex refinement of a two-stage model. For example, suppose we forecast that a biotech company will experience supernormal growth of 25% for three years, then 15% growth for five years, and finally slow down to a stable, long-run rate of 3% (see Figure 29.3). Alternatively, in stage 2, the growth rate may also linearly decay to the stage 3 stable, long-run growth rate.

Figure 29.3: Example of a Three-Stage DDM

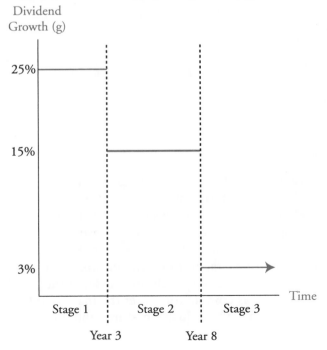

©2018 Kaplan, Inc.

Spreadsheet modeling: The two and three stage models we've discussed so far are really just models in which we've simplified the growth pattern to make the calculations doable. Obviously that's an important consideration on the exam. However, in practice we can use spreadsheets to model any pattern of dividend growth we'd like with different growth rates for each year because the spreadsheet does all the calculations for us. Spreadsheet modeling is applicable to firms about which you have a great deal of information and can project different growth rates for differing periods, such as construction firms and defense contractors with many long-term contracts. Figure 29.4 is an example of three different spreadsheet models.

Figure 29.4: Examples of Spreadsheet Modeling

| | Growth Rates | | | | | | |
Year	1	2	3	4	5	6	7 and after
Scenario 1	20%	19%	13%	5%	5%	5%	5%
Scenario 2	20%	19%	13%	11%	5%	5%	5%
Scenario 3	20%	19%	13%	11%	8%	7%	5%

LOS 29.j: Explain the growth phase, transition phase, and maturity phase of a business.

CFA® Program Curriculum: Volume 4, page 225

While the basic GGM assumes constant growth, most firms go through a pattern of growth that includes several phases:

■ An *initial growth phase*, where the firm has rapidly increasing earnings, little or no dividends, and heavy reinvestment.

■ A *transition phase*, in which earnings and dividends are still increasing but at a slower rate as competitive forces reduce profit opportunities and the need for reinvestment.

■ A *mature phase*, in which earnings grow at a stable but slower rate, and payout ratios are stabilizing as reinvestment matches depreciation and asset maintenance requirements.

The level and pattern of specific fundamental variables during the three phases, as well as the appropriate valuation model to apply in each phase, are shown in Figure 29.5.

Figure 29.5: Growth, Transition, and Maturity Phase

Variable	Growth Phase		
	Initial Growth	Transition	Maturity
Earnings Growth	Very high	Above average but falling	Stable at long-run level
Capital Investment	Significant requirements	Decreasing	Stable at long-run level
Profit Margin	High	Above average but falling	Stable at long-run level
FCFE	Negative	May be positive, and growing	Stable at long-run level
ROE vs. Required Return	ROE > r	ROE approaching r	ROE = r
Dividend Payout	Low or zero	Increasing	Stable at long-run level
Appropriate Model	Three-stage	Two-stage	Gordon growth

This pattern is not predestined because many firms are successful in constantly adapting and entering into new growth opportunities. Mature firms may develop technology that forms the basis for a whole new product and market. The point is that a multistage model is required in order to value many firms. Fortunately, the GGM is easily adaptable to multistage growth.

LOS 29.k: Describe terminal value and explain alternative approaches to determining the terminal value in a DDM.

CFA® Program Curriculum: Volume 4, page 228

No matter which dividend discount model we use, we have to estimate a terminal value at some point in the future. There are two ways to do this: using the Gordon growth model and using the market multiple approach.

The most common method (on the exam) is to estimate the terminal value with the Gordon growth model. In other words, at some point in the future, we assume dividends will begin to grow at a constant, long-term rate. Then the terminal value at that point is just the value derived from the Gordon growth model.

Many analysts also use market price multiples to estimate the terminal value rather than use the GGM method of discounting dividends. For example, we could forecast earnings and a P/E ratio at the forecast horizon and then estimate the terminal value as the P/E multiplied by the earnings estimate.

EXAMPLE: Estimating terminal value

Level Partners is expected to have earnings in ten years of $12 per share, a dividend payout ratio of 50%, and a required return of 11%. At that time, the dividend growth rate is expected to fall to 4% in perpetuity, and the trailing P/E ratio is forecasted to be eight times earnings. Estimate the terminal value at the end of ten years using the Gordon growth model and the P/E multiple.

Answer:

The dividend at the end of ten years is expected to be $6 ($12 multiplied by 50%). The dividend in Year 11 is then $6.00 × 1.04 = $6.24. The terminal value using the Gordon growth model is therefore:

$$\text{terminal value in Year 10} = \frac{D_{10} \times (1+g)}{r-g} = \frac{D_{11}}{r-g} = \frac{\$6.24}{0.11 - 0.04} = \$89.14$$

The terminal value given forecasted earnings of $12 and a P/E ratio of 8 is:

$$\text{terminal value in Year 10 (trailing P/E multiple)} = \$12.00 \times 8 = \$96.00$$

LOS 29.1: Calculate and interpret the value of common shares using the two-stage DDM, the H-model, and the three-stage DDM.

CFA® Program Curriculum: Volume 4, page 226

Valuation Using the Two-Stage Model

The two-stage fixed growth rate model is based on the assumption that the firm will enjoy an initial period of high growth, followed by a mature or stable period in which growth will be lower but sustainable:

$$V_0 = \left[\sum_{t=1}^{n} \frac{D_0 (1+g_S)^t}{(1+r)^t} \right] + \left[\frac{D_0 \times (1+g_S)^n \times (1+g_L)}{(1+r)^n \times (r-g_L)} \right]$$

where:
g_S = short-term growth rate
g_L = long-term growth rate
r = required return
n = length of high growth period

EXAMPLE: Calculating value with a two-stage DDM

Sea Island Recreation currently pays a dividend of $1.00. An analyst forecasts growth of 10% for the next three years, followed by 4% growth in perpetuity thereafter. The required return is 12%. Calculate the current value per share.

Answer:

We could solve the problem by plugging the appropriate numbers into the formula as follows:

$$V_0 = \left[\sum_{t=1}^{3} \frac{\$1.00 \times (1.10)^t}{(1.12)^t}\right] + \left[\frac{\$1.00 \times (1.10)^3 \times (1.04)}{(1.12)^3 (0.12 - 0.04)}\right]$$

$$V_0 = \frac{\$1.00 \times (1.10)^1}{(1.12)^1} + \frac{\$1.00 \times (1.10)^2}{(1.12)^2} + \frac{\$1.00 \times (1.10)^3}{(1.12)^3} + \frac{\$1.00 \times (1.10)^3 \times (1.04)}{(1.12)^3 \times (0.12 - 0.04)}$$

$$V_0 = \frac{\$1.10}{(1.12)^1} + \frac{\$1.21}{(1.12)^2} + \frac{\$1.331}{(1.12)^3} + \frac{\$1.3842}{(1.12)^3 \times (0.12 - 0.04)}$$

$$V_0 = \$15.21$$

If we were robots instead of humans, this would be fine. However, because we are human beings (and not mindless machines), it might be better to actually try to understand what we are doing, limit the need to remember yet another formula, and reduce the possibility of error. This can be accomplished by drawing a time line and placing the appropriate cash flows on the line, followed by the fairly straightforward computation on our financial calculators that we did earlier (in the multiperiod DDM). The forecasted dividends are shown in the following figure.

Dividend Cash Flows

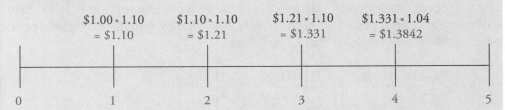

Constant growth at 4% begins after the third year, and we can employ the DDM to determine the value of the stock at time t = 3. Accordingly:

$$V_3 = \frac{D_3 \times (1 + g)}{r - g} = \frac{D_4}{r - g} = \frac{\$1.3842}{0.12 - 0.04} = \$17.30$$

Now the problem is exactly like the three-period DDM we solved in an earlier LOS: we know the dividends in years 1, 2, and 3, the terminal value in Year 3, and the discount rate. The cash flows that we need to solve the problem are shown in the following figure.

Dividend and Terminal Value Cash Flows

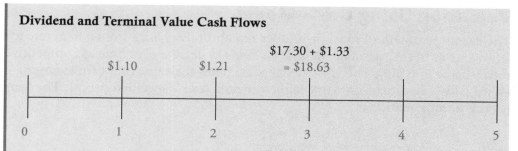

$17.30 + $1.33
= $18.63

$1.10 $1.21

0   1   2   3   4   5

The financial calculator does the hard work for us: CF0 = 0; C01 = 1.10; C02 = 1.21; C03 = 18.63; I = 12; CPT → NPV = 15.21.

We arrived at an estimated value of $15.21 using the calculator, which is exactly the same answer we got with the ugly formula. After a bit of practice, you should find that the calculator method is easier than the complicated formula, and, just as importantly, it will be less prone to error.

The value of a firm that doesn't currently pay a dividend is a simple version of the two-stage DDM, where the firm pays no dividends in the first stage. Therefore, the value of the firm is just the present value of the terminal value computed at the point in time at which dividends are projected to start.

EXAMPLE: Valuing a non-dividend-paying stock

Arena Distributors is a new company and currently pays no dividends. The company recently reported earnings of $1.50 per share and is expected to grow at a 15% rate for the next four years. Beginning in Year 5, Arena is expected to distribute 20% of its earnings in the form of dividends and to have a constant growth rate of 5%. The required rate of return is 12%. Calculate the value of Arena shares today.

Answer:

First forecast the earnings in Year 5. Then calculate the dividends in Year 5 as 20% of Year 5 earnings. Applying the Gordon growth model to the Year 5 dividend gives us an estimate of the terminal value in Year 4. The terminal value discounted back four years is the current value of the stock.

$$E_4 = \$1.50 \times (1.15)^4 = \$2.62$$

$$E_5 = \$2.62 \times 1.05 = \$2.75$$

$$D_5 = \$2.75 \times 0.20 = \$0.55$$

$$V_4 = \frac{\$0.55}{0.12 - 0.05} = \$7.86$$

$$V_0 = \frac{\$7.86}{1.12^4} = \$5.00$$

Valuation Using the H-Model

The earnings growth of most firms does not abruptly change from a high rate to a low rate as in the two-stage model but tends to decline over time as competitive forces come into play. The H-model approximates the value of a firm assuming that an initially high rate of growth declines linearly over a specified period. The formula for this approximation is:

$$V_0 = \frac{D_0 \times (1 + g_L)}{r - g_L} + \frac{D_0 \times H \times (g_S - g_L)}{r - g_L}$$

where:

$H = \left(\frac{t}{2}\right)$ = half-life (in years) of high-growth period

t = length of high growth period

g_S = short-term growth rate

g_L = long-term growth rate

r = required return

Note that the first term is what the shares would be worth if there were no high-growth period and the perpetual growth rate was g_L. The second term is an approximation of the additional value that results from the high-growth period.

> **EXAMPLE: Calculating value with the H-model**
>
> Omega Foods currently pays a dividend of €2.00. The growth rate, which is currently 20%, is expected to decline linearly over the next ten years to a stable rate of 5% thereafter. The required return is 12%. Calculate the current value of Omega.
>
> **Answer:**
>
> $$V_0 = \frac{€2.00 \times 1.05}{0.12 - 0.05} + \frac{€2.00 \times \left(\frac{10}{2}\right) \times (0.20 - 0.05)}{0.12 - 0.05} = €30.00 + €21.43 = €51.43$$
>
> Remember that the H-model provides only an approximation of the value of Omega shares. To find the exact answer, we'd have to forecast each of the first ten dividends, applying a different growth rate to each, and then discount them back to the present at 12%. In general, the H-value approximation is more accurate the shorter the high-growth period, t, and/or the smaller the spread between the short-term and long-term growth rates, $g_S - g_L$.

Valuation Using the Three-Stage DDM

A *three-stage model* can be used to estimate the value of a firm that is projected to have three stages of growth with a fixed rate of growth for each stage. The approach is the same as the two-stage model, with the projected dividends and the terminal value of the shares discounted to their present value at the required rate of return. Again, a time line or an equivalent cash flow table will help the intuition. Your speed and accuracy will develop with practice.

EXAMPLE: Calculating value with the three-stage DDM

R&M has a current dividend of $1.00 and a required rate of return of 12%. A dividend growth rate of 15% is projected for the next two years, followed by a 10% growth rate for the next four years before settling down to a constant 4% growth rate thereafter. Calculate the current value of R&M.

Answer: Relevant Cash Flows for R&M Example

Time	Value	Calculation	D_t or V_t
1	D_1	$1.00(1.15)	$1.150
2	D_2	$1.150(1.15)	$1.323
3	D_3	$1.323(1.10)	$1.455
4	D_4	$1.455(1.10)	$1.600
5	D_5	$1.600(1.10)	$1.760
6	D_6	$1.760(1.10)	$1.936
6	V_6	[$1.936(1.04)] / (0.12 − 0.04)	$25.168

Now we enter the cash flows into our calculator, noting that the total cash flow at Time 6 is $1.936 + $25.168 = $27.104: CF0 = 0; C01 = 1.150; C02 = 1.323; C03 = 1.455; C04 = 1.600; C05 = 1.760; C06 = 27.104; I = 12; CPT → NPV = 18.864.

According to the three-stage model, R&M is worth $18.864 today. This question is tedious, but it is not a question to be feared, as long as your calculator batteries hold up.

EXAMPLE: Three-stage growth model with linear growth decline in stage 2

As an analyst, you have gathered the following information on a company you are tracking. The current annual dividend is $0.75. Dividends are expected to grow at a rate of 12% over the next three years, decline linearly to 4% over the next six years, and then remain at a long-term equilibrium growth rate of 4% in perpetuity. The required return is 9%. Calculate the value of the company.

Answer:

Let's start by valuing the last two stages using the H-model. We know that:

$$V_3 = \frac{\left[D_3 \times (1 + g_L)\right] + \left[D_3 \times H(g_S - g_L)\right]}{r - g_L}$$

$$D_3 = D_0(1 + g_S)^3 = \$0.75(1.12)^3 = \$1.0537$$

It follows that:

$$V_3 = \frac{[\$1.0537 \times (1.04)] + \left[\$1.0537 \times \frac{6}{2} \times (0.12 - 0.04)\right]}{0.09 - 0.04} = \$26.9747$$

Now we have a series of three cash flows to discount in order to find the current value of the stock, and our financial calculator does the rest of the work.

CF0 = 0; C01 = D_1 = $0.75(1.12) = $0.84; C02 = D_2 = $0.75(1.12)^2 = $0.9408; and C03 = D_3 + V_3 = $1.0537 + $26.9747 = $28.0284; I = 9; CPT → NPV = 23.2056.

The price of the stock is $23.2056.

Valuation Models Using Spreadsheets

If you have been calculating along with the examples, you already recognize that the use of these models can be computationally intensive, though the formulas are straightforward. These characteristics make DDM models ideally suited to being solved with spreadsheet software. A spreadsheet allows the analyst to easily calculate values based on models with many stages, growth rates, and required rates of return.

LOS 29.m: Estimate a required return based on any DDM, including the Gordon growth model and the H-model.

CFA® Program Curriculum: Volume 4, page 239

We have been using DDMs to determine the value of a stock, assuming that we know the dividends and required rates of return. The models are just as useful in determining the required rate of return, given the current value and dividends of a stock. No matter which model you're using (whether it's a two-stage DDM, an H-model, a three-stage DDM, or a spreadsheet model), in theory this is easy: *Given all the other inputs to the model, we can back into the expected return that makes the present value of the forecasted dividend stream equal to the current market price.*

For example, if the dividend growth rate is constant forever, we can use the Gordon growth model to calculate the implied expected return given the expected dividend, the current market price, and the expected growth rate:

$$r = \frac{D_1}{P_0} + g$$

> **EXAMPLE: Calculating expected return with the Gordon growth model**
>
> Smyth & Weston Explosives' stock is expected to pay a dividend of $1.60, has a current price of $40.00, and has a projected growth rate of 9%. Calculate S&W's implied required return.
>
> **Answer:**
>
> $$r = \frac{\$1.60}{\$40.00} + 0.09 = 0.13 = 13\%$$

The H-model can be rewritten in terms of *r* and used to solve for *r* given the other model inputs:

$$r = \left[\left(\frac{D_0}{P_0} \right) \times \left\{ (1 + g_L) + [H \times (g_S - g_L)] \right\} \right] + g_L$$

> **EXAMPLE: Solving for expected return with the H-model**
>
> Beluga Fisheries, Inc., just paid a current dividend of $0.75, which has been growing at a rate of 10%. This growth rate is expected to decline to 5% over the next five years and then remain at 5% indefinitely. Calculate the implied required return for Beluga based on the current price of $30.00.

Answer:

$$r = \left(\frac{\$0.75}{\$30.00}\right) \times \left\{(1 + 0.05) + \left[\left(\frac{5}{2}\right) \times (0.10 - 0.05)\right]\right\} + 0.05 = 0.0794 = 7.94\%$$

Using the general two-stage model is more difficult because we have to solve for r with an iterative process because there is no closed-form solution. Here is an example of how to approach the problem using the two-stage DDM.

EXAMPLE: Solving for expected return with the two-stage DDM

Ozone Laboratories, Inc., recently paid a dividend of $1.00. Dividends are expected to grow at a rate of 11% for the next two years and 8% thereafter. The implied required return for Ozone based on the current price of $36.00 is *closest* to:

A. 9.5%.

B. 10.0%.

C. 11.2%.

Answer:

We have to solve for r in the following equation:

$$\frac{\$1.00 \times 1.11}{1 + r} + \frac{\$1.00 \times 1.11^2}{(1 + r)^2} + \left(\frac{\$1.00 \times 1.11^2 \times 1.08}{r - 0.08}\right)\left(\frac{1}{(1 + r)^2}\right) = \$36.00$$

This actually requires an iterative process. The easiest way to do this is to start with the middle value from the three answer choices (10%, in this case):

terminal value in Year 2 estimate

$$= \$34.00 = \frac{D_3}{0.10 - 0.08} = \frac{(\$1.00) \times (1.11)^2 \times (1.08)}{0.10 - 0.08}$$

$$= \frac{\$1.331}{0.10 - 0.08} = 66.55$$

Use your calculator to value the stock:

CF0 = 0, C01 = 1.11, C02 = 1.23 + 66.55 = 67.78

NPV (I = 10%) = $57.03 (too high relative to the given market price of $36)

Hence, the discount rate has to be higher. The only higher value (from the multiple choices) is 11.2%.

Let's confirm:

P$_2$ = 1.331 / (0.112 − 0.08) = 41.59

CF0 = 0, C01 = 1.11, C02 = 1.23 + 41.59 = 42.82

PV (I = 10%) = $36.40 (close enough)

LOS 29.n: Explain the use of spreadsheet modeling to forecast dividends and to value common shares.

CFA® Program Curriculum: Volume 4, page 237

We have previously noted that, in practice, financial analysts are much more likely to use a spreadsheet than any of the stylized models presented here when valuing equity securities. The reason for this is the inherent flexibility and computational accuracy of spreadsheet modeling.

A firm's dividends (or cash flows) often do not grow at a smooth rate for an extended period. When changes in dividends can be predicted, there can obviously be more than two or three stages of change involved. Moreover, there are often idiosyncratic events that, even if they can be predicted, do not fit neatly into any of the patterns required by these models. Using a spreadsheet is relatively straightforward and can accommodate nearly any pattern that the analyst can imagine.

Step 1: Establish the base level of cash flows or dividends. In the case of dividends, this would ordinarily be either the amount paid over the preceding year or some normalized level based upon projected firm earnings.

Step 2: Estimate changes in the firm's dividends for the foreseeable future (also known as the supernormal growth period) and project future cash dividends on the basis of these estimates. Because the spreadsheet can be programmed in a virtually infinite series of combinations, any dividend pattern desired can be achieved.

Step 3: Because an equity security has an infinite life, the analyst needs to estimate what normalized level of growth will occur at the end of the supernormal growth period. This allows for an estimate of a terminal value, representing the cash flow (i.e., the firm's value if sold at this time) to be received at the end of the supernormal growth period.

Step 4: Discount all projected dividends and the terminal value back to today to obtain an estimate of the firm's current value.

The last step is where the use of the spreadsheet really pays off. The analyst is in position to conduct detailed scenario analyses wherein the model inputs can be altered to see how changes in the pattern of future dividends, interest rates, and firm risk affect firm valuation estimates.

The bottom line is that performing the analysis just listed for a period of 10 or 20 years is relatively easy with a spreadsheet but would be all but impossible with any of the stylized models presented.

LOS 29.o: Calculate and interpret the sustainable growth rate of a company and demonstrate the use of DuPont analysis to estimate a company's sustainable growth rate.

CFA® Program Curriculum: Volume 4, page 241

The sustainable growth rate (SGR) is the rate at which earnings (and dividends) can continue to grow indefinitely, assuming that the firm's debt-to-equity ratio is unchanged and it doesn't issue new equity. SGR is a simple function of the earnings retention ratio and the return on equity:

$$SGR = b \times ROE$$

where:

b = earnings retention rate = 1 − dividend payout rate
ROE = return on equity

The SGR is important because it tells us how quickly a firm can grow with internally generated funds.

> **EXAMPLE: Calculating SGR**
>
> Biotechnica, Inc., is growing earnings at an annual rate of 9%. It currently pays out dividends equal to 20% of earnings. Biotechnica's ROE is 15%. Calculate its SGR.
>
> **Answer:**
>
> $$g = (1 - 0.20) \times (15\%) = 12\%$$

A firm's rate of growth is a function of both its earnings retention and its return on equity. ROE can be estimated with the DuPont formula, which presents the relationship between margin, sales, and leverage as determinants of ROE:

$$ROE = \frac{net\,income}{stockholders'\,equity} = \left(\frac{net\,income}{sales}\right) \times \left(\frac{sales}{total\,assets}\right) \times \left(\frac{total\,assets}{stockholders'\,equity}\right)$$

If the other factors remain constant, we can see that the growth of a firm's earnings (and dividends) is a function of its ROE and its retention rate:

$$g = \left(\frac{net\,income - dividends}{net\,income}\right) \times \left(\frac{net\,income}{sales}\right) \times \left(\frac{sales}{total\,assets}\right) \times \left(\frac{total\,assets}{stockholders'\,equity}\right)$$

This has also been called the *PRAT* model, where SGR is a function of the profit margin (P), the retention rate (R), the asset turnover (A), and financial leverage (T). Two of these factors are functions of the firm's financing decisions (leverage and earnings retention), and two are functions of performance (return on assets equals profit margin multiplied by asset turnover). These factors can be used as building blocks in developing an estimate of a firm's growth. If the actual growth rate is forecasted to be greater than SGR, the firm will have to issue equity unless the firm increases its retention ratio, profit margin, total asset turnover, or leverage.

PROFESSOR'S NOTE

Technically, the correct way to calculate sustainable growth rate is with ROE based on beginning shareholders' equity. However, it is often done with average equity as an approximation. On the exam, use whichever method is specified in the question.

EXAMPLE: Calculating ROE and SGR

Halo Construction has been successful in a mature industry. Over the last three years, Halo has averaged a profit margin of 10%, a total asset turnover of 1.8, and a leverage ratio of 1.25. Assuming Halo continues to distribute 40% of its earnings as dividends, calculate its long-term SGR.

Answer:

$$g = P \times R \times A \times T$$
$$g = 0.10 \times (1 - 0.4) \times 1.8 \times 1.25 = 0.135 = 13.5\%$$

PROFESSOR'S NOTE

Sustainable growth rate is a very, very important topic. Make sure you know how to calculate ROE and SGR given a balance sheet and an income statement, as in the following example.

EXAMPLE: Calculating ROE and SGR

Given the following partial balance sheets and income statement for Far Horizons Company, calculate three components of the ROE (using the DuPont model) and the sustainable growth rate for 2018 based on beginning balance sheet values. Use a dividend payout ratio of 30%. All values are in millions of USD.

Far Horizons Income Statement

Income statement for fiscal year 2018	
Sales	$40.0
Net income	$1.8

Far Horizons Balance Sheet

Balance sheet fiscal year end 2017 and 2018					
	2017	**2018**		**2017**	**2018**
Assets	$30.0	$50.0	Liabilities	$10.0	$20.0
			Equity	20.0	30.0
Total	$30.0	$50.0	Total	$30.0	$50.0

Answer:

$$\text{profit margin} = \frac{\$1.80}{\$40.00} = 0.045 = 4.5\%$$

$$\text{asset turnover} = \frac{\$40.00}{\$30.00} = 1.333$$

$$\text{financial leverage} = \frac{\$30.00}{\$20.00} = 1.5$$

$$\text{ROE} = (0.045) \times (1.333) \times (1.5) = 0.09 = 9.0\%$$

$$\text{g} = \text{ROE} \times \text{b} = 9.0\% \times (1 - 0.30) = 6.3\%$$

LOS 29.p: Evaluate whether a stock is overvalued, fairly valued, or undervalued by the market based on a DDM estimate of value.

CFA® Program Curriculum: Volume 4, page 234

If a stock is trading at a price (market price) higher than the price implied by a dividend discount model (model pri.e., the stock is considered to be **overvalued**. Similarly, if the market price is lower than the model price, the stock is considered to be **undervalued**, and if the model price is equal to the market price, the stock is considered to be **fairly valued**.

PROFESSOR'S NOTE

Overpriced means overpriced <u>in the market</u>.

In other words: market price > calculated value.

MODULE QUIZ 29.3

To best evaluate your performance, enter your quiz answers online.

1. Aerosail Company exhibits the following fundamental characteristics:
    - Profit margins are higher than the industry average but have fallen over the last four years from 45% to 32%.

    - Free cash flow to equity is positive and has grown 18% in the last two years.

    - Dividend payout has increased from 5% to 15% in the last three years.

    What phase of the life cycle is Aerosail *most likely* in, and which dividend discount model is *most appropriate* to value the company's common stock?

Phase	Model
A. Transition	Gordon growth
B. Transition	Multistage
C. Growth	Gordon growth

2. An analyst forecasts dividends over the next three years for Aerosail Company of $1.00, $2.00, and $2.50. He forecasts a terminal value in three years of $52.00. Aerosail is currently selling for $39.71. The implied required return based on the analyst forecast is *closest* to:
   A. 10.2%.
   B. 13.5%.
   C. 14.8%.

Use the following information to answer Questions 3 through 7.

Jamie Johnson, CFA, has been asked by her supervisor to evaluate the value of two stocks in the recreational vehicle industry, AAA Motorhomes (AAA) and Three Star Travelers (TST). Johnson compiled analyst information for the two companies in Table 1. The expected return on the market is 11%, and the risk-free rate is 4%. Johnson's supervisor has requested that Johnson focus on dividends in estimating the value of the two firms.

TABLE 1	AAA	TST
Current Roe	0.30	0.22
Current EPS	$2.50	$4.60
Retention Ratio	0.40	0.30
Beta	1.2	0.9

TABLE 2	Risk Premiums	Factor Sensitivities	
		AAA	TST
Confidence Risk	0.048	0.63	0.42
Time Horizon Risk	0.031	0.47	0.39
Inflation Risk	0.045	0.70	0.51
Business Cycle Risk	0.038	0.98	0.91
Market Timing Risk	–0.018	0.05	0.21

3. The sustainable growth rates for each firm are *closest* to:

	AAA	TST
A.	18.0%	6.6%
B.	12.0%	6.6%
C.	12.0%	15.4%

4. Johnson decides to start by estimating the value of the two stocks using the constant growth dividend discount model and estimating the required rate of returns using the capital asset pricing model (CAPM). Both firms are expected to grow at their sustainable growth rates. The estimated values are *closest* to:

	AAA	TST
A.	$273.54	$92.77
B.	$273.54	$48.57
C.	$420.00	$92.77

5. Johnson believes the estimate for TST using the constant dividend discount model (DDM) is appropriate. However, she believes that AAA is expected to grow at a higher rate of 20% for the next four years and then grow at a rate of 7% after that. Using the two-stage model, and CAPM for the required rate of return, the current value of AAA is *closest* to:
   A. $45.69.
   B. $58.00.
   C. $61.62.

6. After further consideration, Johnson feels the growth rates of AAA and TST are more likely to gradually decline over the next four years and therefore considers the H-model. She estimates TST growth will decline from current 15% to long-term 5% and AAA growth will decline from current 20% to long-term 7%. Johnson estimates the required rate of return for AAA and TST to be 15.3% and 12.6%, respectively. Johnson's estimated values of AAA and TST using the H-model are *closest* to:

AAA	TST
A. $15.35	$52.96
B. $24.04	$35.58
C. $24.04	$52.96

7. Johnson's supervisor also requested a calculation of the justified leading P/E ratios for the two firms using a macroeconomic multifactor model based on the information in Table 2 (on the previous page) to estimate the required returns. Assuming that the earnings and dividends will grow at 5% for TST and 7% for AAA, the justified leading P/E ratios are *closest* to:

AAA	TST
A. 11.11	12.87
B. 7.26	9.21
C. 11.89	13.21

Use the following information to answer Questions 8 and 9.

Sally Curten, CFA, has gathered the following information on Jameston Fiber Optics, Inc., (JFOI) and industry norms.

Selected Financial Data for JFOI (in millions)

Total sales:	$2,044	(fiscal year 2016)
Total assets:	$1,875	(FYE 2015)
Net income:	$322	(fiscal year 2016)
Total debt:	$1,465	(FYE 2015)

Industry ratios:	Net profit margin	= 15.7%
	Total asset turnover	= 1.1
	Return on equity	= 40.5%

8. The return on equity for JFOI is *closest* to:
   A. 17.2%.
   B. 37.4%.
   C. 78.5%.

9. Using DuPont analysis, Curten determines that the *most influential* factor(s) that management used to increase the ROE for JFOI compared to the industry is:
   A. asset efficiency.
   B. profitability.
   C. leverage.

Use the following information to answer Questions 10 and 11.

Lisa Design pays a current annual dividend of €2.00 and is currently growing at a rate of 20%. This rate is expected to decline to 10% over four years and remain at that level indefinitely. The required rate of return for an investment in Lisa Design is 18%.

10. The current estimated value of Lisa Design using the H-model is *closest* to:
    A. €24.22.
    B. €29.78.
    C. €32.50.

11. Suppose instead that the 20% growth rate is expected to persist for four years and then decline immediately to 10%, at which level it will remain indefinitely. The current estimated value of Lisa Design is *closest* to:
    A. €31.99.
    B. €32.50.
    C. €37.76.

12. Jill Smart is an analyst with Allenton Partners. Jill is reviewing the valuation of three companies (P, Q, and R) using the dividend discount model (DDM) and their corresponding current market prices.

    The information below summarizes the findings:

	Stock		
	P	Q	R
Market price	35	40	38
DDM price	40	35	38

    Based on the above information, which statement best describes the market's valuation of P, Q, and R?
    A. P is overvalued, Q is undervalued, and R is fairly valued.
    B. P is undervalued, Q is fairly valued, and R is overvalued.
    C. P is undervalued, Q is overvalued, and R is fairly valued.

KEY CONCEPTS

LOS 29.a

In stock valuation models, there are three predominant definitions of future cash flows: dividends, free cash flow, and residual income.

Dividends are appropriate when:

- The company has a history of dividend payments.
- The dividend policy is clear and related to the earnings of the firm.
- The asset is being valued from the position of a minority shareholder.

Free cash flow is appropriate when:

- The company does not have a dividend payment history or has a dividend payment history that is not related to earnings.
- The free cash flow corresponds with the firm's profitability.
- The asset is being valued from the position of a controlling shareholder.

Residual income is most appropriate for firms that:

- Do not have dividend payment histories.
- Have negative free cash flow for the foreseeable future.
- Have transparent financial reporting and high-quality earnings.

LOS 29.b

Stock valuation can be approached using DDMs for single periods, two periods, and multiple holding periods. No matter what the holding period, the stock price is the present value of the forecasted dividends plus the present value of the estimated terminal value, discounted at the required return.

LOS 29.c

The Gordon growth model assumes that:

- Dividends grow at a constant growth rate.
- Dividend policy is related to earnings.
- Required rate of return r is greater than the long-term constant growth rate g.

$$V_0 = \frac{D_0 \times (1 + g)}{r - g} = \frac{D_1}{r - g}$$

LOS 29.d

If P_0 is fairly priced:

$$P_0 = V_0 = D_1 / (r - g)$$
$$g = r - (D_1 / P_0)$$

LOS 29.e

The value of an asset is equal to the current earning stream divided by the required return, plus the present value of growth opportunities (PVGO):

$$\text{value} = \frac{\text{earnings}}{\text{required return}} + \text{PVGO}$$

LOS 29.f

The Gordon growth model can also be used to estimate justified leading and trailing P/E ratios based on the fundamentals of the firm:

$$\text{justified leading P/E} = \frac{P_0}{E_1} = \frac{1-b}{r-g}$$

$$\text{justified trailing P/E} = \frac{P_0}{E_0} = \frac{(1-b) \times (1+g)}{r-g}$$

LOS 29.g

The value of a fixed-rate perpetual preferred stock is equal to the dividend divided by the required return:

$$\text{value of perpetual preferred shares} = \frac{D_p}{r_p}$$

LOS 29.h

The GGM has a number of characteristics that make it useful and appropriate for many applications:

- Very applicable to stable, mature dividend-paying firms.
- Can be applied to indices very easily.
- Easily communicated and explained because of its straightforward approach.
- Useful in determining price-implied growth rates, required rates of return, and value of growth opportunities.
- Can be added to other more complex valuations.

There are also some characteristics that limit the applications of the Gordon model:

- Valuations are very sensitive to estimates of growth rates and required rates of return, both of which are difficult to estimate with precision.
- The model cannot be easily applied to non-dividend-paying stocks.
- Unpredictable growth patterns of some firms would make using the model difficult.

LOS 29.i, 29.l

Multistage growth models have a number of strengths and a few limitations.

Strengths:

- Multiple-stage DDMs are flexible.

- The models can be used to estimate values given assumptions of growth and required return or to derive required returns and projected growth rates implied by market prices.

- The models enable the analyst to review all of the assumptions built into the models and to consider the impact of different assumptions.

- The models are very easily constructed and computed with the use of spreadsheet software.

Limitations:

- The estimates are only as good as the assumptions and projections used as inputs.

- A model must be fully understood in order for the analyst to arrive at accurate estimates. Without a clear understanding of the model, the effects of assumptions cannot be determined.

- The estimates of value are very sensitive to the assumptions of growth and required return.

- Formulas and data input can lead to errors that are difficult to identify.

There are several multistage growth models, with the most appropriate being the one that most closely matches the firm's actual growth pattern. The terminal value for multistage models is estimated using the Gordon growth model or market price multiples.

- The two-stage model has two distinct stages with a stable rate of growth during each stage.

- The H-model also has two stages but assumes that the growth rate declines at a constant linear rate during the first stage and is stable in the second stage:

$$V_0 = \frac{D_0 \times (1 + g_L)}{r - g_L} + \frac{D_0 \times H \times (g_S - g_L)}{r - g_L}$$

- The three-stage model can either have stable growth rates in each of the three stages or have a linearly declining rate in the second stage.

- The spreadsheet model can incorporate any number of stages with specified rates of growth for each stage. This is most easily modeled with a computer spreadsheet.

LOS 29.j

Most firms go through a pattern of growth that includes three stages:

■ An initial growth stage, where the firm has rapidly increasing earnings, little or no dividends, and heavy reinvestment.

■ A transition stage, in which earnings and dividends are still increasing but at a slower rate as competitive forces reduce profit opportunities and the need for reinvestment.

■ A mature stage, in which earnings grow at a stable but slower rate, and payout ratios are stabilizing as reinvestment matches depreciation and asset maintenance requirements.

LOS 29.k

No matter which dividend discount model we use, we have to estimate a terminal value using either the Gordon growth model or the market multiple approach. The Gordon growth model assumes that in the future, dividends will begin to grow at a constant, long-term rate. Then the terminal value at that point is just the value derived from the Gordon growth model.

Using market price multiples to estimate the terminal value involves, for example, forecasting earnings and a P/E ratio at the forecast horizon and then estimating the terminal value as the P/E multiplied by the earnings estimate.

LOS 29.m

Given all of the other inputs to the Gordon growth model or H-model, we can rearrange the formula to back into the expected return that makes the present value of the forecasted dividend stream equal to the current market price:

GGM:

$$r = \frac{D_1}{P_0} + g$$

H-Model:

$$r = \left[\left(\frac{D_0}{P_0} \right) \times \left\{ (1 + g_L) + [H \times (g_S - g_L)] \right\} \right] + g_L$$

LOS 29.n

In practice, financial analysts are much more likely to use a spreadsheet than any of the stylized models present here when valuing equity securities. The reason for this is the inherent flexibility and computational accuracy of spreadsheet modeling. Steps include:

■ Establish the base level of cash flows or dividends.

■ Estimate changes in the firm's dividends for the foreseeable future.

■ Estimate what normalized level of growth will occur at the end of the supernormal growth period, allowing for an estimate of a terminal value.

■ Discount and sum all projected dividends and the terminal value back to today.

LOS 29.o

The SGR is defined as the rate that earnings (and dividends) can continue to grow indefinitely, assuming that a firm's debt-to-equity ratio is unchanged and it doesn't issue any new equity. It can be derived from the relationship between the firm's retention rate and ROE as determined by the DuPont formula:

$$g = \left(\frac{\text{net income} - \text{dividends}}{\text{net income}}\right) \times \left(\frac{\text{net income}}{\text{sales}}\right) \times \left(\frac{\text{sales}}{\text{total assets}}\right) \times \left(\frac{\text{total assets}}{\text{stockholders' equity}}\right)$$

This has also been called the PRAT model, where SGR is a function of the profit margin (P), the retention rate (R), the asset turnover (A), and the degree of financial leverage (T). Use beginning-of-period balance sheet values unless otherwise instructed.

LOS 29.p

If the model price is lower than (higher than, equal to) the market price, the stock is considered overvalued (undervalued, fairly valued).

Study Session 10

ANSWER KEY FOR MODULE QUIZZES

Module Quiz 29.1

1. **C** Residual income models are the best valuation method if the firm does not pay dividends, has negative free cash flow over the forecast horizon, and has transparent financial reporting and high earnings quality. (LOS 29.a)

2. **A** EBEE's stock price today can be calculated using the two-stage model. Start by finding the value of the dividends during the high-growth period of five years.

$$D_1 = D_0(1 + g)^1 = \$2.50(1.30)^1 = \$3.25$$
$$D_2 = D_0(1 + g)^2 = \$2.50(1.30)^2 = \$4.225$$
$$D_3 = D_0(1 + g)^3 = \$2.50(1.30)^3 = \$5.493$$
$$D_4 = D_0(1 + g)^4 = \$2.50(1.30)^4 = \$7.140$$
$$D_5 = D_0(1 + g)^5 = \$2.50(1.30)^5 = \$9.282$$

(Alternatively, you could use your financial calculator to solve for the future value to find D_1, D_2, D_3, D_4, and D_5.)

Next find the value of the stock at the beginning of the constant growth period using the constant growth model: $P_5 = \dfrac{D_6}{r - g}$

CAPM: $r = 0.05 + (1.2 \times 0.06) = 0.122$

$$D_6 = D_5 \times (1 + g) = \$9.282 \times 1.07 = \$9.932$$

$$P_5 = \frac{D_6}{r - g} = \frac{\$9.932}{0.122 - 0.07} = \$191.00$$

The easiest way to proceed is to use the NPV function on the financial calculator.

$CF_0 = 0$; $CF_1 = 3.25$; $CF_2 = 4.225$; $CF_3 = 5.493$; $CF_4 = 7.140$; $CF_5 = 9.282 + 191.00 = 200.282$

$I = 12.2$; $NPV = 127.28$

The value of the firm today is \$127.28 per share. (LOS 29.b)

Module Quiz 29.2

1. **A** The value of a perpetuity (equal payments forever) is equal to annual cash flow divided by required return:

$$V = \frac{C\$5.00}{0.09} = C\$55.56$$

(LOS 29.g)

2. **C** The constant DDM can be used to solve for the required rate of return:

$$r = \frac{D_0 \times (1+g)}{P_0} + g = \frac{\$2.50 \times 1.08}{\$89} + 0.08 = 0.110 = 11.0\%$$

(LOS 29.c)

3. **B** Solve the following equation for g:

$$30.28 = \frac{2(1+g)}{0.13-g}$$

$30.28(0.13 - g) = 2(1 + g)$

$3.9364 - 30.28g = 2 + 2g$

$1.9364 = 32.28g$

$g = 6\%$

(LOS 29.c)

4. **A** The growth rate is –3%. Therefore,

$$\text{stock value} = \frac{D_1}{r-g} = \frac{\$4.00}{0.09 - (-0.03)} = \$33.33.$$

(LOS 29.c)

5. **A** We calculate the value of the expected cash flows at nine years because the formula uses the value of the dividend of t + 1 and then discounts that value to the present at the required rate of return of 12%.

$$V_9 = \frac{\$1.25}{0.12-0.04} = \$15.63$$

$$V_0 = \frac{\$15.63}{1.12^9} = \$5.64$$

(LOS 29.c)

6. **C** The PVGO must be less than zero because the ROE is less than the required return, but the firm is still retaining and reinvesting its cash flow. That means it is destroying value!

$$D_1 = \$4.50 \times 0.40 = \$1.80$$

$$g = 0.0833 \times (1-0.4) = 0.05 = 5\%$$

$$V_0 = \frac{\$1.80}{0.15-0.05} = \$18.00$$

$$V_0 = \frac{E}{r} + PVGO$$

$$PVGO = V_0 - \frac{E}{r} = \$18.00 - \frac{\$4.50}{0.15} = \$18.00 - \$30.00 = -\$12.00$$

(LOS 29.e)

Module Quiz 29.3

1. **B** Based on its fundamentals, Aerosail is most appropriately categorized as being in the transition phase. Multistage models are most appropriate for firms in the transition phase. (LOS 29.j)

2. **B** Solve for the internal rate of return of the expected cash flows.
   CF0 = −39.71
   C01 = 1.00
   C02 = 2.00
   C03 = 54.50 = 52.00 + 2.50 CPT → IRR 13.5% (LOS 29.l)

3. **B** Sustainable growth is equal to return on equity multiplied by retention ratio:

   SGR(AAA) = 0.30 × 0.40 = 0.120 = 12.0%

   SGR(TST) = 0.22 × 0.30 = 0.66 = 6.6%

   (LOS 29.o)

4. **C** The required returns for the two companies based on the CAPM are calculated below.

   AAA: r = 0.04 + 1.2(0.11 − 0.04) = 0.04 + 0.084 = 0.124

   TST: r = 0.04 + 0.9(0.11 − 0.04) = 0.04 + 0.063 = 0.103

   The current values of the two stocks using the constant DDM are calculated next.

   Sustainable growth is equal to return on equity multiplied by retention ratio:

   SGR(AAA) = 0.30 × 0.40 = 0.120 = 12.0%

   SGR(TST) = 0.22 × 0.30 = 0.66 = 6.6%

   Current dividend is current EPS multiplied by payout ratio:

   D_0(AAA) = $2,50 × (1 − 0.4) = $1.50

   D_0(TST) = $4.60 × (1 − 0.3) = $3.22

   Value is calculated with the Gordon constant growth model:

   $$P_0\left(AAA\right) = \frac{\$1.50 \times 1.12}{0.124 - 0.12} = \$420.00$$

   $$P_0\left(TST\right) = \frac{\$3.22 \times 1.066}{0.103 - 0.066} = \$92.77$$

   (LOS 29.b)

5. **A** AAA's stock price today can be calculated using the two-stage model. Start by finding the value of the dividends during the high growth period of five years.

D_0 = (current EPS)(1 – retention ratio) = $2.50 \times (1 - 0.40) = \$1.50$

$D_1 = D_0(1 + g)^1 = \$1.50(1.2)^1 = \$1.800$

$D_2 = D_0(1 + g)^2 = \$1.50(1.2)^2 = \$2.160$

$D_3 = D_0(1 + g)^3 = \$1.50(1.2)^3 = \$2.592$

$D_4 = D_0(1 + g)^4 = \$1.50(1.2)^4 = \$3.110$

Next, find the value of the stock at the beginning of the constant growth period using the constant dividend discount model: $P_4 = \dfrac{D_5}{r-g}$

CAPM: $r = 0.04 + (1.2 \times 0.07) = 0.124$

$D_5 = D_4 \times (1+g) = \$3.11 \times 1.07 = \$3.3277$

$$P_4 = \frac{D_5}{r-g} = \frac{\$3.3277}{0.124 - 0.07} = \$61.624$$

The easiest way to proceed is to use the NPV function in the financial calculator.

$CF_0 = 0$; $CF_1 = 1.8$; $CF_2 = 2.16$; $CF_3 = 2.592$; $CF_4 = 3.110 + 61.624 = 64.734$

$I = 12.4$; NPV = 45.69

The value of the firm today is $45.69 per share. (LOS 29.l)

6. **C** The estimated value of AAA using the H-model is calculated as follows:

$$V_0 = \frac{(\$1.50 \times 1.07) + \left[\$1.50 \times \dfrac{4}{2} \times (0.20 - 0.07)\right]}{0.153 - 0.07} = \$24.04$$

The estimated value of TST using the H-model is calculated as follows:

$$V_0 = \frac{(\$3.22 \times 1.05) + \left[\$3.22 \times \dfrac{4}{2} \times (0.15 - 0.05)\right]}{0.126 - 0.05} = \$52.96$$

(LOS 29.l)

7. **B** Required rate of return from the macroeconomic multifactor model:

    AAA: $0.04 + (0.048 \times 0.63) + (0.031 \times 0.47) + (0.045 \times 0.70) + (0.038 \times 0.98) + (-0.018 \times 0.05) = 0.1527$

    TST: $0.04 + (0.048 \times 0.42) + (0.031 \times 0.39) + (0.045 \times 0.51) + (0.038 \times 0.91) + (-0.018 \times 0.21) = 0.126$

    $$\text{Justified leading P/E (AAA)} = \frac{1-b}{r-g} = \frac{0.6}{0.1527-0.07} = 7.26$$

    $$\text{Justified leading P/E (TST)} = \frac{1-b}{r-g} = \frac{0.7}{0.126-0.05} = 9.21$$

    (LOS 29.f)

8. **C** $\text{ROE} = \dfrac{\$322}{\$1,875-\$1,465} = 78.5\%$ (LOS 29.o)

9. **C** The higher ROE for JFOI is largely due to higher leverage. Assets-to-equity for the industry is calculated as:

    $0.405 = 0.1570 \times 1.1 \times (\text{assets/equity}) \Rightarrow (\text{assets/equity}) = 2.35$

    The ratios for JFOI are calculated as:

    $$(\text{NI/sales}) = \frac{\$322}{\$2,044} = 0.1575$$

    $$(\text{sales/assets}) = \frac{\$2,044}{\$1,875} = 1.09$$

    $$(\text{assets/equity}) = \frac{\$1,875}{\$1,875-\$1,465} = \frac{\$1,875}{\$410} = 4.57$$

    The comparison of DuPont equations for JFOI and the industry are shown below.

    ROE = profitability × asset efficiency × leverage

    ROE = NI/sales × sales/assets × assets/equity

    Industry: $0.405 = 0.1570 \times 1.1 \times 2.35$

    JFOI: $0.785 = 0.1575 \times 1.09 \times 4.57$

    Therefore, the higher leverage resulted in a larger ROE for JFOI relative to the industry. (LOS 29.o)

10. **C** The H-model uses a half-life factor equal to one-half of the declining stage in years. This approach values the dividend growth at the long-term rate and adds an estimate for the additional value of the supernormal growth during the first stage.

    $$V = \frac{\left[€2.00 \times (1.10) \right] + \left[€2.00 \times \left(\frac{4}{2}\right) \times (0.20-0.10) \right]}{(0.18-0.10)} = €32.50$$

    (LOS 29.m)

11. **C** $D_1 = 2(1.20) = €2.40$; $D_2 = 2(1.20)^2 = €2.88$; $D_3 = 2(1.20)^3 = 3.46$;
$D_4 = 2(1.20)^4 = €4.15$

$$P_4 = \frac{D_5}{r-g} = \frac{2(1.20)^4(1.10)}{0.18-0.10} = €57.02$$

$PV(D_1, D_2, D_3, D_4 + P_4; r = 18\%) = €37.76$

(LOS 29.l)

12. **C** Stock P has model price higher than the market price and hence is undervalued by the market. Stock Q has model price lower than the market price and hence is overvalued. Stock R has model price equal to the market price and hence is fairly valued. (LOS 29.p)

The following is a review of the Equity Valuation (3) principles designed to address the learning outcome statements set forth by CFA Institute. Cross-Reference to CFA Institute Assigned Reading #30.

READING 30

Free Cash Flow Valuation

Study Session 11

EXAM FOCUS

This topic review introduces the concept of free cash flow. The value of a firm's stock is calculated by forecasting free cash flow to the firm (FCFF) or free cash flow to equity (FCFE) and discounting these cash flows back to the present at the appropriate required rate of return. FCFF or FCFE are the appropriate models to use when (1) the firm doesn't pay dividends at all or pays out fewer dividends than dictated by its cash flow, (2) free cash flow tracks profitability, or (3) the analyst takes a corporate control perspective. Make sure you see the parallels between the free cash flow framework and the discounted dividend framework (i.e., the basic free cash flow model is analogous to the Gordon growth model). Memorize the formulas for FCFF and FCFE. This is a very important test topic, as many analysts prefer free cash flow models to dividend discount models.

MODULE 30.1: FCF COMPUTATION

Video covering this content is available online.

Warm-Up: Free Cash Flow

Forget about all the complicated financial statement relationships for a minute and simply picture the firm as a cash *processor*. Cash flows into the firm in the form of revenue as it sells its product, and cash flows out as it pays its cash operating expenses (e.g., salaries and taxes, but not interest expense, which is a financing and not an operating expense). The firm takes the cash that's left over and makes short-term net investments in working capital (e.g., inventory and receivables) and long-term investments in property, plant, and equipment (PP&E). The cash that remains is available to pay out to the firm's investors: bondholders and common shareholders (let's assume for the moment that the firm has not issued preferred stock). That pile of remaining cash is called **free cash flow to the firm** (FCFF) because it's *free* to pay out to the firm's investors (see Figure 30.1). The formal definition of FCFF is the cash available to all of the firm's investors, including stockholders and bondholders, after the firm buys and sells products, provides services, pays its cash operating expenses, and makes short- and long-term investments.

PROFESSOR'S NOTE

Taxes paid are included in the definition of cash operating expenses for purposes of defining free cash flow, even though taxes aren't generally considered a part of operating income.

What does the firm do with its FCFF? First, it takes care of its bondholders because common shareholders are paid after all creditors. So it makes interest payments to bondholders and borrows more money from them or pays some of it back. However, making interest payments to bondholders has one advantage for common shareholders: it reduces the tax bill.

The amount that's left after the firm has met all its obligations to its other investors is called **free cash flow to equity** (FCFE), as can be seen in Figure 30.1. However, the board of directors still has discretion over what to do with that money. It could pay it all out in dividends to its common shareholders, but it might decide to only pay out some of it and put the rest in the bank to save for next year. That way, if FCFE is low the next year, it won't have to cut the dividend payment. So FCFE is the cash available to common shareholders after funding capital requirements, working capital needs, and debt financing requirements.

PROFESSOR'S NOTE

You need to know these general definitions. We will explore how these two cash flow measures are estimated using accounting data, and in the process we'll throw a lot of formulas at you. It's much easier to remember these formulas and repeat them on the exam if you have a conceptual understanding of what FCFF and FCFE represent. That way if, for example, you happen to forget the FCFE formula on exam day, you still have a chance to reconstruct it by thinking through what FCFE really is.

Figure 30.1: FCFF and FCFE

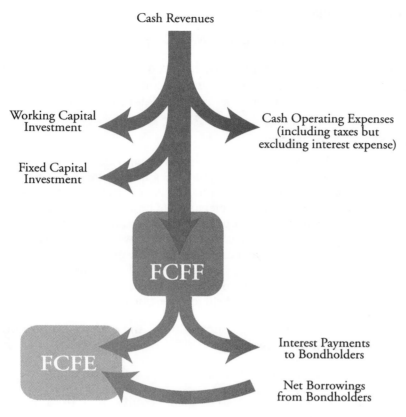

 PROFESSOR'S NOTE

You may be wondering, why does net borrowing affect FCFE but not FCFF? Think of FCFF as the cash flow generated by the firm's core business. Borrowing isn't generated by the firm's core business, so net borrowing has no impact on FCFF. On the other hand, think of FCFE as cash that could be given to shareholders, if management wanted to. Net borrowing increases FCFE.

LOS 30.a: Compare the free cash flow to the firm (FCFF) and free cash flow to equity (FCFE) approaches to valuation.

CFA® Program Curriculum: Volume 4, page 285

We will use the typical discounted cash flow technique for free cash flow valuation, in which we estimate value today by discounting expected future cash flows at the appropriate required return. What makes this complicated is that we'll end up with two values we want to estimate (firm value and equity value), two cash flow definitions (FCFF and FCFE), and two required returns [weighted average cost of capital (WACC) and required return on equity]. The key to this question on the exam is knowing which *cash flows* to discount at which *rate* to estimate which *value*.

The value of the *firm* is the present value of the expected future *FCFF* discounted at the *WACC* (this is so important we're going to repeat it as a formula):

firm value = FCFF discounted at the WACC

The weighted average cost of capital is the required return on the firm's assets. It's a weighted average of the required return on common equity and the after-tax required return on debt. The formula is presented later in this topic review.

 PROFESSOR'S NOTE

Technically, what we've called firm value is actually the value of the operating assets (the assets that generate cash flow). Significant nonoperating assets, such as excess cash (not total cash on the balance sheet), excess marketable securities, or land held for investment should be added to this estimate to calculate total firm value. Most of the time, the value of these assets is small in relation to the present value of the FCFFs, so we don't lose much by ignoring it. If you are asked to calculate the value of the firm using the FCFF approach, calculate the present value of the FCFFs and then look for any additional information in the problem that specifically says "excess cash and marketable securities" or "land held for investment."

The value of the firm's *equity* is the present value of the expected future *FCFE* discounted at the *required return on equity*:

equity value = FCFE discounted at the required return on equity

Given the value of the firm, we can also calculate equity value by simply subtracting out the market value of the debt:

equity value = firm value − market value of debt

Details of the calculations are discussed later in this topic review. However, this is an extremely important concept, so memorize it now.

 PROFESSOR'S NOTE

A very common mistake is to use the wrong discount rate or the wrong cash flow definition. Remember, always discount FCFF at the WACC to find firm value and FCFE at the required return on equity to estimate equity value.

The differences between FCFF and FCFE account for differences in capital structure and consequently reflect the perspectives of different capital suppliers. FCFE is easier and more straightforward to use in cases where the company's capital structure is not particularly volatile. On the other hand, if a company has negative FCFE and significant debt outstanding, FCFF is generally the best choice. We can always estimate equity value indirectly by discounting FCFF to find firm value and then subtracting out the market value of debt to arrive at equity value.

LOS 30.b: Explain the ownership perspective implicit in the FCFE approach.

CFA® Program Curriculum: Volume 4, page 285

The ownership perspective in the free cash flow approach is that of an acquirer who can change the firm's dividend policy, which is a control perspective, or for minority shareholders of a company that is *in-play* (i.e., it is a takeover target with potential bidders). The ownership perspective implicit in the dividend discount approach is that of a minority owner who has no direct control over the firm's dividend policy. If investors are willing to pay a premium for control of the firm, there may be a difference between the values of the same firm derived using the two models.

Analysts often prefer to use free cash flow rather than dividend-based valuation for the following reasons:

■ Many firms pay no, or low, cash dividends.

■ Dividends are paid at the discretion of the board of directors. It may, consequently, be poorly aligned with the firm's long-run profitability.

■ If a company is viewed as an acquisition target, free cash flow is a more appropriate measure because the new owners will have discretion over its distribution (control perspective).

■ Free cash flows may be more related to long-run profitability of the firm as compared to dividends.

 MODULE QUIZ 30.1

To best evaluate your performance, enter your quiz answers online.

1. Chamber Group is analyzing the potential takeover of Outmenu, Inc. Chamber has gathered the following data on Outmenu. All figures are in millions of dollars.

	2016	2015	2014	2013
Net income	–$26	$34	$18	$26
FCFE	–$1	–$23	$14	–$15
FCFF	$3	$4	$6	$8
Dividends	$5	$5	$4	$4
Debt-to-equity	93%	91%	78%	84%

The *most appropriate* model for valuing Outmenu is the:
A. free cash flow to equity model.
B. dividend discount H-model.
C. free cash flow to the firm model.

2. Suppose an analyst uses the statement of cash flows to calculate free cash flow to the firm (FCFF) as cash flow from operations less fixed capital investment, and free cash flow to equity (FCFE) as FCFF plus net borrowing. The firm has short- and long-term debt on its balance sheet. Has the analyst correctly stated, overstated, or understated FCFF and FCFE?

	FCFF	FCFE
A.	Overstated	Correct
B.	Understated	Understated
C.	Understated	Correct

3. An analyst calculates firm value using a single-stage model on December 31, 2017, as:

$$\text{value of the firm} = \frac{\text{FCF E}_{2018}}{r - g} + \text{MVD}$$

where:

FCF E$_{2018}$ = free cash flow to equity forecast for 2018

r = required return on equity

g = growth rate in FCFE

MVD = market value of debt on 12/31/2017

Assuming there are no nonoperating assets on the balance sheet, the analyst has *most likely*:
A. correctly calculated firm value.
B. incorrectly calculated firm value. The weighted average cost of capital should be substituted for the required return on equity.
C. incorrectly calculated firm value. The weighted average cost of capital should be substituted for the required return on equity, and FCFE$_{2017}$(1 + g) should be substituted for FCFE$_{2018}$.

MODULE 30.2: FIXED AND WORKING CAPITAL COMPUTATION

Video covering this content is available online.

LOS 30.c: Explain the appropriate adjustments to net income, earnings before interest and taxes (EBIT), earnings before interest, taxes, depreciation, and amortization (EBITDA), and cash flow from operations (CFO) to calculate FCFF and FCFE.

CFA® Program Curriculum: Volume 4, page 289

You may feel overwhelmed by the formulas in this topic review. We'll show you the ones you need to know for this LOS without showing you the derivations. The basic idea is that we can arrive at FCFF by starting with one of four different financial statement items (net income, EBIT, EBITDA, or cash flow from operations [CFO]) and then making the appropriate adjustments. Then we can calculate FCFE from FCFF or by starting with net income or CFO.

Calculating FCFF from net income. FCFF is calculated from net income as:

$$FCFF = NI + NCC + [Int \times (1 - \text{tax rate})] - FCInv - WCInv$$

where:
NI = net income
NCC = noncash charges
Int = interest expense
FCInv = fixed capital investment (capital expenditures)
WCInv = working capital investment

Notice that net income does not represent free cash flows defined as FCFF, so we have to make four important adjustments to net income to get to FCFF: noncash charges, fixed capital investment, working capital investment, and interest expense.

Noncash charges. Noncash charges are added back to net income to arrive at FCFF because they represent expenses that reduced reported net income but didn't actually result in an outflow of cash. The most significant noncash charge is usually depreciation. Here are some other examples of noncash charges that often appear on the cash flow statement:

- Amortization of intangibles should be added back to net income, much like depreciation.

- Provisions for restructuring charges and other noncash losses should be added back to net income. However, if the firm is accruing these costs to cover future cash outflows, then the forecast of future free cash flow should be reduced accordingly. Gains or losses on sale of long-term assets are also removed (they would be accounted for under fixed capital investment).

- Income from restructuring charge reversals and other noncash gains should be subtracted from net income.

- For a bond issuer, the amortization of a bond discount should be added back to net income, and the accretion of the bond premium should be subtracted from net income to calculate FCFF.

- Deferred taxes, which result from differences in the timing of reporting income and expenses for accounting versus tax purposes, must be carefully analyzed. Over time, differences between book and taxable income should offset each other and have no significant effect on overall cash flows. If, however, the analyst expects deferred tax liabilities to continue to increase (i.e., not reverse), increases in deferred tax liabilities should be added back to net income. Increases in deferred tax assets that are not expected to reverse should be subtracted from net income.

Fixed capital investment. Investments in fixed capital do not appear on the income statement, but they do represent cash leaving the firm. That means we have to subtract them from net income to estimate FCFF. Fixed capital investment is a net amount: it is equal to the difference between capital expenditures (investments in long-term fixed assets) and the proceeds from the sale of long-term assets:

$$FCInv = \text{capital expenditures} - \text{proceeds from sales of long-term assets}$$

Both capital expenditures and proceeds from long-term asset sales (if any) are likely to be reported on the firm's statement of cash flows. If no long-term assets were sold

Study Session 11

during the year, then capital expenditures will also equal the change in the gross PP&E account from the balance sheet.

So what is the Level II candidate supposed to do on exam day to calculate FCInv? Let's examine two cases: first, if no long-term assets were sold during the year, and second, if the company did sell long-term assets.

If no long-term assets were sold during the year:

FCInv = ending net PP&E − beginning net PP&E + depreciation

If long-term assets were sold during the year, then:

- Determine capital expenditures from either (1) an item in the statement of cash flows called something like "purchase of fixed assets" or "purchases of PP&E" under cash flow from investing activities, or (2) data provided in the vignette.

- Determine proceeds from sales of fixed assets from either (1) an item in the statement of cash flows called something like "proceeds from disposal of fixed assets," or (2) data provided in the vignette.

- Calculate FCInv = capital expenditures − proceeds from sale of long-term assets.

- If capital expenditures or sales proceeds are not given directly, find gain (loss) on asset sales from the income statement and PP&E figures from balance sheet. Calculate FCInv = ending net PP&E − beginning net PP&E + depreciation − gain on sale. If there is a loss on sale of assets, add that instead of deducting it.

EXAMPLE: Calculating FCInv with no long-term asset sales

Airbrush, Inc. financial statements for 2017 include the following information:

Selected Financial Data

	2017	2016
Gross PP&E	$5,000	$4,150
Accumulated depreciation	$1,500	$1,200
Net PP&E	$3,500	$2,950

There were no sales of PP&E during the year; depreciation expense was $300. Calculate Airbrush's FCInv for 2017.

Answer:

$$\begin{aligned} \text{FCInv} &= \text{capital expenditures} \\ &= \text{ending net PP\&E} - \text{beginning net PP\&E} + \text{depreciation} \\ &= \$3,500 - \$2,950 + \$300 = \$850 \end{aligned}$$

EXAMPLE: Calculating FCInv with long-term asset sales

Suppose that Air Brush reports capital expenditures of $1,400, long-term asset sales of $600, and depreciation expense of $850. The long-term assets sold were fully depreciated. Calculate Airbrush's revised FCInv for 2017.

Answer:

$$\text{revised FCInv} = \text{capital expenditures} - \text{proceeds from sales of long-term assets}$$
$$= \$1,400 - \$600 = \$800$$

Working capital investment. The investment in net working capital is equal to the change in working capital, *excluding cash, cash equivalents, notes payable, and the current portion of long-term debt.* Note that there would be a + sign in front of a *reduction* in working capital; we would add it back because it represents a cash inflow.

MODULE QUIZ 30.2

To best evaluate your performance, enter your quiz answers online.

1. The Anderson Door Co. earned C$30 million before interest and taxes on revenues of C$80 million last year. Capital expenditures were C$20 million, and depreciation was C$15 million. The additions to working capital were C$6 million. The firm's weighted average cost of capital is 12.45%, the marginal tax rate is 40%, and the expected cash flow growth is 5%. The market value of debt is C$25 million. The value of the firm's equity is *closest* to:
    A. C$73.70.
    B. C$93.96.
    C. C$98.70.

2. Imagine that we are provided the following information for a firm:
    - Net income = $50.

    - Working capital investment = $4.

    - Beginning gross fixed assets = $90; ending gross fixed assets = $136.

    - Beginning accumulated depreciation = $30; ending accumulated depreciation = $40.

    - Depreciation expense = $27.

    - Net borrowing = $0.

    In addition, a piece of equipment with an original book value of $19 was sold for $10. The equipment had a book value at the time of the sale of $2. The gain was classified as unusual. Free cash flow to equity is *closest* to:
    A. $6.
    B. $10.
    C. $18.

MODULE 30.3: NET BORROWING AND VARIATIONS OF FORMULAE

Video covering this content is available online.

Interest expense. Interest was expensed on the income statement, but it represents a financing cash flow to bondholders that is available to the firm *before* it makes any payments to its capital suppliers. Therefore, we have to add it back. However, we don't add back the entire interest expense, only the after-tax interest cost because paying interest reduces our tax bill. For example, if the marginal tax rate is 30%, every dollar of interest paid reduces the tax bill by 30 cents. The net effect on free cash flow is an increase in the after-tax interest cost of 70 cents.

Study Session 11

Figure 30.2: Calculating FCFF and FCFE Using the Statement of Cash Flows

Statement of Cash Flows	FCFF and FCFE	
Net income (NI)	Net income (NI)	
+ Noncash charges (NCC)	+ Noncash charges (NCC)	
– WCInv	– WCInv	
Cash flow from operations (CFO)	Cash flow from operations (CFO)	After-tax
	+ Int (1 – tax rate) ⟶	interest
– FCInv	– FCInv	expense is
		classified as
		financing
(Almost) FCFF	**(Actual) FCFF**	outflow
+ Net borrowing	+ Net borrowing	rather than
	– Int (1 – tax rate) ◀	operating
		outflow
FCFE	**FCFE**	
– Dividends	– Dividends	
+/– Common stock issues (repurchases)	+/– Common stock issues (repurchases)	
Net change in cash	Net change in cash	

Unfortunately, you have to memorize a number of free cash flow formulas to be fully prepared for the exam. However, we can use the statement of cash flows (as it is required to be reported under U.S. GAAP) as a framework to provide some intuition concerning the free cash flow formulas and perhaps make it a little easier to remember these formulas.

Given our conceptual discussion of FCFF and FCFE, it would make sense to define them as shown in the first column of Figure 30.2.

PROFESSOR'S NOTE

Depreciation is added back in full because we will claim it on our taxes, yet it doesn't represent an actual cash flow. Interest isn't added back in full, because if we retain that cash, we'll have lower interest expense, and thus higher tax.

Free cash flow to the firm is the operating cash flow left after the firm makes working capital and fixed capital investment. Therefore, we can get close to the actual calculation by using the first column in Figure 30.2:

$$\text{(Almost) FCFF} = (\text{NI} + \text{NCC} - \text{WCInv}) - \text{FCInv}$$
$$= \text{CFO} - \text{FCInv}$$

We're not quite there, however, because of one unique feature of the statement of cash flows: interest expense is considered an operating cash flow, whereas we'd like to call it a financing cash flow. Because interest is tax deductible, the after-tax interest expense [interest × (1 – tax rate)] reduces net income; but, we want to add it back to net income and then subtract it out as a financing cash outflow. By doing that, we go from our (almost) definition to the actual formula for FCFF (as shown in the second column in Figure 30.2):

$$\text{(Actual) FCFF} = (\text{NI} + \text{NCC} - \text{WCInv}) + \text{Int}(1 - \text{tax rate}) - \text{FCInv}$$
$$= \text{CFO} + \text{Int}(1 - \text{tax rate}) - \text{FCInv}$$

We can also use the second column format to calculate FCFE directly from FCFF:

$$\text{FCFE} = \text{FCFF} - \text{Int}(1 - \text{tax rate}) + \text{net borrowing}$$

Notice that any financial decisions that affect cash flows below FCFE (e.g., dividends, share repurchases, and share issues) do not affect FCFF or FCFE.

Calculating FCFF from EBIT. FCFF can also be calculated from earnings before interest and taxes (EBIT):

$$\text{FCFF} = [\text{EBIT} \times (1 - \text{tax rate})] + \text{Dep} - \text{FCInv} - \text{WCInv}$$

where:
EBIT = earnings before interest and taxes
Dep = depreciation

If we start with earnings before interest and taxes (EBIT), we have to add back depreciation because it was subtracted out to get to EBIT. However, because EBIT is before interest and taxes, we don't have to take out interest (remember that it's a financing cash flow). We do have to adjust for taxes, though, by computing after-tax EBIT, which is EBIT multiplied by one minus the tax rate. We also make the same adjustments as we did before by subtracting out fixed capital and working capital investment.

PROFESSOR'S NOTE

Because many noncash adjustments occur on the income statement below EBIT, we don't need to adjust for them when calculating free cash flow if we start with EBIT. We assume that the only noncash charge that appears above EBIT is depreciation in the equation "FCFF from EBIT." In general, however, the rule is to adjust for any noncash charge that appears on the income statement abo ve the income statement item you're starting with.

Calculating FCFF from EBITDA. We can also start with earnings before interest, taxes, depreciation, and amortization (EBITDA) to arrive at FCFF:

$$\text{FCFF} = [\text{EBITDA} \times (1 - \text{tax rate})] + (\text{Dep} \times \text{tax rate}) - \text{FCInv} - \text{WCInv}$$

where:
EBITDA = earnings before interest, taxes, depreciation, and amortization

Remember that EBITDA is before depreciation, so we only have to add back the depreciation tax shield, which is depreciation multiplied by the tax rate. Even though depreciation is a noncash expense, the firm reduces its tax bill by expensing it, so the free cash flow available is increased by the taxes saved.

Calculating FCFF from CFO. Finally, FCFF can also be estimated by starting with cash flow from operations (CFO) from the statement of cash flows:

$$FCFF = CFO + [Int \times (1 - tax\ rate)] - FCInv$$

where:
CFO = cash flow from operations

Cash flow from operations is equal to net income plus noncash charges less working capital investment. We have to add back to CFO the after-tax interest expense to get to FCFF because interest expense (and the resulting tax shield) was reflected on the income statement to arrive at net income. We also have to subtract out fixed capital investment since CFO only includes changes in working capital investment.

PROFESSOR'S NOTE

Which formula should you use on the exam? I suggest that, at a minimum, you memorize the first one (that starts with net income) and the last one (that starts with cash flow from operations). That way, given either an income statement or a cash flow statement, you can calculate FCFF. However, don't be surprised if you're required to know the other two as well.

Calculating FCFE from FCFF. Calculating FCFE is easy once we have FCFF:

$$FCFE = FCFF - [Int \times (1 - tax\ rate)] + net\ borrowing$$

where:
net borrowing = long- and short-term new debt issues − long- and short-term
debt repayments

If we start with FCFF, we have to adjust for the two cash flows to bondholders to calculate FCFE: the after-tax interest expense and any new long- or short-term borrowings. We only subtract the after-tax interest expense because paying interest reduces the firm's tax bill and reduces the cash available to the shareholders by the interest paid minus the taxes saved.

Calculating FCFE from net income. We can also calculate FCFE from net income by making some of the usual adjustments. The two differences between this "FCFE from net income" formula and the "FCFF from net income formula" are (1) after-tax interest expense is not added back and (2) net borrowing is added back.

$$FCFE = NI + NCC - FCInv - WCInv + net\ borrowing$$

Calculating FCFE from CFO. Finally, we can calculate FCFE from CFO by subtracting out fixed capital investment (which reduces cash available to shareholders) and adding back net borrowing (which increases the cash available to shareholders).

$$FCFE = CFO - FCInv + net\ borrowing$$

Free Cash Flow With Preferred Stock

The FCFF and FCFE formulas assume that the company uses only debt and common equity to raise funds. The use of preferred stock requires the analyst to revise the FCFF and FCFE formulas to reflect the payment of preferred dividends and any issuance or repurchase of such shares. *Remember to treat preferred stock just like debt, except preferred dividends are not tax deductible.*

Specifically, any preferred dividends should be added back to the FCFF, just as after-tax interest charges are in the net income approach to generating FCFF. This approach assumes that *net income* is net income to common shareholders after preferred dividends have been subtracted out. The WACC should also be revised to reflect the percent of total capital raised by preferred stock and the cost of that capital source. The only adjustment to FCFE would be to modify net borrowing to reflect new debt borrowing and net issuances by the amount of the preferred stock. Keep in mind that relatively few firms issue preferred stock.

MODULE QUIZ 30.3

To best evaluate your performance, enter your quiz answers online.

Use the following information to answer Questions 1 through 3.

Meyer Henderson, CFA, is analyzing the financials of Roth Department Stores. He intends to use a free cash flow to the firm (FCFF) model to value Roth's common stock. In the 2016 financial statements and footnotes he has identified the following items:

- Item #1: Roth reported depreciation and software amortization of $23 million in 2016.

- Item #2: The deferred tax liability increased by $17 million in 2016.

- Item #3: Roth reported income of $6 million in 2016 from the reversal of previous restructuring charges related to store closings in 2015.

- Item #4: Net income totaled $173 million in 2016.

- Item #5: The net increase in noncash net working capital accounts was $47 million in 2016.

- Item #6: Net capital spending totaled $86 million in 2016.

- Item #7: Roth reported interest expense of $19 million.

Henderson estimated Roth's marginal tax rate to be 35%. He also expects Roth to be profitable for the foreseeable future, so he does not expect the deferred tax liability to reverse. As the base-year projection for his FCFF valuation, Henderson calculates FCFF for 2016 as:

$$\text{FCFF}_{2016} = \$173 + \$23 + \$6 + \$17 + [\$19(1 - 0.35)] - \$86 - \$47$$
$$= \$98.35 \text{ million}$$

1. In implementing the FCFF model to value Roth, did Henderson correctly treat Items #1 and #2?
   A. Both items were treated correctly.
   B. One item was treated correctly and the other incorrectly.
   C. Neither item was treated correctly.

2. In implementing the FCFF model to value Roth, did Henderson correctly treat Items #3 and #4?
   A. Both items were treated correctly.
   B. One item was treated correctly and the other incorrectly.
   C. Neither item was treated correctly.

3. In implementing the FCFF model to value Roth, did Henderson correctly treat Items #5 and #7?
   A. Both items were treated correctly.
   B. One item was treated correctly and the other incorrectly.
   C. Neither item was treated correctly.

MODULE 30.4: EXAMPLE

Video covering this content is available online.

LOS 30.d: Calculate FCFF and FCFE.

CFA® Program Curriculum: Volume 4, page 289

Let's try an example to see if all these formulas really work.

> **EXAMPLE: Calculating FCFF and FCFE**
>
> Anson Ford, CFA, is analyzing the financial statements of Sting's Delicatessen. He has a 20X6 income statement and balance sheet, as well as 20X7 income statement, balance sheet, and cash flow from operations forecasts (as shown in the following tables). Assume there will be no sales of long-term assets in 20X7. Calculate forecasted free cash flow to the firm (FCFF) and free cash flow to equity (FCFE) for 20X7.
>
> **Sting's Income Statement**
>
> | Income Statement | | |
> |---|---|---|
> | | **20X7 Forecast** | **20X6 Actual** |
> | Sales | $300 | $250 |
> | Cost of goods sold | 120 | 100 |
> | Gross profit | 180 | 150 |
> | SG&A | 35 | 30 |
> | Depreciation | 50 | 40 |
> | EBIT | 95 | 80 |
> | Interest expense | 15 | 10 |
> | Pre-tax earnings | 80 | 70 |
> | Taxes (at 30%) | 24 | 21 |
> | Net income | $56 | $49 |

Sting's Balance Sheet

Balance Sheet		
	20X7 Forecast	**20X6 Actual**
Cash	$10	$5
Accounts receivable	30	15
Inventory	40	30
Current assets	$80	$50
Gross property, plant, and equipment	400	300
Accumulated depreciation	(190)	(140)
Total assets	$290	$210
Accounts payable	$20	$20
Short-term debt	20	10
Current liabilities	$40	$30
Long-term debt	114	100
Common stock	50	50
Retained earnings	86	30
Total liabilities and owners' equity	$290	$210

Sting's Cash Flow From Operations Forecast

Cash Flow From Operations Forecast for 20X7	
Net income	$56
+ depreciation	50
– WCInv	25
Cash flow from operations	$81

Answer:

Fixed capital investment is equal to capital expenditures (because there are no asset sales), which is equal to the change in net PP&E plus depreciation:

Net PP&E 20X6 = (gross PP&E) – (accumulated depreciation) = 300 – 140
 = 160

FCInv = (210 – 160) + 50
 = 100

Working capital investment is the change in the working capital accounts, excluding cash and short-term borrowings:

$$\text{WCInv} = (\text{AcctsRec}_{20X7} + \text{Inv}_{20X7} - \text{AcctsPay}_{20X7}) -$$
$$(\text{AcctsRec}_{20X6} + \text{Inv}_{20X6} - \text{AcctsPay}_{20X6})$$

$$\text{WCInv} = (30 + 40 - 20) - (15 + 30 - 20) = 50 - 25 = 25$$

Given that depreciation is the only noncash charge, we can calculate FCFF from net income:

$$\begin{aligned} \text{FCFF} &= \text{NI} + \text{NCC} + [\text{Int} \times (1 - \text{tax rate})] - \text{FCInv} - \text{WCInv} \\ &= 56 + 50 + [15 \times (1 - 0.3)] - 100 - 25 = -8.5 \\ &= 56 + 50 + 10.5 - 100 - 25 = -8.5 \end{aligned}$$

It's entirely possible that FCFF can be negative in the short term. We'll talk more later about how to value firms with negative FCFF.

Net borrowing is the difference between the new debt issues, and debt repayments:

$$\begin{aligned} \text{net borrowing} &= (\text{long- and short-term new debt issues}) - (\text{long- and} \\ &\qquad \text{short-term debt repayments}) = (114 + 20) - (100 + 10) = 24 \end{aligned}$$

$$\begin{aligned} \text{FCFE} &= \text{FCFF} - [\text{Int}(1 - \text{tax rate})] + \text{net borrowing} \\ &= -8.5 - 10.5 - 24 = 5 \end{aligned}$$

EXAMPLE: Calculating FCFF and FCFE with the other formulas

Calculate FCFF starting with EBIT, EBITDA, and CFO, and calculate FCFE starting with NI and CFO.

Answer:

$$\begin{aligned} \text{FCFF} &= [\text{EBIT} \times (1 - \text{tax rate})] + \text{Dep} - \text{FCInv} - \text{WCInv} \\ &= [95 \times (1 - 0.3)] + 50 + -100 - 25 = -8.5 \end{aligned}$$

$$\begin{aligned} \text{FCFF} &= [\text{EBITDA} \times (1 - \text{tax rate})] + (\text{Dep} \times \text{tax rate}) - \text{FCInv} - \text{WCInv} \\ &= [145 \times (1 - 0.3)] + (50 \times 0.3) - 100 - 25 = -8.5 \end{aligned}$$

$$\begin{aligned} \text{FCFF} &= \text{CFO} + [\text{Int} \times (1 - \text{tax rate})] - \text{FCInv} \\ &= 81 + [15 \times (1 - 0.3)] - 100 = -8.5 \end{aligned}$$

$$\begin{aligned} \text{FCFE} &= \text{NI} + \text{Dep} - \text{FCInv} - \text{WCInv} + \text{net borrowing} \\ &= 56 + 50 - 100 - 25 + 24 = 5 \end{aligned}$$

$$\begin{aligned} \text{FCFE} &= \text{CFO} - \text{FCInv} + \text{net borrowing} \\ &= 81 - 100 + 24 = 5 \end{aligned}$$

EXAMPLE: Calculating FCFF and FCFE using the statement of cash flows

In order to see how all these formulas fit together, reconstruct the framework from Figure 30.2 using the actual numbers from the previous example.

Answer:

Net income	$56.0	
+ noncash charges	+ 50.0	
− WCInv	− 25.0	
Cash flow from operations		$81.0
+ Int (1 − tax rate)	+ 10.5	
− FCInv	− 100.0	
FCFF		**−$8.5**
+ net borrowing	+ 24.0	
− Int (1 − tax rate)	− 10.5	
FCFE		**+$5.0**

An analyst may also be concerned about the uses of cash flow. Typically, this is done to verify the FCFF calculation, as FCFF sources must always equal FCFF uses, and FCFE sources must always equal FCFE uses.

Uses FCFF = changes in cash balances
+net payments to debt providers
+net payments to equity stakeholders

Uses FCFE = changes in cash balances
+net payments to equity stakeholders

MODULE QUIZ 30.4

To best evaluate your performance, enter your quiz answers online.

1. The adjustments to cash flow from operations necessary to obtain free cash flow to the firm (FCFF) are:
   A. add noncash charges, subtract fixed capital investment, and subtract working capital investment.
   B. add after-tax interest expense and subtract fixed capital investment.
   C. add net borrowing and subtract fixed capital investment.

Video covering this content is available online.

MODULE 30.5: FCF OTHER ASPECTS

LOS 30.e: Describe approaches for forecasting FCFF and FCFE.

CFA® Program Curriculum: Volume 4, page 310

Two approaches are commonly used to forecast future FCFF and FCFE.

The first method is to calculate *historical free cash flow* and apply a growth rate under the assumptions that growth will be constant and fundamental factors will be maintained. For example, we could calculate free cash flow in the most recent year and then forecast it to grow at 8% for four years and 4% forever after that. This is the same method we used for dividend discount models. Note that the growth rate for FCFF is usually different than the growth rate for FCFE.

The second method is to forecast the underlying *components of free cash flow* and calculate each year separately. This is a more realistic, more flexible, and more complicated method because we can assume that each component of free cash flow is growing at a different rate over some short-term horizon. This often ties sales forecasts to future capital expenditures, depreciation expenses, and changes in working capital. Importantly, capital expenditures have two dimensions: outlays that are needed to maintain *existing capacity* and marginal outlays that are needed to support *growth*. Thus, the first type of outlay is related to the current level of sales, and the second type depends on the predicted sales growth.

In forecasting FCFE with the second method, it is common to assume that the firm maintains a *target debt-to-asset ratio* for net new investment in fixed capital and working capital. For example, if the target debt ratio is 40% and fixed capital investment is $60 million, $24 million (0.40 multiplied by $60 million) is assumed to be financed with debt and $36 million with equity. Thus, net borrowing may be expressed without having to specifically forecast underlying debt issuance or repayment. This implies that we can forecast FCFE with the following formula:

$$FCFE = NI - [(1 - DR) \times (FCInv - Dep)] - [(1 - DR) \times WCInv]$$

where:
DR = target debt-to-asset ratio

LOS 30.f: Compare the FCFE model and dividend discount models.

CFA® Program Curriculum: Volume 4, page 315

The free cash flow to equity approach takes a control perspective that assumes that recognition of value should be immediate. Dividend discount models take a minority perspective, under which value may not be realized until the dividend policy accurately reflects the firm's long-run profitability.

LOS 30.g: Explain how dividends, share repurchases, share issues, and changes in leverage may affect future FCFF and FCFE.

CFA® Program Curriculum: Volume 4, page 315

This is a deceptively simple LOS. The short answer is that dividends, share repurchases, and share issues have *no effect* on FCFF and FCFE; changes in leverage have only a minor effect on FCFE and no effect on FCFF.

The reason is very straightforward. FCFF and FCFE represent cash flows available to investors and shareholders, respectively, before any payout decisions. Dividends and share repurchases, on the other hand, represent *uses* of those cash flows; as such, these financing decisions don't affect the level of cash flow *available*. Changes in leverage will have a small effect on FCFE. For example, a decrease in leverage through a repayment of debt will decrease FCFE in the current year and increase forecasted FCFE in future years as interest expense is reduced.

LOS 30.h: Evaluate the use of net income and EBITDA as proxies for cash flow in valuation.

CFA® Program Curriculum: Volume 4, page 316

Net income is a poor proxy for FCFE. We can see that by simply examining the formula for FCFE in terms of NI.

Once again, we have not burdened you with the derivation:

$$FCFE = NI + NCC - FCInv - WCInv + net\ borrowing$$

Net income includes noncash charges like depreciation that have to be added back to arrive at FCFE. In addition, it ignores cash flows that don't appear on the income statement, such as investments in working capital and fixed assets as well as net borrowings.

EBITDA is a poor proxy for FCFF. We can also see this from the formula relating FCFF to EBITDA (which you've already seen):

$$FCFF = [EBITDA \times (1 - tax\ rate)] + (Dep \times tax\ rate) - FCInv - WCInv$$

EBITDA doesn't reflect the cash taxes paid by the firm, and it ignores the cash flow effects of the investments in working capital and fixed capital.

LOS 30.i: Explain the single-stage (stable-growth), two-stage, and three-stage FCFF and FCFE models and select and justify the appropriate model given a company's characteristics.

CFA® Program Curriculum: Volume 4, page 320

Single-Stage FCFF Model

The single-stage FCFF model is analogous to the Gordon growth model discussed in the previous topic review on dividend valuation models. The single-stage FCFF model is useful for stable firms in mature industries. The model assumes that (1) FCFF grows at a constant rate (g) forever, and (2) the growth rate is less than the weighted average cost of capital (WACC).

The formula should look familiar; it's the Gordon growth model with FCFF replacing dividends and WACC replacing required return on equity.

$$\text{value of the firm} = \frac{\text{FCFF}_1}{\text{WACC} - g} = \frac{\text{FCFF}_0 \times (1 + g)}{\text{WACC} - g}$$

where:
FCFF_1 = expected free cash flow to the firm in one year

FCFF_0 = starting level of FCFF

g = constant expected growth rate in FCFF

WACC = weighted average cost of capital

The WACC is the weighted average of the rates of return required by each of the capital suppliers (usually just equity and debt) where the weights are the proportions of the firm's total market value from each capital source:

$$\text{WACC} = \left(w_e \times r_e\right) + \left[w_d \times r_d \times (1 - \text{tax rate})\right]$$

where :

$$w_e = \frac{\text{market value of equity}}{\text{market value of equity} + \text{market value of debt}}$$

$$w_d = \frac{\text{market value of debt}}{\text{market value of equity} + \text{market value of debt}}$$

It is assumed that payments to stockholders are *not* tax deductible, and payments to debtholders are tax deductible. Thus, the after-tax cost of debt is the before-tax rate of return on debt multiplied by one minus the firm's marginal tax rate. WACC will change over time as the firm's capital structure changes. Therefore, analysts usually use target capital structure weights rather than actual weights. On the exam, use target weights if they are given in the problem; otherwise use actual market-value weights.

Single-Stage FCFE Model

The single-stage constant-growth FCFE valuation model is analogous to the single-stage FCFF model, with FCFE instead of FCFF and required return on equity instead of WACC:

$$\text{value of equity} = \frac{FCFE_1}{r - g} = \frac{FCFE_0 \times (1 + g)}{r - g}$$

where:
$FCFE_1$ = expected free cash flow to equity in one year

$FCFE_0$ = starting level of FCFE

g = constant expected growth rate in FCFE

r = required return on equity

PROFESSOR'S NOTE

It's quite likely that a firm's growth rate in FCFF will be different than its FCFE growth rate.

The single-stage FCFE model is often used in international valuation, especially for companies in countries with high inflationary expectations when estimation of nominal growth rates and required returns is difficult. In those cases, real (i.e., inflation-adjusted) values are estimated for the inputs to the single-stage FCFE model: FCFE, the growth rate, and the required return.

Multistage Models: How Many Variations Are There?

This is where things get a little complicated. If we analyze every possible permutation of multistage free cash flow models that might appear on the exam, you would be overwhelmed. There are at least three important ways that these models can differ. Let's take them one at a time, but keep in mind the basic valuation principle at work here: *value is always estimated as the present value of the expected future cash flows discounted at the appropriate discount rate.*

FCFF versus FCFE: Remember that the value of the firm is the present value of the FCFF discounted at the WACC; the value of equity is the present value of the FCFE discounted at the required return on equity.

Two-stage versus three-stage models: We can model the future growth pattern in two stages or three. There are several variations of each approach depending on how we model growth within the stages.

Forecasting growth in total free cash flow (FCFF or FCFE) versus forecasting the growth rates in the components of free cash flow: The simple free cash flow model, in which we forecast total FCFE or FCFF, looks a lot like the multistage dividend discount models. The benefit of using free cash flow models, however, is when we refine our approach by forecasting the values and/or growth rates in the components of free cash flow over the first stage and then calculate free cash flow in each year using one of our formulas. There are even variations of this approach in which we start with earnings per share instead of sales.

Model Assumptions and Firm Characteristics

The assumptions for the two- and three-stage free cash flow models are simply the assumptions we make about the projected pattern of growth in free cash flow. We would use a two-stage model for a firm with two stages of growth: a short-term supernormal growth phase and a long-term stable growth phase. For example, a firm with a valuable patent that expires in seven years might experience a high growth rate for seven years and then immediately drop to a long-term, lower growth rate beginning in the eighth year. We would use a three-stage model for a firm that we expect to have three distinct stages of growth (e.g., a growth phase, a mature phase, and a transition phase).

Examples of Two-Stage Models

Let's discuss some examples of two-stage models. We're going to wait until the next LOS, however, to start doing the number crunching. For now, concentrate on the differences in the assumptions: FCFF versus FCFE, growth pattern in the first stage, and forecasting total free cash flow versus forecasting its components.

We could analyze a:

- Two-stage FCFF model in which FCFF is projected to grow at 20% for the first four years and then 4% every year thereafter.

- Two-stage FCFE model in which FCFE declines from 20% to 4% over four years and then stays at 4% forever.

- Two-stage FCFE model in which sales grow at 20% for four years, the net profit margin is constant at 8%, fixed capital investment is equal to 60% of the dollar increase in sales, working capital investment is equal to 25% of the dollar increase in sales, and the debt ratio is 50%. Given a starting value for sales, we have all we need to forecast FCFE for the first four years.

Remember that we also need a terminal value at the end of the first growth stage for each of these examples. The most common method for estimating terminal value is to apply a single-stage free cash flow model at the point in time when growth settles down to its long-run level. This is the same method we used in the last topic review with dividend discount models.

Examples of Three-Stage Models

Three-stage models have all the complications of the two-stage models, with an additional growth stage to consider. Keep in mind, however, that what we're trying to do is forecast FCFF or FCFE over some interim period with three distinct stages of growth, estimate the terminal value, and then estimate the value of the firm or the value of the equity today as the present value of those cash flows discounted at the appropriate required return. For example, we could analyze a:

- Three-stage FCFE model in which FCFE grows at 30% for two years (stage 1), 15% for four years (stage 2), and then 5% forever (stage 3).

■ Three-stage FCFF model in which FCFF grows at 25% for three years (stage 1), declines to 4% over next the five years (stage 2), then stays at 4% forever (stage 3).

■ Three-stage FCFE model in which we forecast the components of FCFE over three different stages.

LOS 30.j: Estimate a company's value using the appropriate free cash flow model(s).

CFA® Program Curriculum: Volume 4, page 320

We've already discussed free cash flow models, so now let's get to the hard work: actually calculating value using these models. We won't go through every different possible example, but we will give you a range of examples that cover nearly every important concept.

Single-Stage FCFF Model

The first example is a basic single-stage FCFF model where we first calculate WACC as the appropriate required return.

> **EXAMPLE: Calculating firm value with a single-stage FCFF model**
>
> Knappa Valley Winery's (KVW) most recent FCFF is $5,000,000. KVW's target debt-to-equity ratio is 0.25. The market value of the firm's debt is $10,000,000, and KVW has 2,000,000 shares of common stock outstanding. The firm's tax rate is 40%, the shareholders require a return of 16% on their investment, the firm's before-tax cost of debt is 8%, and the expected long-term growth rate in FCFF is 5%. Calculate the value of the firm and the value per share of the equity.
>
> **Answer:**
>
> Note that the problem gives the FCFF in the most recent year ($FCFF_0$). Therefore, you need to increase $FCFF_0$ at the growth rate by one year (at the 5% rate) to get $FCFF_1$.
>
> Let's calculate the WACC. The target debt-to-equity ratio is 0.25. This implies that for every $1 of debt, there is $4 of equity, for total capital of $5. Since total assets equals total capital, it follows that the target debt-to-asset ratio is 1/5, or 20%, and the target equity-to-asset ratio is 4/5, or 80%. The WACC is:
>
> $$\text{WACC} = (w_e \times r_e) + [w_d \times r_d \times (1 - \text{tax rate})]$$
>
> $$= (0.8 \times 0.16) + [0.20 \times 0.08(1 - 0.40)] = 0.1376 = 13.76\%$$
>
> We can now calculate the value of the firm as:
>
> $$\text{value of firm} = \frac{\$5,000,000 \times 1.050}{0.1376 - 0.050} = \$59,931,507$$
>
> Given that debt is worth $10,000,000, the implied total value of the equity is:
>
> value of equity = $59,931,507 − $10,000,000 = $49,931,507

With 2,000,000 shares outstanding, the value of the equity per share is:

$$\frac{\$49,931,507}{2,000,000} = \$24.97$$

Notice that the actual debt-to-equity ratio (10,000,000 / 49,931,507 = 0.20) does not equal the target ratio of 0.25. There is nothing inconsistent in this example. WACC is usually calculated using target capital weights.

Single-Stage FCFE Model

EXAMPLE: Calculating value with a single-stage FCFE model

Ridgeway Construction has an FCFE of 2.50 Canadian dollars (C$) per share and is currently operating at a target debt-to-equity ratio of 0.4. The expected return on the market is 9%, the risk free rate is 4%, and Ridgeway has a beta of 1.5. The expected growth rate of FCFE is 4.5%. Calculate the value of Ridgeway stock.

Answer:

Begin by computing the required return on equity with the CAPM:

$$r = 0.04 + [1.50 \times (0.09 - 0.04)] = 0.115 = 11.5\%$$

Note that the problem gives FCFE in the most recent year ($FCFE_0$). The model calls for the FCFE *next* year, which is $FCFE_1$. Therefore, you need to multiply $FCFE_0$ by one plus the growth rate to get $FCFE_1$. The equity value per share is:

$$\text{equity value per share} = \frac{\text{C\$2.50} \times 1.045}{0.115 - 0.045} = \text{C\$37.32}$$

PROFESSOR'S NOTE

In the first example, we calculated total value and then equity value per share by dividing total value by the number of shares. In the second example we were given FCFE per share, so we could calculate value per share directly. Read the questions on the exam carefully to make sure you use the correct approach given the information in the problem.

Two-Stage FCFF Model

The first two-stage example requires the FCFF model and a forecast of the components of FCFF during the high-growth stage.

EXAMPLE: Calculating value with a two-stage FCFF model

The Prentice Paint Company earned a net profit margin of 20% on revenues of $20 million this year. Fixed capital investment was $2 million, and depreciation was $3 million. Working capital investment equals 7.5% of sales every year. Net income, fixed capital investment, depreciation, interest expense, and sales are expected to grow at 10% per year for the next five years. After five years, the growth in sales, net income, fixed capital investment, depreciation, and interest expense will decline to a stable 5% per year. The tax rate is 40%, and Prentice has 1 million shares of common stock outstanding and long-term debt paying 12.5% interest trading at its par value of $32 million. Calculate the value of the firm and its equity using the FCFF model if the WACC is 17% during the high-growth stage and 15% during the stable stage.

Answer:

The components of FCFF are calculated in the following table.

FCFF for Years 0 Through 6 (in per-share amounts of $)

	0	1	2	3	4	5	6
Sales ($)	20.00	22.00	24.20	26.62	29.28	32.21	33.82
Net Income	4.00	4.40	4.84	5.32	5.86	6.44	6.76
Interest (1 − T)	2.40	2.64	2.90	3.19	3.51	3.87	4.06
Depreciation	3.00	3.30	3.63	3.99	4.39	4.83	5.07
FCInv	2.00	2.20	2.42	2.66	2.93	3.22	3.38
WCInv	1.50	1.65	1.82	2.00	2.20	2.42	2.54
FCFF	**$5.90**	**$6.49**	**$7.13**	**$7.84**	**$8.63**	**$9.50**	**$9.97**

Let's demonstrate the calculation of the FCFF in Year 0:

net income	$= \$20.00 \times 0.20 = \$4.00$
interest	$= \$32.00 \times 0.125 = \$4.00$
interest(1 − T)	$= \$4.00 \times (1 - 0.40) = \$2.40$
WCInv	$= \$20.00 \times 0.075 = \$1.50$
FCFF	$= \$4.00 + \$2.40 + \$3.00 - \$2.00 - \$1.50 = \$5.90$

In Year 1, sales grow by 10% to $22.00 per share. Following five years of 10% growth, the growth of each component falls to 5%.

The terminal value (as of Year 5, discounted at the stable WACC of 15%) is:

$$\text{terminal value} = \frac{\text{FCFF}_6}{\text{WACC} - g} = \frac{\$9.97}{0.15 - 0.05} = \$99.70$$

We can place the cash flows to be evaluated on a time line, such as the one in the following figure, to get a clearer picture of what we need to evaluate.

FCFF Timeline

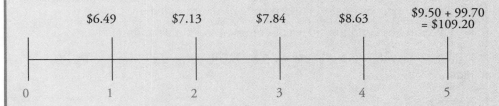

Notice that the WACC in the high-growth stage (17%) is different than the stable stage (15%).

We calculated terminal value in Year 5 using 15%, but we'll calculate the present value today of the high-growth cash flows and the terminal value at 17%. The total of the firm today is:

$$\text{value of firm} = \frac{\$6.49}{1.17^1} + \frac{\$7.13}{1.17^2} + \frac{\$7.84}{1.17^3} + \frac{\$8.63}{1.17^4} + \frac{\$109.20}{1.17^5} = \$70.06$$

To perform this calculation quickly and accurately, use the following keystrokes on your financial calculator:

$CF_0 = 0$; $C01 = 6.49$; $C02 = 7.13$; $C03 = 7.84$; $C04 = 8.63$; $C05 = 109.20$
$I = 17$; $CPT \rightarrow NPV = 70.06$

Thus, given that the value of the firm's debt is $32 per share, the value of equity per share is $70.06 - $32.00 = $38.06.

It is uncommon for growth rates to drop as drastically and quickly from stage 1 to stage 2 as shown in the previous example. It is more likely to find a gradual decline in the growth rate as a company matures and attracts more competition that will decrease its profit margin and its sustainable growth rate. This next two-stage example is an FCFE model with declining growth rates in stage 1 and constant growth in stage 2.

EXAMPLE: Two-stage FCFE model with declining growth in stage 1

Consider a rival to the Prentice Paint Company presented in the previous example. Suppose that Sioux Falls Decor also has revenues of $20 million this year. However, we assume that its future performance will be tracked relative to sales as follows:

■ Sales growth and the net profit margin are projected by year as shown in the following table:

Sales and Net Margin Forecasts

Year	1	2	3	4	5	6
Sales growth	30%	25%	20%	15%	10%	5%
Net profit margin	8.0%	7.5%	7.0%	6.0%	5.5%	5.0%

■ Fixed capital investment *net of depreciation* is projected to be 30% of the sales increase in each year.

■ Working capital requirements are 7.0% of the projected dollar increase sales in each year.

■ Debt will finance 40% of the investments in net capital and working capital.

■ The company has a 12% required rate of return on equity.

■ The firm has 1 million shares of common stock outstanding.

Calculate the value of the equity of Sioux Falls using the two-stage FCFE model.

Answer:

Recognize that the target debt-to-asset ratio (DR) is 0.40. The following table shows the FCFE for years 1 through 6 ($ amounts are per share).

Calculating FCFE for Years 1 Through 6

Year	1	2	3	5	6
Sales growth	30%	25%	20%	10%	5%
Net profit margin	8.0%	7.5%	7.0%	5.5%	5.0%
Sales	$26.00	$32.50	$39.00	$49.335	$51.802
Net income	2.08	2.44	2.73	2.71	2.59
FCInv – Dep	1.80	1.95	1.95	1.346	0.74
WCInv	0.42	0.455	0.455	0.314	0.171
Debt financing*	0.888	0.962	0.962	0.664	0.364
FCFE	$0.748	$0.997	$1.287	$1.714	$2.043

* Debt will finance 40% of the investment in net capital and working capital.

debt financing = (debt-to-asset ratio) × [(FCInv − Dep) + WCInv]

So for year 3:

debt financing = (0.4) × [(1.95) + 0.455] = 0.962

Let's demonstrate the calculation of the cash flow components in Year 1:

sales $\qquad$ = $20.00 × 1.30 = $26.00
net income $\quad$ = $26.00 × 0.08 = $2.08
net FCInv $\quad$ = ($26.00 − $20.00) × 0.30 = $1.80
WCInv $\qquad$ = ($26.00 − $20.00) × 0.07 = $0.42
FCFE $\qquad$ = NI − [(1 − DR) × (FCInv − Dep)] − [(1 − DR) × WCInv]
$\qquad\qquad$ = $2.08 − [(1 − 0.4) × $1.80] − [(1 − 0.4) × $0.42] = $0.748

Terminal value (as of Year 5, assuming 5% stable long-term growth) is equal to:

$$\text{terminal value} = \frac{\$2.043}{0.12 - 0.05} = \$29.186$$

Total current value of equity:

$$\text{value of equity} = \frac{\$0.748}{1.12^1} + \frac{\$0.997}{1.12^2} + \frac{\$1.287}{1.12^3} + \frac{\$1.391}{1.12^4} + \frac{\$1.714 + \$29.186}{1.12^5} = \$20.80$$

As usual, we would rely on the cash flow keys of our financial calculator to perform the above calculation:

$CF_0 = 0$; $C01 = 0.748$; $C02 = 0.997$; $C03 = 1.287$; $C04 = 1.391$; $C05 = 30.90$

$I = 12$; CPT → NPV = 20.80

Three-Stage FCFE Model

The following example of a three-stage FCFE model is a little different than the last two examples because we're given growth in total FCFE in each of three stages, rather than the growth rates in the components. Growth in the first and third stage is constant, while growth in the second stage is declining. There is one tricky feature to this problem—the required return in each of the three growth stages is different.

> **EXAMPLE: Three-stage FCFE model with forecast growth in total FCFE**
>
> Medina Classic Furniture, Inc. is expected to experience growth in three distinct stages in the future. Its most recent FCFE is 0.90 Canadian dollars (C$) per share. The following information has been compiled:
>
> *High-growth period:*
>
> ■ Duration = 3 years.
>
> ■ FCFE growth rate = 30%.
>
> ■ Shareholders' required return = 20%.
>
> *Transitional period:*
>
> ■ Duration = 3 years.
>
> ■ FCFE growth will decline by 9% per year down to the indicated stable growth rate.
>
> ■ Shareholders' required return = 15%.
>
> *Stable-growth period:*
>
> ■ FCFE growth rate = 3%.
>
> ■ Shareholders' required return = 10%.
>
> Calculate the value of the firm's equity using the three-stage FCFE model.
>
> **Answer:**
>
> The annual FCFE and the associated present value are presented in the table:
>
> **FCFE and PV**
>
> | High-Growth Period | Year 1 | Year 2 | Year 3 |
> |---|---|---|---|
> | Growth rate | 30% | 30% | 30% |
> | FCFE | C$1.170 | C$1.521 | C$1.977 |
> | PV (@ 20%) | C$0.975 | C$1.056 | C$1.144 |
>
> | Transitional Period | Year 4 | Year 5 | Year 6 |
> |---|---|---|---|
> | Growth rate | 21% | 12% | 3% |
> | FCFE | C$2.393 | C$2.680 | C$2.760 |
> | PV | C$1.204 | C$1.173 | C$1.050 |
>
> The transitional present values are computed using a combination of the 20% initial discount rate and the transitional 15% rate. For example, the present value of $FCFE_5$ is computed as:
>
> $$C\$1.173 = \frac{C\$2.680}{1.20^3 \times 1.15^2}$$

We can calculate the terminal value of the stock as of Year 6 using the FCFE projected for Year 7. Notice that we use the stage 3 required return of 10%.

$$\text{terminal value} = \frac{\$2.760 \times 1.03}{0.10 - 0.03} = \$40.611$$

The value of Medina stock is:

$$\text{value per share} = 0.975 + 1.056 + 1.144 + 1.204 + 1.173 + 1.050 + \left(\frac{40.611}{1.20^3 \times 1.15^3}\right)$$
$$= \text{C}\$22.055$$

The changing discount rates were important here for a couple of reasons. First, the terminal value in Year 6 had to be discounted for three years at 20% and for three years at 15%. Second, due to the changing discount rates, our financial calculator was not as helpful as it was in other multiple cash flow calculations. It simply cannot handle the changing discount rates in one easy set of calculations.

LOS 30.k: Explain the use of sensitivity analysis in FCFF and FCFE valuations.

CFA® Program Curriculum: Volume 4, page 321

Sensitivity analysis shows how sensitive an analyst's valuation results are to changes in each of a model's inputs. Some variables have a greater impact on valuation results than others. The importance of various forecasting errors can be assessed through comprehensive sensitivity analysis.

PROFESSOR'S NOTE

On the exam, it is unlikely that you will be asked to conduct a comprehensive sensitivity analysis that includes numerous calculations. However, a few key calculations and/or an interpretation of a sensitivity analysis are quite possible.

There are two major sources of error in valuation analysis:

- Estimating the future *growth* in FCFF and FCFE. Growth forecasts depend on a firm's future profitability, which in turn depends on sales growth, changes in profit margin, position in the life cycle, its competitive strategy, and the overall profitability of the industry.

- The chosen *base years* for the FCFF or FCFE growth forecasts. A representative base year must be chosen, or all of the subsequent analysis and valuation will be flawed.

For example, suppose an analyst is conducting a sensitivity analysis on the value of a beverage stock using the FCFE approach. She provides high and low estimates of the following variables consistent with their forecasted ranges in her model: FCFE, beta, risk-free rate of return, equity risk premium, and the FCFE growth rate. This produces a series of value estimates that reveal the sensitivity of her valuation estimate to variations in her underlying inputs.

LOS 30.l: Describe approaches for calculating the terminal value in a multistage valuation model.

CFA® Program Curriculum: Volume 4, page 323

There are two basic approaches for calculating terminal value: using a single-stage model or a multiple approach. All of our examples used the first approach, in which we forecasted an FCFF or FCFE at the point in time at which cash flows begin to grow at the long-term, stable growth rate, and then we estimated terminal value using a single-stage model.

The other way to do this is to use valuation multiples (like P/E ratios) to estimate terminal value. The terminal value in year *n* in terms of P/E, for example, would be expressed as:

terminal value in year *n* = (trailing P/E) × (earnings in year n)
terminal value in year *n* = (leading P/E) × (forecasted earnings in year n+1)

> **EXAMPLE: Estimating terminal value with a P/E multiple**
>
> An analyst estimates the EPS of Polar Technology in five years to be $2.10, the EPS in six years to be $2.32, and the median trailing industry P/E to be 35. Calculate the terminal value in Year 5.
>
> **Answer:**
>
> terminal value in Year 5 = 35 × $2.10 = $73.50

LOS 30.m: Evaluate whether a stock is overvalued, fairly valued, or undervalued based on a free cash flow valuation model.

CFA® Program Curriculum: Volume 4, page 334

If a stock is trading at a price (market price) higher than the price implied by a free cash flow valuation model (model price), the stock is considered to be **overvalued**. Similarly, if the market price is lower than the model price, the stock is considered to be **undervalued**, and if the model price is equal to the market price, the stock is considered to be **fairly valued**.

MODULE QUIZ 30.5

To best evaluate your performance, enter your quiz answers online.

1. The Gray Furniture Co. earned £3.50 per share last year. Investment in fixed capital was £2.00 per share, depreciation was £1.60, and the investment in working capital was £0.50 per share. Gray is currently operating at its target debt-to-asset ratio of 40%. Thus, 40% of annual investments in working capital and fixed capital will be financed with new borrowings. Shareholders require a return of 14% on their investment, and the expected growth rate is 4%. The value of Gray's stock is *closest* to:
   A. £27.04.
   B. £29.90.
   C. £30.78.

Use the following information to answer Questions 2 through 4.

The Sanford Software Co. earned $20 million before interest and taxes on revenues of $60 million last year. Investment in fixed capital was $12 million, and depreciation was $8 million. Working capital investment was $3 million. Sanford expects earnings before interest and taxes (EBIT), investment in fixed and working capital, depreciation, and sales to grow at 12% per year for the next five years. After five years, the growth in sales, EBIT, and working capital investment will decline to a stable 4% per year, and investments in fixed capital and depreciation will offset each other. Sanford's tax rate is 40%. Suppose that the weighted average cost of capital (WACC) is 11% during the high growth stage and 8% during the stable stage. The calculation of FCFF in years 1 through 5 is shown in the following table:

Year	0	1	2	3	4	5
Sales	60.00	67.20	75.26	84.30	94.41	105.74
EBIT	20.00	22.40	25.09	28.10	31.47	35.25
EBIT(1 − T)	12.00	13.44	15.05	16.86	18.88	21.15
Dep	8.00	8.96	10.04	11.24	12.59	14.10
FCInv	12.00	13.44	15.05	16.86	18.88	21.15
WCInv	3.00	3.36	3.76	4.21	4.72	5.29
FCFF	5.00	5.60	6.28	7.03	7.87	8.81

2. Free cash flow to the firm (FCFF) in Year 6 is *closest* to:
    A. $14.14.
    B. $16.49.
    C. $18.26.

3. The terminal value in Year 5 is *closest* to:
    A. $206.12.
    B. $220.25.
    C. $412.25.

4. The value of the firm using a FCFF model is *closest* to:
    A. $149.04.
    B. $265.17.
    C. $270.35.

Use the following information to answer Questions 5 through 9.

An analyst following Barlow Energy has compiled the following information in preparation for additional analysis she has to include in a report she has been asked to produce (data is in hundreds of millions of $):

Security Type	Market Value	Before-Tax Required Return
Preferred stock	$200	7.0%
Bonds	$600	7.5%
Common stock	$700	14.0%
Total	$1,500	

- Bonds are trading at par.
- Preferred share dividends: $14
- Net income available to common: $125

- Investment in working capital: $30
- Investment in fixed capital: $100
- Net new borrowing: $40
- Depreciation: $50
- Tax rate: 40%
- Long-term growth rate of FCFF: 4%
- Long-term growth rate of FCFE: 4%
- WACC: 9.27%

5. The current FCFF for Barlow Energy is *closest* to:
   A. $36.
   B. $62.
   C. $86.

6. The total value of Barlow Energy using a single-stage FCFF model is *closest* to:
   A. $894.40.
   B. $1,631.88.
   C. $1,697.15.

7. The value of Barlow Energy's equity using a single-stage FCFF model is *closest* to:
   A. $897.15.
   B. $1,097.15.
   C. $1,497.15.

8. The current FCFE using the information for Barlow Energy is *closest* to:
   A. $45.
   B. $85.
   C. $99.

9. The value of Barlow Energy's equity using a single-stage model and the current FCFE is *closest* to:
   A. $468.
   B. $850.
   C. $884.

10. Which of the following is the *best* estimate of the cash flows available to the firm's investors before any financing decisions?
    A. EBITDA × (1 − tax rate).
    B. EBITDA × (1 − tax rate) + (Dep × tax rate) − FCInv − WCInv.
    C. EBITDA × (1 − tax rate) + (Dep × tax rate) − FCInv − WCInv + Int × (1 − tax rate).

Use the following information to answer Questions 11 and 12.

Rachel Keimmel, CFA, is researching the MWC Corporation, a U.S.-based automobile parts manufacturing firm. MWC has recently entered into a long-term agreement with a German automobile company to be the sole supplier of an innovative suspension system that will be used with a newly designed, moderately priced sports car. Keimmel believes that this new agreement will favorably impact MWC's stock price. To support her belief, Keimmel reviewed MWC's financial statements and sales forecasts and reached the following conclusions:

- MWC's earnings and FCFE growth will be 15% per year for two years, then stabilize at 8% per year.
- MWC will maintain its current dividend payout ratio.

- MWC has a beta of 1.2.
- Government bonds yield 6.4%, and the market equity risk premium is 5.5%.
- The most recent dividend paid to MWC shareholders was $2.30.

Keimmel also has MWC's current cash flow statement, which follows.

MWC Incorporated
Statement of Cash Flows, December 31, 2017
($ Thousands)

Cash Flow from Operating Activities

Net income		29,960
Depreciation		8,400

Changes in Working Capital

(Increase) Decrease in receivables	(4,000)	
(Increase) Decrease in inventories	(6,400)	
Increase (Decrease) in payables	4,800	
Increase (Decrease) in other current liabilities	1,200	
Net change in working capital		(4,400)
Net cash from operating activities		33,960

Cash Flow from Investing Activities

Purchase of fixed assets (PP&E)	(12,000)	
Net cash from investing activities		(12,000)

Cash Flow from Financing Activities

Change in debt outstanding	3,200	
Payment of cash dividends	(23,920)	
Net cash from financing activities		(20,720)
Net change in cash and cash equivalents		1,240
Beginning-of-period cash		8,760
End-of-period cash		10,000

11. The value of MWC's common stock using the two-stage dividend discount model is *closest* to:
   A. $56.33.
   B. $61.55.
   C. $65.88.

12. The value of MWC's common stock using the two-stage FCFE approach is *closest* to:
    A. $55.09.
    B. $59.10.
    C. $68.24.

13. The Hoffman Card Co. earned £1.50 per share last year. Investment in fixed capital was £0.80 per share, and depreciation was £0.30. Investment in working capital was £0.20 per share. Hoffman expects earnings to grow at 15% per year for the next five years and that investment in fixed capital, depreciation, and investment in working capital will grow at the same rate. After five years, the growth in earnings and working capital requirements will decline to a stable 5% per year, and investment in fixed capital and depreciation will offset each other (i.e., they will be equal). Hoffman's target debt ratio is 30%. The shareholders require a return of 17% on their investment during the high-growth stage and a return of 10% on their investment during the stable stage. The FCFE in Year 6 and the value per share of Hoffman's common stock are *closest* to:

	FCFE in Year 6	Share value
A.	£2.03	£31.08
B.	£2.88	£31.08
C.	£2.88	£57.60

14. Suppose an analyst estimates equity value by discounting free cash flow to equity (FCFE) at the weighted average cost of capital (WACC) in the FCFE model and estimates firm and equity value by discounting free cash flow to the firm (FCFF) at the required return on equity in the FCFF model. The analyst would *most likely*:
    A. overestimate equity value with the FCFE model and underestimate firm value and equity value with the FCFF model.
    B. underestimate equity value with the FCFE model and overestimate firm value and equity value with the FCFF model.
    C. underestimate equity value with the FCFE model and underestimate firm value and equity value with the FCFF model.

Use the following information to answer Questions 15 and 16.

At the end of 2017, Meyer Henderson, CFA, also prepared a 10-year forecast of free cash flow to equity (FCFE) and free cash flow to the firm (FCFF) from 2018 to 2027 for Trammel Medical Supplies. In early 2018, Trammel unexpectedly announced a new 15-year issue of senior debt. The proceeds are expected to be used to repurchase common stock in the open market during 2018.

15. As a result of the unexpected debt issue, Henderson should *most likely*:
    A. increase his FCFE forecast for 2018 and decrease his FCFE forecast for 2019 through 2027.
    B. decrease his FCFE forecast for 2018 and increase his FCFE forecast for 2019 through 2027.
    C. increase his FCFE forecast for 2018 and not change his FCFE forecast for 2019 through 2027.

16. As a result of the unexpected debt issue, Henderson should *most likely*:
    A. increase his FCFF forecast for 2018 and decrease his FCFF forecast for 2019 through 2027.
    B. decrease his FCFF forecast for 2018 and increase his FCFF forecast for 2019 through 2027.
    C. not change his FCFF forecast for 2018 and also not change his FCFF forecast for 2019 through 2027.

KEY CONCEPTS

LOS 30.a

FCFF is the cash available to all of the firm's investors, including stockholders and bondholders, after the firm buys and sells products, provides services, pays its cash operating expenses, and makes short- and long-term investments. FCFE is the cash available to common shareholders after funding capital requirements, working capital needs, and debt financing requirements.

The value of the firm is the present value of the expected future FCFF discounted at the WACC. The value of the firm's equity is the present value of the expected future FCFE discounted at the required return on equity.

FCFE is easier and more straightforward to use in cases where the company's capital structure is not particularly volatile. On the other hand, if a company has negative FCFE and significant debt outstanding, FCFF is generally the best choice.

LOS 30.b

Analysts prefer to use either FCFF or FCFE as a measure of value if:

- The firm does not pay dividends.
- The firm pays dividends, but the dividends do not reflect the company's long-run profitability.
- The analyst takes a control perspective.

Thus, in valuation, the use of free cash flows reflects a control perspective while the use of dividends reflects a minority common stockholder's perspective. The ownership perspective in the free cash flow approach is that of an acquirer who can change the firm's dividend policy, which is a control perspective.

LOS 30.c, 30.d

FCFF and FCFE may be calculated starting either from net income, cash flows from operations, EBIT, or EBITDA. You need to know how to calculate the following measures using financial data:

$$FCFE = NI + NCC + [Int \times (1 - tax\ rate)] - FCInv - WCInv$$
$$FCFE = [EBIT \times (1 - tax\ rate)] + Dep - FCInv - WCInv$$
$$FCFE = [EBITDA \times (1 - tax\ rate)] + (Dep \times tax\ rate) - FCInv - WCInv$$
$$FCFE = CFO + [Int \times (1 - tax\ rate)] - FCInv$$
$$FCFE = FCFF - [Int \times (1 - tax\ rate)] + net\ borrowing$$
$$FCFE = NI + NCC - FCInv - WCInv + net\ borrowing$$
$$FCFE = CFO - FCInv + net\ borrowing$$

LOS 30.e

For forecasting FCFE, use:

$$FCFE = NI - [(1 - DR) \times (FCInv - Dep)] - [(1 - DR) \times WCInv]$$

©2018 Kaplan, Inc.

LOS 30.f

The free cash flow to equity approach takes a control perspective, which assumes that recognition of value should be immediate. Dividend discount models take a minority perspective, under which value may not be realized until the dividend policy accurately reflects the firm's long-run profitability.

LOS 30.g

Dividends, share repurchases, and share issues have no effect on FCFF and FCFE; changes in leverage have only a minor effect on FCFE and no effect on FCFF.

LOS 30.h

Net income is a poor proxy for FCFE. Net income includes noncash charges (e.g., depreciation) that have to be added back to arrive at FCFE. In addition, it ignores cash flows that don't appear on the income statement, such as investments in working capital and fixed assets as well as net borrowings. This can be seen by simply examining the formula for FCFE in terms of NI:

$$FCFE = NI + NCC - FCInv - WCInv + \text{net borrowing}$$

EBITDA is a poor proxy for FCFF. The following equation makes this point clear:

$$FCFF = EBITDA\,(1 - \text{tax rate}) + (Dep \times \text{tax rate}) - FCInv - WCInv$$

EBITDA doesn't reflect the cash taxes paid by the firm, and it ignores the cash flow effects of the investments in working capital and fixed capital.

LOS 30.i, 30.j

The single-stage free cash flow models are useful for stable firms in mature industries. The models assume free cash flows grow at a constant rate, g, forever and that the growth rate is less than the required return (WACC for FCFF models and required return on equity for FCFE models).

$$\text{value of the firm} = \frac{FCFF_1}{WACC - g}$$

$$\text{value of equity} = \frac{FCFE_1}{r - g}$$

The assumptions for the two- and three-stage free cash flow models are simply the assumptions we make about the projected pattern of growth in free cash flow. We'd use a two-stage model for a firm with two stages of growth: a short-term supernormal growth phase and a long-term stable growth phase. We'd use a three-stage model for a firm that we expect to have three distinct stages of growth (e.g., a growth phase, a mature phase, and a transition phase).

LOS 30.k

Sensitivity analysis shows how sensitive an analyst's valuation results are to changes in each of a model's inputs. Some variables have a greater impact on valuation results than others. The importance of various forecasting errors can be assessed through comprehensive sensitivity analysis.

LOS 30.l

There are two basic approaches for calculating terminal value: using a single-stage model or a multiple approach. The multiple approach uses valuation multiples (like P/E ratios) to estimate terminal value.

LOS 30.m

If a stock's model price is lower than (higher than, equal to) the market price, the stock is considered overvalued (undervalued, fairly valued).

ANSWER KEY FOR MODULE QUIZZES

Module Quiz 30.1

1. **C** Dividend discount models like the Gordon growth model and the dividend discount H-model are not appropriate in this case for two reasons: (1) dividends are not related to the firm's earnings stream, and (2) this is a takeover situation in which a free cash flow model is more appropriate.

   The FCFF model is preferred to the FCFE model because (1) FCFE is negative and volatile and (2) leverage is relatively high. (LOS 30.a)

2. **C** The firm must have interest expense on its income statement because of the debt on its balance sheet. By ignoring the after-tax interest cash flow, the analyst has understated FCFF, which is actually equal to CFO plus after-tax interest cash flow less fixed capital investment. He has, however, calculated FCFE correctly because FCFE is equal to CFO less fixed capital investment (his incorrect FCFF calculation) plus net borrowing. (LOS 30.c)

3. **A** Although the calculation is a bit unusual (we usually calculate firm value as the present value of FCFF discounted at the weighted average cost of capital), the analyst has correctly calculated firm value. The first term is equal to the market value of equity on 12/31/2017; firm value is equal to the market value of equity plus the market value of debt. (LOS 30.a)

Module Quiz 30.2

1. **A**

$$FCFF_0 = [EBIT \times (1 - \text{tax rate})] + Dep - FCInv - WCInc$$

$$FCFF_0 (\text{in millions}) = [C\$30 \times (1 - 0.40)] + C\$15 - C\$20 - C\$6 = C\$7.0$$

$$\text{value of firm} (\text{in millions}) = \frac{C\$7.0 \times 1.05}{0.1245 - 0.05} = C\$98.7$$

$$\text{value of equity} (\text{in millions}) = C\$98.7 - C\$25.0 = C\$73.7$$

(LOS 30.c)

2. **B** <u>Given</u>: NI = $50; depreciation = $27; ending net PP&E = ending gross fixed assets – ending accumulated depreciation = $136 – $40 = $96; beginning net PP&E = beginning gross fixed assets – beginning accumulated depreciation = $90 – $30 = $60; WCInv = $4; net borrowings = $0; gains on sale of equipment = $8.

   FCInv = ending net PPE – beginning net PPE + depreciation – gain on sale
   = 96 – 60 + 27 – 8 = $55

   NCC = depreciation – gain = 27 – 8 = $19

   FCFE = NI + NCC – FCInv – WCInv + net borrowings
   = 50 + 19 – 55 – 4 + 0 = $10

   (LOS 30.c)

Module Quiz 30.3

For Questions 1 through 3, items #1, 2, 4, 5, 6, and 7 were applied correctly. Only item #3 related to the reversal of restructuring charges was applied incorrectly: income from restructuring charge reversals is a noncash gain that should be subtracted from net income to calculate FCFF. Depreciation and software amortization should be added back to net income, after-tax interest should be added back, and the increase in deferred taxes should be added back (because it is not expected to reverse in the foreseeable future). Net working capital and fixed capital investments should be subtracted from net income to arrive at FCFF. The correct calculation of FCFF is

$$FCFF_{2016} = \$173 + \$23 - \$6 + \$17 + [\$19(1 - 0.35)] - \$86 - \$47$$
$$= \$86.35 \text{ million}$$

1. **A** See answer explanation above for Questions 1 through 3. (LOS 30.c)

2. **B** See answer explanation above for Questions 1 through 3. (LOS 30.c)

3. **A** See answer explanation above for Questions 1 through 3. (LOS 30.c)

Module Quiz 30.4

1. **B** Free cash flow to the firm is equal to cash flow from operations plus after-tax interest expense [interest(1 − tax rate)] minus fixed capital investment. (LOS 30.d)

Module Quiz 30.5

1. **C**

$$FCFE = NI - (1 - DR)(FCInv - Dep) - (1 - DR)(WCInv)$$
$$= £3.50 - [(1 - 0.4)(£2.00 - £1.60)] - [(1 - 0.4)(£0.50)] = £2.96$$

$$\text{equity value per share} = \frac{£2.96 \times 1.04}{0.14 - 0.04} = £30.78$$

(LOS 30.e)

©2018 Kaplan, Inc.

2. **B** The following table shows FCFF for years 0 through 6 (in $):

Year	0	1	2	3	4	5	6
Sales	60.00	67.20	75.26	84.30	94.41	105.74	109.97
EBIT	20.00	22.40	25.09	28.10	31.47	35.25	36.66
EBIT(1 − T)	12.00	13.44	15.05	16.86	18.88	21.15	21.99
Dep	8.00	8.96	10.04	11.24	12.59	14.10	—
FCInv	12.00	13.44	15.05	16.86	18.88	21.15	—
WCInv	3.00	3.36	3.76	4.21	4.72	5.29	5.50
FCFF	5.00	5.60	6.28	7.03	7.87	8.81	16.49

$$\text{FCFF} = \left[\text{EBIT} \times (1 - \text{tax rate})\right] + \text{Dep} - \text{FCInv} - \text{WCInv}$$

$$\text{FCFF}_6 = 21.99 + 0 + 0 - 5.50 = 16.49$$

(LOS 30.c)

3. **C** The terminal value (as of Year 5) is found by using the FCFF in Year 6 and WACC of 8% and growth rate of 4% in the stable growth stage:

$$\text{terminal value}_5 = \frac{\$16.49}{0.08 - 0.04} = \$412.25$$

(LOS 30.j)

4. **C** The value of the firm today is the present value of the forecasted cash flows, discounted at the WACC during the high-growth stage of 11%:

$$\text{value of firm} = \frac{\$5.60}{1.11} + \frac{\$6.28}{1.11^2} + \frac{\$7.03}{1.11^3} + \frac{\$7.87}{1.11^4} + \frac{\$8.81 + \$412.25}{1.11^5} = \$270.35$$

Using the calculator, enter $CF_0 = 0.00$; C01 = 5.60; C02 = 6.28; C03 = 7.03; C04 = 7.87; C05 = 8.81 + 412.25 = 421.06; I = 11; CPT → NPV = 270.35

(LOS 30.j)

5. **C** With the bonds trading at par, the interest expense is based on the before-tax yield:

$$\text{interest} = \$600 \times 0.075 = \$45$$

Add back preferred dividends to net income available to common to get FCFF:

$$\text{FCFF} = \text{NI}\left(\text{available to common}\right) + \text{NCC} + \left[\text{Int} \times (1 - \text{tax rate})\right]$$
$$+ \text{preferred dividends} - \text{FCInv} - \text{WCInv}$$
$$\text{FCFF} = 125 + 50 + \left[45 \times (1 - 0.40)\right] + 14 - 100 - 30 = \$86$$

(LOS 30.c)

6. **C** The value of the firm is the present value of the constantly growing FCFF. Using single-stage FCFF model we get:

$$\text{value of firm} = \frac{\text{FCFF}_0 \times (1+g)}{\text{WACC} - g} = \frac{\$86 \times 1.04}{0.0927 - 0.04} = \$1,697.15$$

(LOS 30.j)

7. **A** The value of the equity is equal to firm value less the market value of debt and preferred stock:

value of equity = $1,697.15 – $600 – $200 = $897.15

(LOS 30.j)

8. **B** FCFF = 86 (computed earlier).

$$\text{FCFE} = \text{FCFF} - \left[\text{Int} \times (1 - \text{tax rate})\right] - \text{preferred dividends} + \text{net borrowing}$$
$$= 86 - \left[45 \times (1 - 0.4)\right] - 14 + 40 = \$85$$

(LOS 30.c)

9. **C** value of equity $= \dfrac{\$85 \times 1.04}{0.14 - 0.04} = \$884$ (LOS 30.j)

10. **B** Free cash flow to the firm (FCFF) is the estimate of the cash flows available to the firm's investors after the firm buys and sells products, provides services, pays its cash operating expenses, and makes short- and long-term investment decisions, but before the firm makes any financing decisions. EBITDA is a poor proxy for free cash flow. FCFF is calculated as:

FCFF = [EBITDA × (1 – tax rate)] + (Dep × tax rate) – FCInv – WCInv

(LOS 30.h)

11. **A** Based on the CAPM, the required return on MWC's common equity can be computed as follows:

r = 6.4% + (1.2 × 5.5%) = 13%

The current value of MWC common stock can be estimated using the two-stage DDM approach as follows:

$$
\begin{aligned}
g &= 15\% \\
D_{2017} &= \$2.30 \\
D_{2018} &= \$2.30 \times 1.15 = \$2.65 \\
D_{2019} &= \$2.65 \times 1.15 = \$3.05
\end{aligned}
$$

$$\text{terminal value} = \frac{\$3.05 \times 1.08}{(0.13 - 0.08)} = \$65.88$$

$$\text{equity value} = \frac{\$2.65}{1.13} + \frac{\$3.05 + \$65.88}{1.13^2} = \$56.33$$

(LOS 30.j)

12. B The current value of MWC common stock can be estimated using the two-stage FCFE approach as follows:

$$\text{FCFE}_{2017} = \text{CFO} - \text{FCInv} + \text{net borrowing} = 33,960 - 12,000 + 3,200$$
$$= \$25,160$$

$$\text{shares outstanding} = \text{dividends paid / dividends per share} = \frac{\$23,920}{\$2.30} = 10,400$$

$$\text{FCFE}_{2017} \text{ per share} = \frac{\text{FCFE}_{2017}}{10,400} = \frac{\$25,160}{10,400} = \$2.42$$

$$
\begin{aligned}
g & = 15\% \\
\text{FCFE}_{2017} & = \$2.42 \\
\text{FCFE}_{2018} & = \$2.42 \times 1.15 = \$2.78 \\
\text{FCFE}_{2019} & = \$2.78 \times 1.15 = \$3.20
\end{aligned}
$$

$$\text{terminal value} = \frac{\$3.20 \times 1.08}{(0.13 - 0.08)} = \$69.12$$

$$\text{equity value} = \frac{\$2.78}{1.13} + \frac{\$3.20 + \$69.12}{1.13^2} = \$59.10$$

(LOS 30.d)

13. B The following table shows FCFE for years 0 through 6 (in £).

$$\text{FCFE} = \text{NI} - [(1 - \text{DR}) \times (\text{FCInv} - \text{Dep})] - [(1 - \text{DR}) \times \text{WCInv}]$$

	Year 0	Year 1	Year 2	Year 3	Year 4	Year 5	Year 6
NI	1.50	1.73	1.98	2.28	2.62	3.02	3.17
(−) [(1 − DR) (FCInv − Dep)]	0.35	0.40	0.46	0.53	0.61	0.70	0
(−) [(1 − DR) (WCInv)]	0.14	0.16	0.19	0.21	0.24	0.28	0.29
(=) FCFE	1.01	1.17	1.33	1.53	1.76	2.03	2.88

Example of FCFE calculation (Year 1):

$$
\begin{aligned}
\text{FCFE} &= \text{NI} - [(1 - \text{DR}) \times (\text{FCInv} - \text{Dep})] - [(1 - \text{DR}) \times \text{WCInv}] \\
&= 1.73 - [(1 - 0.3) \times (0.92 - 0.35)] - [(1 - 0.3) \times 0.23] \\
&= 1.17
\end{aligned}
$$

Calculate terminal value in year five using FCFE estimate for Year 6, discounted at required return of 10% in the stable growth period.

$$\text{terminal value}_5 = \frac{\pounds 2.88}{0.10 - 0.05} = \pounds 57.60$$

Use the short-term discount rate of 17% to discount the cash flows back to the present:

$$\text{equity value per share} = \frac{1.17}{1.17^1} + \frac{1.33}{1.17^2} + \frac{1.53}{1.17^3} + \frac{1.76}{1.17^4} + \frac{2.03 + 57.60}{1.17^5} = \pounds 31.08$$

Using the calculator, enter the following: $\text{CF}_0 = 0.00$; C01 = 1.17; C02 = 1.34; C03 = 1.54; C04 = 1.76; C05 = 2.03 + 57.60 = 59.63; I = 17; CPT → NPV = 31.08 (LOS 30.j)

14. **A**   WACC is less than required return on equity. Incorrectly using the WACC (which is too low) in the FCFE model will overestimate equity value. Incorrectly using required return on equity (which is too high) in the FCFF model will underestimate firm value and equity value. (LOS 30.j)

15. **A**   The increased net borrowing for 2018 will cause the forecasted free cash flow to *equity* (FCFE) to increase in 2018. However, in future years, the higher interest expense associated with the debt issue will cause the FCFE forecast to decrease. (LOS 30.g)

16. **C**   Free cash flow to the *firm* (FCFF) represents cash flow available to all investors before any financing cash flows, including interest payments. Changes in leverage are uses of cash (i.e., financing decisions) that do not affect FCFF. (LOS 30.g)

READING 31

Market-Based Valuation: Price and Enterprise Value Multiples

Study Session 11

EXAM FOCUS

This topic review covers the estimation of P/E, P/B, PEG, P/S, P/CF, and enterprise value/EBITDA ratios. The justified price multiple models draw heavily on the previous two topic reviews on dividend discount models and free cash flow models. You should be able to estimate justified price multiples for individual firms and to apply the method of comparables to estimate their (relative) values.

MODULE 31.1: P/E MULTIPLE

Warm-Up: Multiples

Video covering this content is available online.

Price multiples are among the most widely used tools for valuation of equities. Comparing stocks' price multiples can help an investor judge whether a particular stock is overvalued, undervalued, or properly valued in terms of measures such as earnings, sales, cash flow, or book value per share. **Enterprise value multiples** relate the total value of a company, as reflected in the market value of its capital from all sources, to a measure of operating earnings generated, such as earnings before interest, taxes, depreciation, and amortization. **Momentum indicators** compare a stock's price or a company's earnings to their values in earlier periods.

LOS 31.a: Distinguish between the method of comparables and the method based on forecasted fundamentals as approaches to using price multiples in valuation, and explain economic rationales for each approach.

CFA® Program Curriculum: Volume 4, page 379

The **method of comparables** values a stock based on the average price multiple of the stock of similar companies. The economic rationale for the method of comparables is the Law of One Price, which asserts that two similar assets should sell at comparable price multiples (e.g., price-to-earnings). This is a relative valuation method, so we can only assert that a stock is over- or undervalued *relative* to benchmark value.

The **method of forecasted fundamentals** values a stock based on the ratio of its value from a discounted cash flow (DCF) model to some fundamental variable (e.g., earnings per share). The economic rationale for the method of forecasted fundamentals is that the value used in the numerator of the justified price multiple is derived from a DCF model: value is equal to the present value of expected future cash flows discounted at the appropriate risk-adjusted rate of return.

EXAMPLE: Method of comparables

MK Technologies shares are selling for $50. Earnings for the last 12 months were $2 per share. The average trailing P/E ratio for firms in MK's industry is 32 times. Determine whether MK is over- or undervalued using the method of comparables.

Answer:

MK's trailing P/E is:

$$\frac{\$50}{\$2} = 25 \text{ times}$$

MK is relatively undervalued because its observed trailing P/E ratio (25 times) is less than the industry average trailing P/E ratio (32 times).

EXAMPLE: Method of forecasted fundamentals

Shares of Comtronics, Inc. are selling for $30. The mean analyst earnings per share forecast for next year is $4.00, and the long-run growth rate is 5%. Comtronics has a dividend payout ratio of 60%. The required return is 14%. Calculate the fundamental value of Comtronics using the Gordon growth model and determine whether Comtronics shares are over- or undervalued using the method of forecasted fundamentals.

Answer:

The fundamental value according to the Gordon growth model is:

$$V_0 = \frac{D_1}{r - g} = \frac{(0.6 \times \$4.00)}{0.14 - 0.05} = \$26.67$$

The fair value P/E ratio based on forecasted fundamentals is:

$$\frac{\$26.67}{\$4.00} = 6.67 \text{ times}$$

The observed leading P/E ratio based on the current market price is:

$$\frac{\$30.00}{\$4.00} = 7.50 \text{ times}$$

Comtronics is overvalued because the observed P/E multiple of 7.5 is greater than the fair value P/E ratio of 6.67. Notice that we would have come to the same conclusion by comparing market price ($30.00) to intrinsic value ($26.67).

LOS 31.b: Calculate and interpret a justified price multiple.

LOS 31.c: Describe rationales for and possible drawbacks to using alternative price multiples and dividend yield in valuation.

LOS 31.d: Calculate and interpret alternative price multiples and dividend yield.

CFA® Program Curriculum: Volume 4, pages 382 and 384–385

Price multiples are ratios of a common stock's market price to some fundamental variable. The most common example is the price-to-earnings (P/E) ratio. A **justified price multiple** is what the multiple *should be* if the stock is fairly valued. If the actual multiple is greater than the justified price multiple, the stock is overvalued; if the actual multiple is less than the justified multiple, the stock is undervalued (all else equal).

P/E Ratio

There are a number of rationales for using price-to-earnings (P/E) ratio in valuation:

- Earnings power, as measured by earnings per share (EPS), is the primary determinant of investment value.
- The P/E ratio is popular in the investment community.
- Empirical research shows that P/E differences are significantly related to long-run average stock returns.

On the other hand, P/E ratios have a number of shortcomings:

- Earnings can be *negative*, which produces a meaningless P/E ratio.
- The volatile, transitory portion of earnings makes the interpretation of P/Es difficult for analysts.
- Management discretion within allowed accounting practices can distort reported earnings, and thereby lessen the comparability of P/Es across firms.

We can define two versions of the P/E ratio: trailing and leading P/E. The difference between the two is how earnings (the denominator) are calculated. *Trailing P/E* uses earnings over the *most recent* 12 months in the denominator. *Leading P/E ratio* (a.k.a. forward or prospective P/E) uses next year's expected earnings, which is defined as either expected earnings per share (EPS) for the next four quarters, or expected EPS for the next fiscal year.

$$\text{trailing P/E} = \frac{\text{market price per share}}{\text{EPS over previous 12 months}}$$

$$\text{leading P/E} = \frac{\text{market price per share}}{\text{forecasted EPS over next 12 months}}$$

Trailing P/E is not useful for forecasting and valuation if the firm's business has changed (e.g., as a result of an acquisition). Leading P/E may not be relevant if earnings are sufficiently volatile so that next year's earnings are not forecastable with any degree of accuracy.

EXAMPLE: Calculating P/E ratio

Byron Investments, Inc., reported €32 million in earnings during the current fiscal year. An analyst forecasts an EPS over the next 12 months of €1.00. Byron has 40 million shares outstanding at a market price of €18.00 per share. Calculate Byron's trailing and leading P/E ratios.

Answer:

$$\text{current-year EPS} = \frac{€32,000,000}{40,000,000} = €0.80$$

$$\text{trailing P/E} = \frac{€18.00}{€0.80} = 22.5$$

$$\text{leading P/E} = \frac{€18.00}{€1.00} = 18.0$$

MODULE QUIZ 31.1

To best evaluate your performance, enter your quiz answers online.

1. The stock of Western Graphics Co. paid a dividend of $0.40 per share *last* year on earnings of $1.00 per share. The firm's earnings and dividends are expected to grow at 5% per year forever. Shareholders require a return of 12% on their investment. The justified trailing and leading P/E multiples are *closest* to:

Trailing P/E	Leading P/E
A. 6.0	5.7
B. 6.0	6.3
C. 5.7	6.3

2. An analyst is valuing an electric utility with a dividend payout ratio of 0.65, a beta of 0.56, and an expected earnings growth rate of 0.032. A regression on other electric utilities produces the following equation:

   predicted P/E = 8.57 + (5.38 × dividend payout) + (15.53 × growth) − (0.61 × beta)

   The predicted P/E on the basis of the values of the explanatory variables for the company is *closest* to:
   A. 12.2.
   B. 15.4.
   C. 20.8.

3. Party Favors, Inc. has a leading P/E of 18.75 and a 5-year consensus growth rate forecast of 15.32%. The median PEG, based on leading P/E, for a group of companies comparable in risk to Party Favors, Inc. is 0.92. The stock appears to be:
   A. overvalued because its PEG ratio is 0.82.
   B. overvalued because its PEG ratio is 1.22.
   C. undervalued because its PEG ratio is 0.82.

4. Consumer Products, Inc. has a trailing P/E of 27.52, while the median peer group P/E is 33.25. Assuming that there are no differences in the fundamentals among the peer firms and Consumer Products, the firm is:
   A. correctly valued.
   B. overvalued.
   C. undervalued.

5. The 12-month trailing EPS for Sample Fabrication Company as of December 31, 2015, is $1.29. Sample stock trades at $42.50 per share as of 12/31/15. In the first quarter of 2015, Sample reported an extraordinary loss of $0.22 per share. In the third quarter, the company reported a loss from the write-down of inventory of $0.04 per share. In the fourth quarter, Sample reported a gain of $0.08 per share from a change in accounting estimate when it increased the estimate of useful life of certain manufacturing equipment. Sample's trailing P/E ratio based on underlying earnings is *closest* to:
   A. 24.6.
   B. 28.9.
   C. 32.9.

6. The average ROE for Lever, Inc. over the last business cycle was 32%. Lever's earnings per share for 2016 is expected to be $5. The dividend payout ratio is 30%, and the current book value per share is $14. Shares are trading in the market at $54. Lever's normalized earnings per share are *closest* to:
   A. $4.48.
   B. $5.00.
   C. $5.26.

7. A firm has a justified price-to-sales ratio of 2.0 times, a net profit margin of 5%, and a long-term growth rate of 4%. The justified leading P/E (based on the Gordon growth model) is *closest* to:
   A. 34.8.
   B. 38.5.
   C. 40.0.

8. At the end of 2015, an analyst estimates the value of Copyright, Inc. common stock to be $84 per share using a two-stage, dividend discount H-model and forecasts earnings for 2016 to be $4.20 per share. Copyright is *most likely*:
   A. underpriced if its actual leading P/E is 15.0 times.
   B. underpriced if its actual leading P/E is 23.0 times.
   C. overpriced if its actual leading P/E is 16.6 times.

MODULE 31.2: P/B MULTIPLE

Video covering this content is available online.

P/B Ratio

Advantages of using the price-to-book (P/B) ratio include:

■ Book value is a cumulative amount that is usually positive, even when the firm reports a loss and EPS is negative. Thus, a P/B can typically be used when P/E cannot.

■ Book value is more stable than EPS, so it may be more useful than P/E when EPS is particularly high, low, or volatile.

■ Book value is an appropriate measure of net asset value for firms that primarily hold liquid assets. Examples include finance, investment, insurance, and banking firms.

■ P/B can be useful in valuing companies that are expected to go out of business.

■ Empirical research shows that P/Bs help explain differences in long-run average stock returns.

Disadvantages of using P/B include:

■ P/Bs do not reflect the value of intangible economic assets, such as human capital.

■ P/Bs can be misleading when there are significant differences in the asset size of the firms under consideration because in some cases the firm's business model dictates the size of its asset base. A firm that outsources its production will have fewer assets, lower book value, and a higher P/B ratio than an otherwise similar firm in the same industry that doesn't outsource.

■ Different accounting conventions can obscure the true investment in the firm made by shareholders, which reduces the comparability of P/Bs across firms and countries. For example, research and development costs (R&D) are expensed in the United States, which can understate investment.

■ Inflation and technological change can cause the book and market values of assets to differ significantly, so book value is not an accurate measure of the value of shareholders' investment. This makes it more difficult to compare P/Bs across firms.

The price-to-book ratio is defined as:

$$\text{P/B ratio} = \frac{\text{market value of equity}}{\text{book value of equity}} = \frac{\text{market price per share}}{\text{book value per share}}$$

where:

book value of equity = common shareholders' equity

= (total assets − total liabilities) − preferred stock

We often make adjustments to book value to create more useful comparisons of P/B ratios across different stocks. A common adjustment is to use tangible book value, which is equal to book value of equity less intangible assets. Examples of intangible assets include goodwill from acquisitions (which makes sense because it is not really an asset) and patents (which is more questionable since the asset and patent are separable). Furthermore, balance sheets should be adjusted for significant off-balance-sheet assets and liabilities and for differences between the fair and recorded value of assets and liabilities. Finally, book values often need to be adjusted to ensure comparability. For example, companies using first in, first out (FIFO) for inventory valuation cannot be accurately compared with peers using last in, first out (LIFO). Thus, book values should be restated on a consistent basis.

> **EXAMPLE: Calculating P/B ratio**
>
> Based on the information in the following figure, calculate the P/B for Crisco Systems, Inc. and Soothsayer Corp. as of the end of 2015.

Data for Crisco Systems, Inc. and Soothsayer Corp.

Company	Book Value of Equity 2015 (millions of $)	Sales 2015 (millions of $)	Shares Outstanding 2015 (millions)	Price FYE 2015 ($)
Crisco Systems, Inc.	$28,039	$18,878	7,001	$17.83
Soothsayer Corp.	$6,320	$9,475	5,233	$12.15

Answer:

Crisco Systems, Inc.:

$$\text{book value per share} = \frac{\text{book value of equity}}{\text{number of shares outstanding}} = \frac{\$28,039}{7,001} = \$4.01$$

$$P/B = \frac{\text{market price per share}}{\text{book value per share}} = \frac{\$17.83}{\$4.01} = 4.45 \text{ times}$$

Soothsayer Corp.:

$$\text{book value per share} = \frac{\text{book value of equity}}{\text{number of shares outstanding}} = \frac{\$6,320}{5,233} = \$1.21$$

$$P/B = \frac{\text{market price per share}}{\text{book value per share}} = \frac{\$12.15}{\$1.21} = 10.04 \text{ times}$$

MODULE QUIZ 31.2

To best evaluate your performance, enter your quiz answers online.

1. Creative Toys recently paid a dividend of $1.35 a share. It has a payout ratio of 67%, a ROE of 23%, and an expected growth rate in earnings and dividends for the foreseeable future of 7.6%. Shareholders require a return of 14% on their investment. The justified price to book value multiple is *closest* to:
   A. 1.22.
   B. 1.19.
   C. 2.41.

MODULE 31.3: P/S AND P/CF MULTIPLE

Video covering this content is available online.

P/S Ratio

The *advantages* of using the price-to-sales (P/S) ratio include:

- P/S is meaningful even for distressed firms, since sales revenue is always positive. This is not the case for P/E and P/B ratios, which can be negative.

- Sales revenue is not as easy to manipulate or distort as EPS and book value, which are significantly affected by accounting conventions.

■ P/S ratios are not as volatile as P/E multiples. This may make P/S ratios more reliable in valuation analysis when earnings for a particular year are very high or very low relative to the long-run average.

■ P/S ratios are particularly appropriate for valuing stocks in mature or cyclical industries and start-up companies with no record of earnings. It is also often used to value investment management companies and partnerships.

■ Like P/E and P/B ratios, empirical research finds that differences in P/S are significantly related to differences in long-run average stock returns.

The *disadvantages* of using P/S ratios include:

■ High growth in sales does not necessarily indicate high operating profits as measured by earnings and cash flow.

■ P/S ratios do not capture differences in cost structures across companies.

■ While less subject to distortion, revenue recognition practices can still distort sales forecasts. For example, analysts should look for company practices that speed up revenue recognition. An example is sales on a bill-and-hold basis, which involves selling products and delivering them at a later date. This practice accelerates sales into an earlier reporting period and distorts the P/S ratio.

P/S multiples are computed by dividing a stock's price per share by sales or revenue per share, or by dividing the market value of the firm's equity by its total sales:

$$\text{P/S ratio} = \frac{\text{market value of equity}}{\text{total sales}} = \frac{\text{market price per share}}{\text{sales per share}}$$

EXAMPLE: Calculating P/S ratio

Based on the information in the following figure, calculate the current P/S for Crisco Systems, Inc. and Soothsayer Corp.

Data for Crisco Systems, Inc. and Soothsayer Corp.

Company	Book Value of Equity 2015 (millions of $)	Sales 2015 (millions of $)	Shares Outstanding 2015 (millions)	Price FYE 2015 ($)
Crisco Systems, Inc.	$28,039	$18,878	7,001	$17.83
Soothsayer Corp.	$6,320	$9,475	5,233	$12.15

Answer:

Crisco Systems, Inc.:

$$\text{sales per share} = \frac{\text{sales}}{\text{number of shares outstanding}} = \frac{\$18,878 \text{ million}}{7,001 \text{ million}} = \$2.70$$

$$\text{P/S} = \frac{\text{market price per share}}{\text{sales per share}} = \frac{\$17.83}{\$2.70} = 6.60 \text{ times}$$

Soothsayer Corp.:

$$\text{sales per share} = \frac{\text{sales}}{\text{number of shares outstanding}} = \frac{\$9,475 \text{ million}}{5,233 \text{ million}} = \$1.81$$

$$\text{P/S} = \frac{\text{market price per share}}{\text{sales per share}} = \frac{\$12.15}{\$1.81} = 6.71 \text{ times}$$

P/CF Ratio

Advantages of using the price-to-cash flow (P/CF) ratio include:

- Cash flow is harder for managers to manipulate than earnings.

- Price to cash flow is more stable than price to earnings.

- Reliance on cash flow rather than earnings handles the problem of differences in the quality of reported earnings, which is a problem for P/E.

- Empirical evidence indicates that differences in price to cash flow are significantly related to differences in long-run average stock returns.

There are two drawbacks to the price-to-cash flow ratio, both of which are related to the definition of cash flow. We discuss the specific cash flow definitions next.

- Items affecting actual cash flow from operations are ignored when the EPS plus noncash charges estimate is used. For example, noncash revenue and net changes in working capital are ignored.

- From a theoretical perspective, free cash flow to equity (FCFE) is preferable to operating cash flow. However, FCFE is more volatile than operating cash flow, so it is not necessarily more informative.

MODULE QUIZ 31.3

To best evaluate your performance, enter your quiz answers online.

1. An analyst researching Blue Ridge Camping has determined that the firm has:
   - A payout ratio of 75%.
   - A return on equity (ROE) of 18%.
   - An earnings per share (EPS) of $5.35.
   - Sales per share of $342.
   - Expected earnings/dividends/sales growth of 4.5%.
   - Shareholders required return of 15%.

   The firm's justified price to sales ratio (P/S) multiple based on the above fundamentals is *closest* to:
   A. 0.0780.
   B. 0.1114.
   C. 0.1164.

Study Session 11

Use the following information to answer Questions 2 through 4.

Company	Book Value of Equity 2015 (millions of $)	Sales 2015 (millions of $)	Shares Outstanding 2015 (millions)	Price ($)
Pfeiffer, Inc.	19,950	32,373	6,162	31.37
Mapps, Inc.	61,020	32,187	10,771	25.63

Peer Group	Mean P/B	Median P/B	Mean P/S (sales in millions of $)	Median P/S (sales in millions of $)
Medical-Drugs	5.622	4.250	8.708	4.530
Applications Software	4.100	2.140	3.420	1.440

Pfeiffer belongs to the Medical-Drugs group and Mapps belongs to the Applications Software group.

2. The current price-to-book and price-to-sales ratios for Pfeiffer are *closest* to:

	P/B	P/S
A.	3.238	5.254
B.	3.238	5.971
C.	9.688	5.971

3. The current price-to-book and price-to-sales ratios for Mapps are *closest* to:

	P/B	P/S
A.	4.524	8.578
B.	5.665	2.988
C.	4.524	2.988

4. Which of the following statements is *most accurate*, given the financial data on Pfeiffer, Mapps, and the two industries?
   A. Both stocks are relatively overvalued.
   B. Both stocks are relatively undervalued.
   C. One stock is relatively overvalued and the other is relatively undervalued.

Study Session 11

Cross-Reference to CFA Institute Assigned Reading #31 – Market-Based Valuation: Price and Enterprise Value Multiples

Study Session 11

5. Jeremiah Claxton, CFA, is a junior portfolio manager for a large university endowment fund. Claxton's supervisor, Joanne LeMonte, has asked him to compare the valuation of Home Decor, Inc. and Lester's Companies, Inc. and make a recommendation for an addition to the fund's retail portfolio. LeMonte has specifically asked Claxton to consider the price-to-cash flow valuation metric when making his recommendation. Claxton has gathered the following information.

Comparison Between Lester's and Home Decor (per share amounts)

	Recent Price	Trailing CF per Share	P/CF	Trailing FCFE per Share	P/FCFE	Consensus 5-Year Growth Forecast	Beta
Lester's	$47.8	$2.00	23.90	$0.36	132.78	17.5%	1.22
Home	$28.4	$1.36	20.88	$0.99	28.69	22.2%	1.36

Claxton has also determined that the CAPM betas of the two firms are not significantly different at the 1% level. Based on the information in the table, which of the following statements is *most accurate*?

A. Only one of the stocks is relatively overvalued.
B. Both stocks are relatively undervalued.
C. Both stocks are relatively overvalued.

Use the following information to answer Questions 6 through 9.

Lois Fischer, CFA, is a senior analyst with Merlin Equity Investors. Fischer believes that the retail industry will perform well over the next several quarters and is interested in selecting a retail stock on the basis of its price-to-book multiple. Fischer's research has resulted in a list of five stocks from which she will make her final selection: Wally's, Home Decor, Redrug, Lester's, and Harmon's (all reporting under U.S. GAAP). The following table contains the information upon which Fischer will base her decision.

P/B Comparables for Retail Firms

	Price-to-Book Value						
	2013	2014	2015	3-Year Average	Current	2-Year ROE Forecast	Beta
Wally's*	9.85	8.01	6.93	8.26	6.53	20.00%	0.98
Harmon's*	6.35	4.60	4.16	5.04	3.29	19.95%	1.02
Redrug**	14.93	11.08	13.32	13.11	5.78	18.20%	0.58
Home Decor***	9.75	7.24	8.88	8.62	3.31	19.29%	1.36
Lester's***	7.65	6.25	6.66	6.85	4.32	18.90%	1.22
*Retail industry (department & discount)					5.75	19.98%	
**Retail industry (drugs)					4.69	15.27%	
***Retail industry (home improvement)					3.62	19.29%	

Annabelle Clementi, CFA, is Fischer's supervisor and has more than 15 years of experience analyzing firms in the retail industry. Clementi typically uses the P/B ratio when comparing retail stocks with the industry and among peers. However, Clementi has concluded that firms in the home improvement segment of the retail industry utilize their assets so efficiently that P/B valuation is not appropriate. Since these firms are typically characterized as having relatively strong cash flows, Clementi has decided to assess them using valuation measures that are based on cash flows and cash flow-related concepts. With this in mind, Clementi has obtained the following financial statements for Lester's, Inc., a major player in the home improvement segment of the retail industry. Other relevant information that will assist her with the valuation of Lester's includes the following:

■ Lester's financial statements are prepared using U.S. GAAP.

■ Actual interest paid for the year was $240 million. The reported cash flow from operating activities includes this effect, net of tax savings.

■ The marginal tax rate is 37%.

■ Lester's is currently trading at $42.10 per share.

Lester's, Inc. Income Statement

Period Ending December 31, 2015

Total Revenue	22,111,108,000
Cost of Revenue	(15,743,267,000)
Gross Profit	$ 6,367,841,000
Operating Expenses	
Depreciation	534,102,000
Selling General and Administrative Expenses	3,379,253,000
Nonrecurring	139,870,000
Other Operating Expenses	516,828,000
Total Operating Expenses	$ 4,570,053,000
Operating Income	1,797,788,000
Total Other Income and Expenses, Net	58,431,000
Earnings Before Interest and Taxes	1,856,219,000
Interest Expense	(231,968,000)
Income Before Tax	$ 1,624,251,000
Income Tax Expense	600,989,000
Equity Earnings or Loss Unconsolidated Subsidiary	N/A
Minority Interest	N/A
Net Income From Continuing Operations	$ 1,023,262,000
Nonrecurring Events	
Discontinued Operations	N/A
Extraordinary Items	N/A
Effect of Accounting Changes	N/A
Other Items	N/A

Lester's, Inc. Income Statement (cont.)

Net Income	1,023,262,000
Preferred Stock and Other Adjustments	N/A
Net Income Applicable to Common Shares	$ 1,023,262,000
Earnings per Common Share	
Basic	$ 1.62
Weighted Average Shares Outstanding	
Basic	631,643,000

Lester's, Inc. Statement of Cash Flows

Period Ending December 31, 2015

Net Income	$ 1,023,262,000
Cash Flow Operating Activities	
Depreciation	534,102,000
Changes in Operating Activities	
Changes in Accounts Receivables	(4,593,000)
Changes in Liabilities	306,869,000
Changes in Inventories	(325,406,000)
Changes in Other Operating Activities	(36,792,000)
Cash Flow From Operating Activities	$ 1,497,442,000
Cash Flow Investing Activities	
Capital Expenditures	(2,199,334,000)
Cash Flows From Investing Activities	$ (2,199,334,000)
Cash Flow Financing Activities	
Dividends Paid	(59,884,000)
Sale (Purchase) of Stock	115,870,000
Net Borrowings	873,480,000
Other Cash Flows From Financing Activities	N/A
Cash Flows From Financing Activities	$ 929,466,000
Effect of Exchange Rate	N/A
Change in Cash and Cash Equivalents	227,574,000
Cash and Cash Equivalents at Beginning of Period	455,658,000
Cash and Cash Equivalents at End of Period	$ 683,232,000

6. Based on the information in the first figure, which of the following statements *least likely* supports Fischer's recommendation of Home Decor over Lester's?
   A. Home Decor's P/B ratio relative to the industry.
   B. Home Decor's P/B ratio relative to Lester's P/B ratio.
   C. Home Decor's historical P/B ratios.

7. Which of the following statements is *least likely* a justification of Fischer's selection of Harmon's over Wally's on the basis of the information in the first figure?
   A. Harmon's level of systematic risk relative to Wally's.
   B. Harmon's P/B ratio relative to the industry.
   C. Wally's P/B ratio relative to the industry.

8. Clementi requests that Fischer calculate several ratios using the previous information. The P/CF for Lester's using earnings-plus-noncash-charges for cash flow is *closest* to:
   A. 15.89.
   B. 17.08.
   C. 25.99.

9. Clementi requests that Fischer calculate the P/CFO for Lester's, using adjusted cash flow from operations for cash flow for comparison with other companies. The adjusted P/CFO for Lester's is *closest* to:
   A. 15.
   B. 17.
   C. 19.

MODULE 31.4: EV AND OTHER ASPECTS
Dividend Yield

Video covering this content is available online.

The dividend yield (D/P) is the ratio of the common dividend to the market price. It is most often used for valuing indexes. *Advantages* of the dividend yield approach include:

■ Dividend yield contributes to total investment return.

■ Dividends are not as risky as the capital appreciation component of total return.

Disadvantages of the dividend yield approach include:

■ The focus on dividend yield is incomplete because it ignores capital appreciation.

■ The dividend displacement of earnings concept argues that dividends paid now displace future earnings, which implies a trade-off between current and future cash flows.

Total return on an investment has two components: dividend yield and capital appreciation. *Dividend yield* (D/P) is the ratio of trailing or leading dividend divided by current market price per share:

$$\text{trailing D/P} = \frac{4 \ \times \ \text{most recent quarterly dividend}}{\text{market price per share}}$$

$$\text{leading D/P} = \frac{\text{forecasted dividends over next four quarters}}{\text{market price per share}}$$

The supposed lower risk of dividends relative to capital appreciation assumes that the market is biased in its risk assessment of the components of return.

> **EXAMPLE: Calculating dividend yield**
>
> OnePrice Inc. just paid a dividend of $0.50 per share. The consensus forecasted dividends for OnePrice Inc. over the next four quarters are $0.50, $0.55, $0.60, and $0.65. The current market price is $47.50. Calculate the leading and trailing dividend yield.
>
> **Answer:**
>
> $$\text{trailing D/P} = \frac{4 \times \$0.50}{\$47.50} = 0.042 = 4.2\%$$
>
> $$\text{leading D/P} = \frac{\$0.50 + \$0.55 + \$0.60 + \$0.65}{\$47.50} = \frac{\$2.30}{\$47.50} = 0.048 = 4.8\%$$

LOS 31.e: Calculate and interpret underlying earnings, explain methods of normalizing earnings per share (EPS), and calculate normalized EPS.

CFA® Program Curriculum: Volume 4, page 386

Underlying Earnings

Calculating the P/E ratio is easy, and estimating the market price is usually straightforward. However, estimating the appropriate earnings measure is crucial to successfully using the P/E ratio in market-based valuation. The key focus of an analyst is estimating **underlying earnings** (a.k.a. persistent, continuing, or core earnings), which are earnings that exclude nonrecurring components, such as gains and losses from asset sales, asset write-downs, provisions for future losses, and changes in accounting estimates.

For comparative purposes, analysts generally use diluted EPS, so that the effect of any dilutive securities is taken into account.

> **PROFESSOR'S NOTE**
>
> There is an important link here to financial statement analysis. The basic inputs to most valuation models (like earnings) are found in the financial statements. However, management has significant discretion in determining reported earnings by classifying specific items as nonrecurring. The analyst's job is to identify the recurring components of earnings that reflect the firm's true earning power.

> **EXAMPLE: Calculating underlying earnings**
>
> Using the data in the following figure, calculate the trailing P/E for Magnolia Enterprises as of September 2014 using underlying earnings.

Study Session 11

Data for Magnolia Enterprises [amounts in Canadian dollars (C$)]				
			Nonrecurring Items	
Quarter Ending	Stock Price (C$)	Reported Diluted EPS (C$)	Gain on Asset Sales (C$)	Extraordinary Expense (C$)
December 2013	38.50	1.45		
March 2014	46.25	1.30	0.30	
June 2014	48.50	1.40		0.55
September 2014	44.85	1.35		

Answer:

12-month EPS = 1.45 + 1.30 + 1.40 + 1.35 = C$5.50

underlying earnings = 5.50 − 0.30 + 0.55 = C$5.75

$$\text{trailing P/E} = \frac{\text{C\$44.85}}{\text{C\$5.75}} = 7.80 \text{ times}$$

Earnings contain a transitory portion that is due to cyclicality. While viewed as currently transitory, business cycles are expected to repeat over the long term. The countercyclical tendency to have high P/Es due to lower EPS at the bottom of the cycle and low P/Es due to high EPS at the top of the cycle is known as the *Molodovsky effect*.

Normalized Earnings

Analysts adjust P/Es for cyclicality by estimating **normalized (or normal) earnings per share**, which is an estimate of EPS in the middle of the business cycle. The following two methods are used to normalize earnings:

1. Under **the method of historical average EPS**, the normalized EPS is estimated as the average EPS over some recent period, usually the most recent business cycle.

2. Under **the method of average return on equity**, normalized EPS is estimated as the average return on equity (ROE) multiplied by the current book value per share (BVPS). Once again, average ROE is often measured over the most recent business cycle. The reliance on BVPS reflects the effect of firm size changes more accurately than does the method of historical average EPS.

The method of historical average EPS ignores size effects, so the method of average ROE is preferred.

EXAMPLE: Calculating normalized earnings

Using the data in the following figure, calculate normalized earnings using the method of historical average EPS and the method of average return on equity for Magnolia Enterprises.

Data for Magnolia Enterprises [amounts in Canadian dollars (C$)]

Year	2012	2013	2014	2015
EPS	C$4.20	C$3.75	C$4.75	C$4.30
BVPS	C$26.02	C$27.78	C$29.25	C$32.29
ROE	14.0%	12.0%	16.0%	14.0%

Answer:

normalized earnings (average EPS approach)

$$= \frac{4.20 + 3.75 + 4.75 + 4.30}{4} = C\$4.25$$

$$\text{average ROE} = \frac{0.14 + 0.12 + 0.16 + 0.14}{4} = 0.14 = 14.00\%$$

normalized earnings (average ROE approach) = average ROE × BVPS$_{2015}$

$$= 0.14 \times C\$32.29$$
$$= C\$4.52$$

Normalized earnings are C$4.25 based on the method of historical average EPS and C$4.52 based on the method of average return on equity.

LOS 31.f: Explain and justify the use of earnings yield (E/P).

CFA® Program Curriculum: Volume 4, page 391

Negative earnings render P/E ratios meaningless. In such cases, it is common to use normalized EPS and/or restate the ratio as the **earnings yield (E/P)** because price is never negative. A high E/P suggests a *cheap* security, and a low E/P suggests an *expensive* security, so securities can be ranked from cheap to expensive based on E/P ratios.

LOS 31.g: Describe fundamental factors that influence alternative price multiples and dividend yield.

LOS 31.h: Calculate and interpret the justified price-to-earnings ratio (P/E), price-to-book ratio (P/B), and price-to-sales ratio (P/S) for a stock, based on forecasted fundamentals.

CFA® Program Curriculum: Volume 4, page 395–396

PROFESSOR'S NOTE

We organized the material related to these two LOS by ratio. We start with the formula for the justified price multiple. If you know the formula, you know the fundamental factors. Notice that the LOS ask us to "describe" all of the justified price multiples plus the dividend yield, but only to "calculate" three: P/E, P/B, and P/S.

Justified P/E Multiple

As we said earlier, the justified P/E price multiple is a P/E ratio with the "P" in the numerator equal to the fundamental value derived from a valuation model. The best way to analyze the fundamental factors that affect the P/E ratio is to use the single-stage Gordon growth model:

$$V_0 = \frac{D_0 \times (1 + g)}{(r - g)} = \frac{D_1}{(r - g)}$$

where:
V_0 = fundamental value
D_0 = dividend just paid
D_1 = dividends expected to be received at end of Year 1
r = required return on equity
g = dividend growth rate

If we express D_0 as the product of current earnings per share (E_0) and the payout ratio (D_0 / E_0) and express the retention rate as b, the previous formula becomes trailing P/E:

$$\text{justified trailing P/E} = \frac{P_0}{E_0} = \frac{D_0 \times (1 + g)/E_0}{r - g} = \frac{(1 - b) \times (1 + g)}{r - g}$$

Recognizing that $E_1 = E_0 (1 + g)$ and $D_1 = D_0 (1 + g)$, the leading P/E is calculated as:

$$\text{justified leading P/E} = \frac{P_0}{E_1} = \frac{D_1/E_1}{r - g} = \frac{1 - b}{r - g}$$

PROFESSOR'S NOTE

Remember that if earnings are expected to grow, E_1 will be greater than E_0, and the justified leading P/E (P_0/E_1) will be smaller than the justified trailing P/E (P_0/E_0) because you're dividing by a larger number when you are calculating leading P/E. In fact, trailing P/E will be larger than leading P/E by a factor of $(1 + g)$: justified trailing P/E = justified leading P/E $\times (1 + g)$.

By examining the formulas for justified (leading and trailing) P/E, we can conclude that the fundamental factors that affect P/E are expected growth rate and required return (which is related to risk). The justified P/E ratio is:

- Positively related to the growth rate of expected cash flows, whether defined as dividends or free cash flows, all else equal.

- Inversely related to the stock's required rate of return, all else equal.

> **EXAMPLE: Calculating justified P/E ratio for Comtronics again**
>
> Shares of Comtronics are selling for $30. The mean analyst earnings per share forecast for next year is $4, and the long-run growth rate is 5%. Comtronics has a dividend payout ratio of 60% and a required return of 14%. Calculate the justified leading P/E ratio.
>
> **Answer:**
>
> $$\text{justified leading P/E} = \frac{1 - b}{r - g} = \frac{0.60}{0.14 - 0.05} = 6.67 \text{ times}$$

Study Session 11

Cross-Reference to CFA Institute Assigned Reading #31 – Market-Based Valuation: Price and Enterprise Value Multiples

This is the same answer we got when we calculated Comtronics' P/E the "long way" in the example at the beginning of this topic review.

> **EXAMPLE: Calculating justified P/E ratio**
>
> A stock has a payout ratio of 40%. The shareholders require a return of 11% on their investment, and the expected growth rate in dividends is 5%. Calculate the trailing and leading P/E multiple based on these forecasted fundamentals.
>
> **Answer:**
>
> $$\text{justified trailing P/E} = \frac{(1-b) \times (1+g)}{r-g} = \frac{0.40 \times 1.05}{0.11 - 0.05} = 7.00$$
>
> $$\text{justified leading P/E} = \frac{1-b}{r-g} = \frac{0.40}{0.11 - 0.05} = 6.67$$
>
> or
>
> $$\text{justified trailing P/E} = 6.67 \times (1.05) = 7.00$$

Justified P/B Multiple

Using the sustainable growth relation of $g = \text{ROE} \times b$ and observing that $E_1 = B_0 \times \text{ROE}$, we can also derive the justified P/B from the Gordon growth model as:

$$\text{justified P/B ratio} = \frac{\text{ROE} - g}{r - g}$$

where:
ROE = return on equity
r   = required return on equity
g   = expected growth rate in dividends and earnings

We can draw two useful conclusions from this formula concerning the fundamentals that influence the P/B ratio:

- P/B increases as ROE increases, all else equal.

- The larger the spread between ROE and *r*, all else equal, the higher the P/B ratio. This makes sense if you remember that ROE is the return on the firm's investment projects and *r* is the required return. The larger the spread, all else equal, the more value the firm is creating through its investment activities and the higher its market value as represented by V_0.

We can then use fundamental forecasts of ROE, *r*, and *g* to find a value for this ratio.

> **EXAMPLE: Calculating justified P/B ratio**
>
> A firm's ROE is 14%, its required rate of return is 8%, and its expected growth rate is 4%. Calculate the firm's justified P/B based on these fundamentals.
>
> **Answer:**
>
> $$\text{justified P/B ratio} = \frac{\text{ROE} - g}{r - g} = \frac{0.14 - 0.04}{0.08 - 0.04} = 2.5$$

Justified P/S Multiple

Since net profit margin (PM_0) is equal to E_0/S_0, we can also restate the Gordon growth model as:

$$\text{justified } \frac{P_0}{S_0} = \frac{\left(E_0/S_0\right) \times (1 - b) \times (1 + g)}{r - g}$$

Net profit margin (E_0/S_0) thus influences P/S directly as well as indirectly through its effect on the sustainable growth rate, g:

$$g = \text{retention ratio} \times \text{net profit margin} \times \left(\frac{\text{sales}}{\text{assets}}\right) \times \left(\frac{\text{assets}}{\text{shareholders' equity}}\right)$$

This means that the P/S ratio will increase, all else equal, if:

■ Profit margin increases.

■ Earnings growth rate increases.

We can also do a little algebra and solve for P/S as a function of trailing P/E, which might be an easier formula to remember:

$$\text{justified } \frac{P_0}{S_0} = \left(E_0/S_0\right) \times \left[\frac{(1 - b) \times (1 + g)}{r - g}\right]$$

$$= \text{net profit margin} \times \text{justified trailing P/E}$$

> **EXAMPLE: Calculating justified P/S ratio**
>
> A stock has a dividend payout ratio of 40%, a return on equity (ROE) of 8.3%, an EPS of $4.25, sales per share of $218.75, and an expected growth rate in dividends and earnings of 5%. Shareholders require a return of 10% on their investment. Calculate the justified P/S multiple based on these fundamentals.
>
> **Answer:**
>
> The ratio E_0/S_0 is the profit margin. In this example, the profit margin is ($4.25 / $218.75) = 0.0194. Therefore, we get:
>
> $$\frac{P_0}{S_0} = \frac{0.0194 \times 0.4 \times 1.05}{0.10 - 0.05} = 0.163 \text{ times}$$

Justified P/CF Multiple

The *justified price to cash flow* based on fundamentals can be calculated by finding the value of the stock using a DCF model and dividing the result by the chosen measure of cash flow. For example, equity value using the single-stage FCFE model is:

$$V_0 = \frac{FCFE_0 \times (1 + g)}{r - g}$$

P/CF will increase, all else equal, if:

■ Required return decreases.

■ Growth rate increases.

Justified EV/EBITDA Multiple

The justified EV/EBITDA based on fundamentals is simply the enterprise value based on a forecast of fundamentals divided by EBITDA forecast based on fundamentals. The ratio is:

- Positively related to the growth rate in FCFF and EBITDA.

- Negatively related to the firm's overall risk level and weighted average cost of capital (WACC).

Justified Dividend Yield

The dividend yield relative to fundamentals may be expressed in terms of the Gordon growth model as:

$$\frac{D_0}{P_0} = \frac{r - g}{1 + g}$$

Dividend yield is:

- Positively related to the required rate of return.

- Negatively related to the forecasted growth rate in dividends. This implies that choosing high dividend yield stocks reflects a value rather than a growth investment strategy.

LOS 31.i: Calculate and interpret a predicted P/E, given a cross-sectional regression on fundamentals, and explain limitations to the cross-sectional regression methodology.

CFA® Program Curriculum: Volume 4, page 397

A **predicted P/E** can be estimated from linear regression of historical P/Es on its fundamental variables, including expected growth and risk. While such empirical analysis can provide an analyst with useful insight, there are three *main limitations*:

- The predictive power of the estimated P/E regression for a different time period and/or sample of stocks is uncertain.

- The relationships between P/E and the fundamental variables examined may change over time.

- Multicollinearity is often a problem in these time series regressions, which makes it difficult to interpret individual regression coefficients.

PROFESSOR'S NOTE

Remember from Study Session 3 that multicollinearity refers to the condition in which a high correlation exists between or among two or more of the independent variables in a multiple regression.

> **EXAMPLE: Calculating predicted P/E**
>
> An analyst is valuing a public utility with a dividend payout ratio of 0.50, a beta of 0.95, and an expected earnings growth rate of 0.06. A regression on other public utilities produces the following regression equation:
>
> predicted P/E = 6.75 + (4.00 × dividend payout) + (12.35 × growth) − (0.5 × beta)
>
> The firm's P/E ratio is 12.0. Calculate the predicted P/E on the basis of the values of the explanatory variables for the company, and determine whether the stock is over- or underpriced.
>
> **Answer:**
>
> predicted P/E = 6.75 + (4.00 × 0.50) + (12.35 × 0.06) − (0.5 × 0.95) = 9.02
>
> Actual P/E is greater than predicted P/E, so the firm is overpriced.

PROFESSOR'S NOTE

This is an example of predicting the value of a dependent variable from an estimated regression equation from Study Session 3. A P/E prediction model like this could form the basis for a quant question on the exam.

Warm-Up: Benchmarks

PROFESSOR'S NOTE

The phrase "benchmark value of a multiple" is another name for the justified price multiple using the method of comparables. We use the term "benchmark" in the discussion that follows to be consistent with the wording of the LOS.

The method of comparables approach to valuation compares a stock's price multiple to a benchmark of the multiple using the following steps:

Step 1: Select and calculate the multiple that will be used.

Step 2: Select the benchmark and calculate the mean or median of its multiple over the group of comparable stocks.

Step 3: Compare the stock's multiple to the benchmark.

Step 4: Examine whether any observed difference between the multiples of the stock and the benchmark are explained by the underlying determinants of the multiple, and make appropriate valuation adjustments.

Frequently encountered P/E benchmarks include:

- P/E of another company's stock in a similar industry with similar operating characteristics.
- Average or median P/E of peer group within the company's industry.
- Average or median P/E for the industry.

- P/E of an equity index.

- Average historical P/E for the stock.

LOS 31.j: Evaluate a stock by the method of comparables and explain the importance of fundamentals in using the method of comparables.

LOS 31.r: Evaluate whether a stock is overvalued, fairly valued, or undervalued based on comparisons of multiples.

CFA® Program Curriculum: Volume 4, page 399, 459

The basic idea of the method of comparables is to compare a stock's price multiple to that of a benchmark portfolio. *Firms with multiples below the benchmark are undervalued, and firms with multiples above the benchmark are overvalued.* However, the fundamentals of the stock should be similar to the fundamentals of the benchmark before we can make direct comparisons and draw any conclusions about whether the stock is overvalued or undervalued. In other words, we have to ensure that we're comparing apples to apples. That's why the fundamental variables (i.e., the fundamentals) that affect each multiple are important in applying the method of comparables.

Let's use the P/E ratio as an example. Remember that justified P/E is positively related to growth rates and negatively related to required rate of return and risk. Suppose we determine that the P/E of our stock is less than the benchmark. There are (at least) three possible explanations for this:

- The stock is undervalued.

- The stock is properly valued, but the stock has a lower expected growth rate than the benchmark, which leads to a lower P/E.

- The stock is properly valued, but it has a higher required rate of return (higher risk) than the benchmark, which leads to a lower P/E.

In order to conclude that the stock is truly undervalued, we have to make sure that the stock is comparable to the benchmark; it should have similar expected growth and similar risk.

> **EXAMPLE: Evaluating P/E ratios with the method of comparables**
>
> An analyst has gathered P/E information on two stocks, Allbright Interiors and Basic Designs.
>
> **Market Data on Allbright Interiors and Basic Designs**
>
> | | Trailing P/E | Leading P/E | 5-Year Growth Rate | Beta |
> |---|---|---|---|---|
> | Allbright | 10.0 | 8.7 | 11.0% | 1.3 |
> | Basic Designs | 14.0 | 12.7 | 9.0% | 1.4 |
> | Peer median | 13.3 | 12.1 | 11.0% | 1.3 |
>
> Evaluate the value and P/E of each stock based on the method of comparables.

Answer:

Allbright has a lower P/E than the peer median, despite the fact that it has a comparable growth rate and beta. This indicates Allbright is undervalued. Basic Designs, on the other hand, has a higher P/E, despite lower expected growth and a higher beta, which suggests it's overvalued relative to the benchmark.

The same steps used in valuing stocks with P/Es apply when using P/Bs. The *major difference* between the approaches is that book value forecasts are not widely disseminated like they are for EPS. Thus, most analysts use *trailing book values* in calculating P/Bs. Relative P/B valuation must consider differences in ROE, risk, and expected growth in making comparisons among stocks.

P/S valuation using the method of comparables follows the same steps as for P/E and P/B. However, P/S ratios are usually calculated based on *trailing sales*. Analysts need to control for profit margin, expected growth, risk, and the quality of accounting data in making comparisons.

EXAMPLE: Evaluating P/B and P/S ratios with the method of comparables

Crisco Systems belongs to the Networking Products industry group, and Soothsayer belongs to the Enterprise Software/Services industry group. Recall that the P/B ratios for Crisco and Soothsayer were 4.45 and 10.04, respectively, and the P/S ratios were 6.60 and 6.71. Determine whether the two stocks are overvalued or undervalued compared to their peer group means and medians.

Basic Data From the Computer Industry

Peer Group	Mean P/B	Median P/B	Mean P/S (sales in millions of $)	Median P/S (sales in millions of $)
Networking Products	2.065	1.170	3.733	0.900
Enterprise Software/ Services	7.866	2.770	3.341	1.920

Answer:

The P/B ratio for Crisco Systems exceeds the mean P/B ratio for the peer group (2.065) as well as the median P/B ratio (1.170) for the peer group; therefore, by this measure the stock would appear to be overvalued. The P/S ratio also exceeds both the mean P/S (3.733) and the median P/S (0.900) for the peer group, which also indicates that the stock is overvalued.

The P/B ratio for Soothsayer exceeds the peer group mean P/B (7.866) as well as the peer group median P/B (2.770) and suggests that the stock is overvalued. Similarly, the P/S ratio for Soothsayer exceeds the peer group mean P/S (3.341) as well as the peer group median P/S (1.920) and indicates that Soothsayer stock is overvalued as well.

Note the significant disparity between the mean and median values for each peer group. This is a clear indication of the presence of outliers in the data.

In line with other valuations by comparables discussed earlier (P/E, P/B, and P/S), a lower EV/EBITDA relative to peer firms indicates relative undervaluation, everything else being equal, and a higher ratio indicates overvaluation.

The process for dividend yield is similar to that for other multiples. An analyst compares the target company's dividend yield with that of peers to assess whether it is attractively priced. This assumes that the peers have been identified on the basis of comparable risk. Particular emphasis should be placed on determining whether any difference in dividend yield is due to expected growth differences. High dividend yield relative to the benchmark indicates undervaluation, all else equal.

The Fed and Yardeni Models

The **Fed model** considers the overall market to be overvalued (undervalued) when the earnings yield (i.e., the E/P ratio) on the S&P 500 Index is lower (higher) than the yield on 10-year U.S. Treasury bonds.

The **Yardeni model** includes expected earnings growth rate in the analysis:

$$CEY = CBY - k \times LTEG + \varepsilon_i$$

where:
CEY = current earnings yield of the market
CBY = current Moody's A-rated corporate bond yield
LTEG = five-year consensus earnings growth rate
k = constant assigned by the market to earnings growth (about 0.20 in recent years).

Taking reciprocals of the Yardeni model (and ignoring the error term), we get:

$$\frac{P}{E} = \frac{1}{CBY - k \times LTEG}$$

This shows that the P/E ratio is negatively related to interest rates and positively related to growth.

LOS 31.k: Calculate and interpret the P/E-to-growth ratio (PEG) and explain its use in relative valuation.

CFA® Program Curriculum: Volume 4, page 403

The relationship between earnings growth and P/E is captured by the **P/E-to-growth** (PEG) **ratio**:

$$PEG \ ratio \ = \ \frac{P/E \ ratio}{g}$$

The PEG is interpreted as P/E per unit of expected growth. Remember that the growth rate is one of the fundamental factors that affect P/E (P/E is directly related to the growth rate). The PEG ratio, in effect, "standardizes" the P/E ratio for stocks with different expected growth rates. The implied valuation rule is that stocks with lower PEGs are more attractive than stocks with higher PEGs, assuming that risk is similar.

> **EXAMPLE:** Calculating and using the PEG ratio
>
> Med-Ready, Inc. has a leading P/E of 28.75 and a 5-year consensus growth rate forecast of 14.5%. The median PEG for a group of companies comparable in risk to Med-Ready is 2.34. Calculate the firm's PEG and explain whether the stock appears to be correctly valued, overvalued, or undervalued.
>
> **Answer:**
>
> The firm's PEG is 28.75 / 14.5 = 1.98. Given the comparable group median PEG of 2.34, it appears that Med-Ready may be undervalued. However, it is important for the analyst to determine whether the peer group PEG is also based on leading P/Es and whether the comparable firms are similar in risk.

There are a number of drawbacks to using the PEG ratio:

- The relationship between P/E and g is not linear, which makes comparisons difficult.

- The PEG ratio still doesn't account for risk.

- The PEG ratio doesn't reflect the duration of the high-growth period for a multistage valuation model, especially if the analyst uses a short-term high-growth forecast.

LOS 31.l: Calculate and explain the use of price multiples in determining terminal value in a multistage discounted cash flow (DCF) model.

CFA® Program Curriculum: Volume 4, page 412

A terminal value that is projected as of the end of the investment horizon should reflect the earnings growth that a firm can sustain over the long run, beyond that point in time. Analysts often use terminal price multiples like P/E, P/B, P/S, and P/CF to estimate terminal value. No matter which ratio is used, terminal value is calculated as the product of the price multiple (e.g., P/E ratio) and the fundamental variable (e.g., EPS).

There are two methods of estimating the price multiple: based on fundamentals and based on comparables. The terminal price multiple based on fundamentals is the product of the justified price multiple and an estimate of the fundamental value. For example, the terminal value based on a justified P/E ratio is:

terminal value in year n

    = (justified leading P/E ratio) × (forecasted earnings in year n + 1)

terminal value in year n

    = (justified trailing P/E ratio) × (forecasted earnings in year n)

The terminal price multiple based on comparables is calculated as the benchmark price multiple and an estimate of the fundamental value. For example, the terminal value based on a benchmark P/E is:

terminal value in year n

> = (benchmark leading P/E ratio) × (forecasted earnings in year n + 1)

terminal value in year n

> = (benchmark trailing P/E ratio) × (forecasted earnings in year n)

The strength of the comparables approach is that it uses market data exclusively. In contrast, the fundamentals approach requires estimates of the growth rate, required rate of return, and payout ratio. One weakness of the comparables approach is that a benchmark marred by mispricing will transfer that error to the estimated terminal value.

> **EXAMPLE:** Calculating terminal value with price multiples
>
> An analyst estimates the EPS of Polar Technology in five years to be C$2.10, the EPS in six years to be C$2.32, and the median trailing industry P/E to be 35. Calculate the terminal value in Year 5.
>
> **Answer:**
>
> terminal value in Year 5
> = (benchmark trailing P/E ratio) × (forecasted earnings in Year 5)
> = 35 × C$2.10 = C$73.50

LOS 31.m: Explain alternative definitions of cash flow used in price and enterprise value (EV) multiples and describe limitations of each definition.

CFA® Program Curriculum: Volume 4, page 433

There are at least four definitions of cash flow available for use in calculating the P/CF ratio: (1) earnings-plus-noncash-charges (CF); (2) adjusted cash flow (adjusted CFO); (3) free cash flow to equity (FCFE); and (4) earnings before interest, taxes, depreciation, and amortization (EBITDA). Expect to see any one of them on the exam.

One commonly used proxy for cash flow is **earnings-plus-noncash-charges** (CF):

> CF = net income + depreciation + amortization

The limitation of this definition, as we mentioned previously, is that it ignores some items that affect cash flow, such as noncash revenue and changes in net working capital.

Another proxy for cash flow is cash flow from operations (CFO) from the cash flow statement. CFO is often adjusted for nonrecurring cash flows. US GAAP requires interest paid, interest received, and dividends received to be classified as operating cash flows. IFRS, however, is more flexible: interest paid may be classified as either an operating or financing cash flow, while interest and dividends received can be classified as either operating or investing cash flows. Thus, care should be taken when comparing firms reporting under different standards.

Analysts also often use **free cash flow to equity** (FCFE) and **earnings before interest, taxes, depreciation, and amortization** (EBITDA) as proxies for cash flow. As we mentioned previously, theory suggests that FCFE is the preferred way to define cash flow, but it is more volatile than straight cash flow.

$$FCFE = CFO - FCInv + \text{net borrowing}$$

where:
FCInv $\quad$ = fixed capital investment
net borrowing = (long- and short-term debt issues) − (long- and short-term debt repayments)

EBITDA is a pretax, pre-interest measure that represents a flow to both equity and debt. Thus, it is better suited as an indicator of total company value than just equity value. More on this point is provided in our discussion of the enterprise value-to-EBITDA ratio.

Analysts typically use *trailing* price to cash flow ratio, which relies on the most recent four quarters of cash flow per share. Given one of the four definitions of cash flow, the P/CF ratio is calculated as:

$$\text{PCF / ratio} = \frac{\text{market value of equity}}{\text{cash flow}} = \frac{\text{market price per share}}{\text{cash flow per share}}$$

where:
cash flow = CF, adjusted CFO, FCFE, or EBITDA

EXAMPLE: Calculating P/CF

Data Management Systems, Inc., (DMS) reported net income of $32 million, depreciation and amortization of $41 million, net interest expense of $12 million, and cash flow from operations of $44 million. The tax rate is 30%. Calculate the P/CF ratio using earnings-plus-non-cash-charges (CF) as a proxy for cash flow. DMS has 25 million shares of common stock outstanding, trading at $47 per share.

Answer:

CF $\qquad$ = $32 million + $41 million = $73 million

market value of equity = 25 million shares × $47 per share = $1,175 million

P/CF $\qquad = \dfrac{\$1,175 \text{ million}}{\$73 \text{ million}} = 16.1$ times

---

Study Session 11

Cross-Reference to CFA Institute Assigned Reading #31 – Market-Based Valuation: Price and Enterprise Value Multiples

LOS 31.n: Calculate and interpret EV multiples and evaluate the use of EV/ EBITDA.

CFA® Program Curriculum: Volume 4, page 440

Because EBITDA is a flow to both equity and debt, it should be related to a numerator that measures total company value. **Enterprise value** (EV) is total company value:

EV = market value of common stock + market value of preferred equity + market value of debt + minority interest – cash and investments

The rationale for subtracting cash and investments is that an acquirer's net price paid for an acquisition target would be lowered by the amount of the target's liquid assets. Thus, EV/EBITDA indicates the value of the overall company, not equity.

PROFESSOR'S NOTE

For our discussion going forward, we will assume minority interest and preferred equity is zero (which is typical). If, on the exam, you are given values for preferred stock and/or minority interest, do include them.

EV/EBITDA is the ratio of enterprise value to EBITDA:

$$\text{EV/EBITDA ratio} = \frac{\text{enterprise value}}{\text{EBITDA}}$$

where:
enterprise value = market value of common stock + marked value of debt – cash and investments
EBITDA = recurring earnings from continuing operations + interest + taxes + depreciation + amortization
or for forecasting
= EBIT + depreciation + amortization

EV/EBITDA is useful in a number of situations:

■ The ratio may be more useful than P/E when comparing firms with different degrees of financial leverage.

■ EBITDA is useful for valuing capital-intensive businesses with high levels of depreciation and amortization.

■ EBITDA is usually positive even when EPS is not.

EV/EBITDA has a number of drawbacks, however:

■ If working capital is growing, EBITDA will overstate CFO. Further, the measure ignores how different revenue recognition policies affect CFO.

■ Because FCFF captures the amount of capital expenditures, it is more strongly linked with valuation theory than EBITDA. EBITDA will be an adequate measure if capital expenses equal depreciation expenses.

Study Session 11

Cross-Reference to CFA Institute Assigned Reading #31 – Market-Based Valuation: Price and Enterprise Value Multiples

EXAMPLE: Calculating EV/EBITDA

An analyst gathered the following data for Boulevard Industries [all amounts in Swiss francs (Sf)]:

Recent share price	Sf 22.50
Shares outstanding	40 million
Market value of debt	Sf 137 million
Cash and marketable securities	Sf 62.3 million
Investments	Sf 327 million
Net income	Sf 137.5 million
Interest expense	Sf 6.9 million
Depreciation and amortization	Sf 10.4 million
Taxes	Sf 95.9 million

Based on this information, calculate the EV/EBITDA ratio for Boulevard Industries.

Answer:

$$\text{EBITDA} = 137.5 + 6.9 + 95.9 + 10.4 = \text{Sf 250.7 million}$$
$$\text{EV} = (22.50 \times 40) + 137 - 62.3 - 327 = \text{Sf 647.7 million}$$
$$\text{EV/EBITDA} = \frac{\text{Sf 647.7 million}}{\text{Sf 250.7 million}} = 2.6 \text{ times}$$

An alternative measure of a company's overall value is **total invested capital** (TIC), sometimes referred to as **market value of invested capital**. Total invested capital is the market value of the company's equity and debt. Unlike enterprise value, TIC includes cash and short-term investments.

In addition to EV/EBITDA and TIC/EBITDA, analysts employ enterprise value ratios with EBIT, FCFF, or other items in the denominator. For example, the *enterprise value to sales* (EV/S) ratio can be used as an alternative to the P/S ratio. The EV/S ratio is appropriate for comparing companies with significantly different capital structures.

LOS 31.o: Explain sources of differences in cross-border valuation comparisons.

CFA® Program Curriculum: Volume 4, page 449

Using relative valuation methods that require the use of comparable firms is challenging in an international context due to **differences in accounting methods, cultures, risk, and growth opportunities**. Further, benchmarking is difficult because P/Es for individual firms in the same industry vary widely internationally and country market P/Es can vary significantly. Common differences in international accounting treatment fall into several categories: goodwill, deferred income taxes, foreign exchange adjustments, R&D, pension expense, and tangible asset revaluations.

The usefulness of all price multiples is affected to some degree by differences in international accounting standards. The least affected is P/FCFE, while P/B, P/E, P/EBITDA, and EV/EBITDA will be more seriously affected because they are more influenced by management's choice of accounting methods and estimates.

LOS 31.p: Describe momentum indicators and their use in valuation.

CFA® Program Curriculum: Volume 4, page 451

Momentum indicators relate either the market price or a fundamental variable like EPS to the time series of historical or expected value. Common momentum indicators include earnings surprise, standardized unexpected earnings, and relative strength.

Unexpected earnings or **earnings surprise** is the difference between reported earnings and expected earnings:

earnings surprise = reported EPS − expected EPS

This is usually scaled by a measure that expresses the variability of analysts' EPS forecasts. The economic rationale for examining earnings surprises is that positive surprises may lead to persistent positive abnormal returns.

Similarly, the **standardized unexpected earnings** (SUE) measure is defined as:

$$\text{standardized unexpected earnings (SUE)} = \frac{\text{earnings surprise}}{\text{standard deviation of earnings surprise}}$$

A given size forecast error is more meaningful the smaller the size of the historical forecast errors.

Relative strength indicators compare a stock's price or return performance during a given time period with its own historical performance or with some group of peer stocks. The economic rationale is that patterns of persistence or reversal may exist in stock returns. These are thought to possibly depend on the length of an investor's time horizon.

LOS 31.q: Explain the use of the arithmetic mean, the harmonic mean, the weighted harmonic mean, and the median to describe the central tendency of a group of multiples.

CFA® Program Curriculum: Volume 4, page 457

The price-to-earnings multiple for a stock index is not equal to the mean or weighted mean of the P/Es of the portfolio stocks. Consider two stocks: one priced at $10 with earnings of $1 per share (P/E = 10) and one priced at $16 with earnings of $2 (P/E = 8). For a portfolio with one share of each stock, earnings per share are 1 + 2 = 3 and the "price" of a portfolio share is 10 + 16 = 26. The portfolio price-to-earnings is 26 / 3 = 8.67.

We will demonstrate that the portfolio or index P/E (as well as other relative value ratios based on price) is best calculated as the **weighted harmonic mean** P/E. With the P/Es denoted by X and the weights as w, we have:

$$\text{weighted harmonic mean} = \frac{1}{\sum_{i=1}^{n} \frac{w_i}{X_i}}$$

Consider the following alternative measures of the mean P/E for the portfolio:

arithmetic mean = (8 + 10) / 2 = 9

weighted mean = (10 / 26) × 10 + (16 / 26) × 8 = 8.76

$$\text{harmonic mean} = \frac{2}{\left(\frac{1}{10}\right) + \left(\frac{1}{8}\right)} = 8.88$$

$$\text{weighted harmonic mean} = \frac{1}{\left(\frac{10}{26}\right)\left(\frac{1}{10}\right) + \left(\frac{16}{26}\right)\left(\frac{1}{8}\right)} = 8.67$$

An analyst must be aware of how portfolio P/Es are calculated to understand them. Note that when there are extreme (high or low) outliers, the arithmetic mean will be the most affected. Analysts should be aware that the harmonic mean puts more weight on smaller values. In this case, the median or weighted harmonic mean with the outliers excluded may be the most appropriate measures of the P/E for a portfolio or index. For an equal weighted portfolio or index, the harmonic mean and weighted harmonic mean will be equal.

PROFESSOR'S NOTE

LOS 31.r was addressed back with LOS 31.j.

MODULE QUIZ 31.4

To best evaluate your performance, enter your quiz answers online.

1. Sabrina Valentine, CFA, has gathered the following data for Carolina Steel, Inc. (CSI):

Recent share price	$31.25
Shares outstanding	30 million
Market value of debt	$115 million
Cash and marketable securities	$47.6 million
Investments	$247 million
Net income	$119.4 million
Interest expense	$5.8 million
Depreciation	$6.9 million
Amortization	$2.3 million
Taxes	$85.9 million

The EV/EBITDA ratio for CSI is *closest* to:
A. 3.44.
B. 4.26.
C. 4.78.

Study Session 11

Cross-Reference to CFA Institute Assigned Reading #31 – Market-Based Valuation: Price and Enterprise Value Multiples

2. Which of the following investment strategies is *most consistent* with choosing high dividend yield stocks?
   A. Growth.
   B. Momentum.
   C. Value.

Study Session 11

Cross-Reference to CFA Institute Assigned Reading #31 – Market-Based Valuation: Price and Enterprise Value Multiples

KEY CONCEPTS

LOS 31.a

The method of comparables uses a price multiple for a similar firm or the average price multiple for a portfolio of stocks or an index as a benchmark value. The underlying economic argument for this method is that the value of a dollar of earnings or a dollar of book value, for example, should be the same across similar stocks or stocks in the same industry. Valuation based on the method of comparables is relative, based on the current market values of other stocks.

Rather than using current price multiples for other stocks, the method of forecasted fundamentals uses price multiples based on forecasted values for fundamental characteristics such as growth, dividend payout, or ROE. Under this method, we are assuming that a particular valuation model gives the stock's intrinsic value. As an example, consider the relation P/E = payout ratio / (required return − growth rate). This is the P/E for the stock if its price is equal to its value calculated using the constant growth model, an estimate of the absolute value of the stock.

LOS 31.b

A justified price multiple can be "justified" by either the method of comparables or by the method of forecasted fundamentals. As an example, consider the P/E justified by the constant growth (Gordon growth) model value. Stocks with P/Es less than their justified P/Es, based on forecasts of the fundamental variables involved, are judged to be undervalued. A similar argument can be made for stocks with P/Es less than that for a similar stock or benchmark P/E determined by the method of comparables.

LOS 31.c

Rationales for using price-to-earnings (P/E) ratio in valuation:

- Earnings power, as measured by earnings per share (EPS), is the primary determinant of investment value.
- The P/E ratio is popular in the investment community.
- Empirical research shows that P/E differences are significantly related to long-run average stock returns.

Disadvantages of using the price-to-earnings ratio include:

- Earnings can be negative.
- The volatile, transitory portion of earnings makes interpretation difficult.
- Management discretion distorts reported earnings.

Rationales for using price-to-book (P/B) ratio in valuation:

- Book value is a cumulative amount that is usually positive, even when the firm reports a loss and EPS is negative. Thus, a P/B can typically be used when P/E cannot.
- Book value is more stable than EPS, so it may be more useful than P/E when EPS is particularly high, low, or volatile.

Study Session 11

Cross-Reference to CFA Institute Assigned Reading #31 – Market-Based Valuation: Price and Enterprise Value Multiples

- Book value is an appropriate measure of net asset value for firms that primarily hold liquid assets. Examples include finance, investment, insurance, and banking firms.

- P/B can be useful in valuing companies that are expected to go out of business.

- Empirical research shows that P/Bs help explain differences in long-run average stock returns.

Disadvantages of using the price-to-book ratio include:

- P/Bs do not recognize the value of nonphysical assets.

- P/Bs can mislead when there are significant size differences.

- Different accounting conventions can obscure the true investment in the firm made by shareholders.

- Inflation and technological change can cause the book and market value of assets to differ significantly.

Rationales for using price-to-sales (P/S) ratio in valuation:

- P/S is meaningful even for distressed firms.

- Sales revenue is not as easy to manipulate or distort as EPS and book value.

- P/S ratios are not as volatile as P/E multiples.

- P/S ratios are particularly appropriate for valuing stocks in mature or cyclical industries and start-up companies with no record of earnings.

- Empirical research finds that differences in P/S are significantly related to differences in long-run average stock returns.

Disadvantages of using the price-to-sales ratio include:

- Higher sales do not necessarily indicate higher operating profits.

- P/S ratios do not capture differences in cost structures across companies.

- While less subject to distortion than earnings, revenue recognition practices can distort sales forecasts.

Rationales for using price-to-cash flow (P/CF) ratio in valuation:

- Cash flow is harder for managers to manipulate than earnings.

- Price to cash flow is more stable than price to earnings.

- Reliance on cash flow rather than earnings handles the problem of differences in the quality of reported earnings, which is a problem for P/E.

- Empirical evidence indicates that differences in price to cash flow are significantly related to differences in long-run average stock returns.

Disadvantages of using the price to cash flow include:

- The EPS plus noncash charges estimate ignores items affecting actual cash flow from operations.

- FCFE is preferred but is more volatile than operating cash flow.

Rationales for using dividend yield in valuation:

- Dividend yield contributes to total investment return.

- Dividends are not as risky as the capital appreciation component of total return.

Disadvantages of using dividend yield include:

- Dividend yield is only one component of the return on a stock.

- All else equal, higher dividends will lead to slower growth, which drives the other component of returns, price appreciation.

LOS 31.d

- The trailing P/E ratio is market price per share divided by earnings per share over the last four reported quarters.

- The leading P/E ratio is market price per share divided by estimated earnings per share for the next four quarters.

- The price/sales ratio is the market price per share divided by sales per share.

- The price/book ratio is the market price per share divided by the book value (shareholders' equity) per share.

- The price/cash flow ratio is the market price per share divided by cash flow per share, which can be calculated in various ways.

- For all of these price ratios, a higher value indicates a greater relative stock value.

- The (expected) dividend yield is the expected dividend over the next four quarters divided by the current market price per share.

LOS 31.e

Underlying earnings are earnings that exclude nonrecurring components. Normalized earnings are earnings adjusted for the business cycle using either the method of historical EPS or the method of average ROE. The method of average ROE is preferred.

LOS 31.f

A high earnings yield (E/P) suggests a cheap security, and a low E/P suggests an expensive security, so securities can be ranked from cheap to expensive based on E/P ratios.

LOS 31.g

All else equal:

- The price-to-earnings ratio will be higher the greater the growth rate of earnings and the lower the required rate of return.

- The price-to-sales ratio will be higher the greater the net profit margin and the lower the required rate of return.

- The price-to-cash flow ratio will be higher the greater the growth rate of free cash flow to equity and the lower the required rate of return.

Study Session 11

Cross-Reference to CFA Institute Assigned Reading #31 – Market-Based Valuation: Price and Enterprise Value Multiples

- The price-to-book ratio will be higher the greater the spread between ROE and the required rate of return.

- The dividend yield will be higher the greater the required rate of return and the lower the growth rate of earnings.

LOS 31.h

Based on discounted cash flow valuation:

- The justified leading price-to-earnings ratio based on forecasted fundamentals can be calculated as:

$$P/E = \frac{P_0}{E_1} = \frac{\text{payout ratio}}{r - g}$$

- The justified price-to-book value ratio based on forecasted fundamentals can be calculated as:

$$\frac{P_0}{B_0} = \frac{ROE - g}{r - g}$$

- The justified price-to-sales ratio based on forecasted fundamentals can be calculated as:

$$\frac{P_0}{S_0} = \frac{(E_0 / S_0) \times (1 - b) \times (1 + g)}{r - g}$$

LOS 31.i

Predicted P/E can be estimated from linear regression of historical P/Es on its fundamental variables. In such a case, P/E is the dependent variable and company fundamentals (e.g., growth rate, beta, etc.) are independent variables.

LOS 31.j

When using the method of comparables to identify attractively priced stocks, the analyst must account for differences in the stocks' fundamentals. A stock with a high P/E ratio may still be attractive because of its rapid growth, while a stock with a high dividend yield (low price-to-dividend) may be unattractive because earnings do not support the dividend and no growth is anticipated.

LOS 31.k

The price earnings-to-growth (PEG) ratio is calculated as PEG ratio $= \dfrac{P/E \text{ ratio}}{g}$.

Lower PEGs are more attractive than stocks with higher PEGs, all else equal.

LOS 31.l

Analysts often use price multiples such as P/E, P/B, P/S, and P/CF to estimate terminal value. No matter which ratio we use, terminal value is calculated as the product of the expected price multiple (e.g., P/E ratio) and the terminal value of the fundamental variable (e.g., EPS).

LOS 31.m

There are four measures of cash flow commonly used for cash flow multiples and enterprise value multiples:

1. Earnings plus noncash charges: EPS plus per-share depreciation, amortization, and depletion.

2. Cash flow from operations (CFO): Often adjusted by subtracting nonrecurring cash flows, and for different classifications of cash flows under differing accounting standards. This measure is more technically correct than earnings plus noncash charges.

3. Free cash flow to equity (FCFE): CFO minus capital expenditures, minus (plus) principal payments to (from) debtholders. Most closely linked to value theory but more volatile than other measures. Consider using average FCFE.

4. Earnings before interest, taxes, depreciation, and amortization (EBITDA): Depreciation and amortization are added to EBIT (for forecasting), or interest, taxes, depreciation, and amortization can be added to recurring earnings from continuing operations (for historical values). As a pre-interest earnings measure, EBITDA is a measure of cash flow to the firm, to both debt and equity holders.

LOS 31.n

Enterprise value (EV) is measured as the market value of debt, common equity, and any preferred equity, minus the value of cash and investments. EV/EBITDA is a commonly used measure of relative company value.

Advantages of EV/EBITDA:

■ It is useful for comparing firms with different degrees of financial leverage.

■ EBITDA is useful for valuing capital-intensive businesses with high depreciation.

■ EBITDA is usually positive even when EPS is not.

Disadvantages of EV/EBITDA:

■ If working capital is growing, EBITDA will overstate CFO.

■ FCFF is more strongly linked with valuation theory than EBITDA.

LOS 31.o

Using relative valuation methods that require the use of comparable firms is challenging in an international context due to differences in accounting methods, cultures, risk, and growth opportunities.

LOS 31.p

Momentum indicators relate either the market price or a fundamental variable-like EPS to the time series of historical or expected value. Common momentum indicators include earnings surprise, standardized unexpected earnings, and relative strength.

LOS 31.q

When calculating the P/E or other price multiple for an index or portfolio, the arithmetic mean may be misleading. The most appropriate measure is the weighted harmonic mean of the individual asset P/Es using the portfolio or index weights.

$$\text{weighted harmonic mean} = \frac{1}{\sum_{i=1}^{n} \frac{w_i}{X_i}}$$

LOS 31.r

The basic idea of the method of comparables is to compare a stock's price multiple to the benchmark. Firms with multiples below the benchmark are undervalued, and firms with multiples above the benchmark are overvalued.

ANSWER KEY FOR MODULE QUIZZES

Module Quiz 31.1

1. **A**

$$\text{trailing P/E} = \frac{P_0}{E_0} = \frac{(1-b)\times(1+g)}{r-g} = \frac{\left(\frac{\$0.40}{\$1.00}\right)\times 1.05}{0.12-0.05} = 6.0$$

$$\text{leading P/E} = \frac{P_0}{E_1} = \frac{1-b}{r-g} = \frac{0.40}{0.12-0.05} = 5.7$$

   (LOS 31.h)

2. **A** Predicted P/E = $8.57 + (5.38 \times 0.65) + (15.53 \times 0.032) - (0.61 \times 0.56)$
   $= 12.2$ (LOS 31.i)

3. **B** The firm's PEG is $18.75 / 15.32 = 1.22$. Given the comparable group median PEG of 0.92, it appears that Party Favors, Inc. may be overvalued. (LOS 31.k)

4. **C** Consumer Products appears to be undervalued with a trailing P/E of 27.52 compared with the benchmark of 33.25. (LOS 31.r)

5. **B** Underlying earnings = $\$1.29 + \$0.22 + \$0.04 - \$0.08 = \$1.47$

$$\text{P/E ratio} = \frac{\$42.50}{\$1.47} = 28.9$$

   (LOS 31.e)

6. **A** Only the average ROE and the book value per share are relevant for calculating normalized earnings:

   $$\text{normalized earnings} = \text{average ROE} \times \text{BVPS} = 0.32 \times \$14$$
   $$= \$4.48 \text{ per share}$$

   (LOS 31.e)

7. **B**

   $$\text{net profit margin} = \frac{\text{trailing earnings}}{\text{sales}} = \frac{E_0}{S}$$

   so

   $$\text{trailing P/E} = \frac{P/S}{E_0/S} = \frac{P/S}{\text{net profit margin}}$$

   $$\text{trailing P/E} = \frac{P/S}{\text{net profit margin}} = \frac{2.0}{0.05} = 40$$

   $$\text{leading P/E} = \frac{\text{trailing P/E}}{1+g} = \frac{40}{1.04} = 38.5$$

   (LOS 31.h)

Study Session 11

Cross-Reference to CFA Institute Assigned Reading #31 – Market-Based Valuation: Price and Enterprise Value Multiples

8. **A** Copyright's justified leading P/E multiple using the valuation from the H-model is $84 / $4.20 = 20 times. The firm is underpriced if its actual P/E is less than 20; it is overpriced if its actual P/E is greater than 20. (LOS 31.r)

Module Quiz 31.2

1. **C** Based on the fundamentals:

$$\frac{P_0}{B_0} = \frac{0.23 - 0.076}{0.14 - 0.076} = 2.41$$

(LOS 31.h)

Module Quiz 31.3

1. **C** Profit margin is measured as E/S. In this example, the profit margin is $5.35 / $342 = 0.0156. Thus:

$$\frac{P_0}{S_0} = \frac{0.0156 \times 0.75 \times 1.045}{0.150 - 0.045} = 0.1164 \text{ times}$$

(LOS 31.h)

2. **C**

$$\text{book value / share} = \frac{\text{book value of equity}}{\text{number of shares outstanding}} = \frac{\$19,950}{6,162} = \$3.238$$

$$\text{P/B} = \frac{\text{market price per share}}{\text{book value per share}} = \frac{\$31.37}{\$3.238} = 9.688$$

$$\text{sales/share} = \frac{\text{sales}}{\text{number of shares outstanding}} = \frac{\$32,373}{6,162} = \$5.254$$

$$\text{P/S} = \frac{\text{market price per share}}{\text{sales per share}} = \frac{\$31.37}{\$5.254} = 5.971$$

(LOS 31.b)

3. **A**

$$\text{book value/share} = \frac{\text{book value of equity}}{\text{number of shares outstanding}} = \frac{\$61,020}{10,771} = \$5.665$$

$$\text{P/B} = \frac{\text{market price per share}}{\text{book value per share}} = \frac{\$25.63}{\$5.665} = 4.524$$

$$\text{sales/share} = \frac{\text{sales}}{\text{number of shares outstanding}} = \frac{\$32,187}{10,771} = \$2.988$$

$$\text{P/S} = \frac{\text{market price per share}}{\text{sales per share}} = \frac{\$25.63}{\$2.988} = 8.578 \quad \text{(LOS 31.b)}$$

4. **A** Both stocks are relatively overvalued. The P/B and P/S ratios for Pfeiffer are 9.688 and 5.971. The P/B ratio for Pfeiffer exceeds the mean P/B ratio for the peer group (5.622) as well as the median P/B ratio (4.250) for the peer group, and therefore, by this measure, the stock would appear to be overvalued.

   The P/S ratio also exceeds the median P/S (4.530) for the peer group, which further suggests that the stock is relatively overvalued. The P/B and P/S ratios for Mapps are 4.524 and 8.578. The P/B ratio for Mapps is greater than the mean P/B ratio for the peer group (4.100), and Mapps's P/B ratio exceeds the median ratio (2.140) for the peer group, and therefore, by this measure, Mapps is overvalued. Mapps's P/S ratio exceeds both the mean P/S (3.420) and the median P/S (1.440) for the peer group. The P/S ratio also indicates that Mapps is relatively overvalued. (LOS 31.r)

5. **A** Home Decor appears to be undervalued relative to Lester's. This conclusion is based on the fact that (1) Home Decor is selling at a P/CF of 20.88, which is 87.4% of the P/CF for Lester's (23.90), and (2) the P/FCFE for Home Decor (28.69) is 21.6% of the P/FCFE for Lester's (132.78). We would expect that Home Decor would have a higher P/CF because of its higher expected growth. However, because P/CF is actually lower, this is an indication that Home Decor is undervalued relative to Lester's. (LOS 31.r)

6. **C** In the home improvement segment of the retail industry, Home Decor appears to be a more attractive investment than Lester's for the following reasons:
   - Home Decor is trading at a P/B that is 91% of the average P/B for the home improvement segment of the retail industry, with a forecasted ROE that is the same as that of the industry. This indicates that Home Decor is undervalued relative to its industry.
   - Home Decor is currently trading at a P/B that is 76.6% of the P/B for Lester's, with an estimated ROE that is slightly greater than the forecasted ROE for Lester's. This indicates that Home Decor is undervalued relative to Lester's.
   - Lester's is trading at a P/B that is 119% of the industry average P/B, with a forecasted ROE that is slightly below the industry's forecasted ROE. This indicates that Lester's is overvalued relative to its industry.
   - It should be noted that Home Decor's higher beta may account for Home Decor's low P/B and high forecast ROE relative to Lester's.

   (LOS 31.r)

7. **A** In the department and discount segment of the retail industry, Harmon's appears to be a more attractive investment than Wally's for the following reasons:
   - Harmon's is trading at a P/B that is 57% of the average P/B for the department and discount store segment of the retail industry with a forecasted ROE that is very close to that of the industry. This indicates that Harmon's is undervalued relative to the industry.

Study Session 11

Cross-Reference to CFA Institute Assigned Reading #31 – Market-Based Valuation: Price and Enterprise Value Multiples

■ Harmon's is currently trading at a P/B that is 50% of the current P/B for Wally's, with an estimated ROE that is just slightly less than the forecasted ROE for Wally's. This indicates that Harmon's is undervalued relative to Wally's. It should be noted that the beta values for Harmon's and Wally's are only slightly different, indicating similar risk.

■ Wally's is trading at a P/B that is 114% of the industry average P/B, with a forecasted ROE that is only slightly above the ROE forecast for the industry. This indicates that Wally's is overvalued relative to its industry.

(LOS 31.r)

8. **B**   P = $42.10/share

CF = net income + depreciation = $1,023,262,000 + $534,102,000
= $1,557,364,000

number of basic shares outstanding = 631,643,000

CF/share = $1,557,364,000 / 631,643,000 = $2.4656

P/CF = $42.10 / $2.4656 = 17.08 times

(LOS 31.m)

9. **B**   It is appropriate to make one adjustment to CFO in this problem to reflect nonrecurring items:

■ The nonrecurring expense of $139,870,000 that appears on the income statement should be added back after adjusting for taxes.

CFO (reflecting nonrecurring items) = $1,497,442,000
+ $139,870,000(1 – 0.37) = $1,585,560,100

adjusted CFO per share = $1,585,560,100 / 631,643,000 = $2.51

adjusted P/CFO = $42.10 / $2.51 = 16.77 or closest to 17

(LOS 31.m)

Module Quiz 31.4

1. **A**

EBITDA $= 119.4 + 5.8 + 85.9 + 6.9 + 2.3 = \$220.3$ million

EV $= (31.25 \times 30) + 115 - 47.6 - 247 = \$757.9$ million

EV/EBITDA $= \dfrac{\$757.9}{\$220.3} = 3.44$

(LOS 31.n)

2. **C**   Dividend yield is positively related to the required rate of return and negatively related to the forecasted growth rate in dividends. Thus, choosing high dividend yield stocks reflects a value- rather than a growth-style orientation. (LOS 31.g)

READING
32

Residual Income Valuation

EXAM FOCUS

This topic review introduces the fourth type of valuation model found in the CFA curriculum: Residual income models. You should understand the differences between these models and the dividend discount, free cash flow, and market multiple models. The successful application of residual income models depends on making the appropriate adjustments to the financial statements, so you also should be able to use the techniques you learned in the financial statement analysis material from Study Sessions 5 and 6 in applying these models. The concept of continuing residual income is also related to the material on industry analysis in Study Session 10. With all these links to other concepts in the Level II curriculum, this material is highly testable.

MODULE 32.1: RESIDUAL INCOME DEFINED

LOS 32.a: Calculate and interpret residual income, economic value added, and market value added.

Video covering this content is available online.

CFA® Program Curriculum: Volume 4, page 493

Residual income (RI), or economic profit, is the net income of a firm less a charge that measures stockholders' opportunity cost of capital. The rationale for the residual income approach is that it recognizes the cost of equity capital in the measurement of income. This concept of economic income is not reflected in traditional accounting income, whereby a firm can report positive net income but not meet the return requirements of its equity investors. Accounting net income includes a cost of debt (i.e., interest expense), but does not reflect dividends or other equity capital-related funding costs. This means that accounting income may overstate returns from the perspective of equity investors. Conversely, residual income explicitly *deducts all capital costs*.

EXAMPLE: Calculating residual income

Madeira Fruit Suppliers, Inc. (MFS) distributes fruit to grocery stores in large U.S. cities. The book value of its assets is $1.4 billion, which is financed with $800 million in equity and $600 million in debt. Its before-tax cost of debt is 3.33%, and its marginal tax rate is 34%. MFS has a cost of equity of 12.3%. MFS's abbreviated income statement is shown in the following figure.

Partial Income Statement for MFS

EBIT	$142,000,000
Less: Interest expense	(20,000,000)
Pretax income	122,000,000
Less: Income tax expense	(41,480,000)
Net income	$80,520,000

Determine whether MFS is profitable by calculating residual income and explaining its relationship to reported accounting income.

Answer:

While the accounting net income of $80,520,000 indicates that MFS is profitable, it remains to be seen whether the firm is profitable after deducting a charge for equity. The dollar-based equity charge is:

$$\text{equity charge} = \text{equity capital} \times \text{cost of equity} = \$800 \text{ million} \times 0.123$$
$$= \$98,400,000$$

RI is calculated as:

Net income	$80,520,000
− Equity charge	98,400,000
Residual income	−$17,880,000

Even though MFS is profitable in the traditional accounting sense, it is economically unprofitable after taking into account the necessary charge to meet stockholders' opportunity cost of supplying capital to the company.

EVA and MVA

Economic value added (EVA®) measures the value added for shareholders by management during a given year. EVA is calculated as:

$$\text{EVA} = \text{NOPAT} - (\text{WACC} \times \text{total capital})$$
$$= [\text{EBIT} \times (1 - t)] - \$\text{WACC}$$

where:

NOPAT	= net operating profit after tax
WACC	= after-tax weighted average cost of capital in decimal terms (e.g, 0.05)
t	= marginal tax rate
$WACC	= dollar cost of capital
total capital	= net working capital + net fixed assets
	= book value of long-term debt + book value of equity

PROFESSOR'S NOTE

Notice the difference in calculation between residual income and EVA. Residual income is net income (after subtracting interest expense) minus a charge for equity capital based on the cost of equity. EVA is NOPAT (before subtracting interest expense minus a charge for debt and equity capital based on the WACC). Conceptually, however, they are both measuring economic income. For the purpose of EVA computation, we use beginning-of-year total capital. Market value added (discussed later) uses end-of-year (the same point at which market value is determined) total capital.

The analyst should make the following adjustments (if applicable) to the financial statements before calculating NOPAT and invested capital:

- Capitalize and amortize research and development charges (rather than expense them), and add them back to earnings to calculate NOPAT.

- Add back charges on strategic investments that will generate returns in the future.

- Eliminate deferred taxes and consider only cash taxes as an expense.

- Treat operating leases as capital leases and adjust nonrecurring items.

- Add LIFO reserve to invested capital and add back change in LIFO reserve to NOPAT.

Market value added (MVA) is the difference between the market value of a firm's long-term debt and equity and the book value of invested capital supplied by investors. It measures the value created by management's decisions since the firm's inception. MVA is calculated as:

$$\text{MVA} = \text{market value} - \text{total capital}$$

> **EXAMPLE: Calculating EVA and MVA**
>
> VBM, Inc., reports NOPAT of $2,100, a WACC of 14.2%, and invested capital of $18,000 at the beginning of the year and $21,000 at the end of the year. The market price (year-end) of the firm's stock is $25 per share, and VBM has 800 shares outstanding. The market value (year-end) of the firm's long-term debt is $4,000. Calculate VBM's EVA and MVA.
>
> **Answer:**
>
> First calculate EVA:
>
> $WACC = 0.142 × $18,000 = $2,556
> EVA = $2,100 − $2,556 = −$456
>
> The market value of the company is the market value of the equity plus the market value of the debt:
>
> MV of company = ($25 × 800) + $4,000 = $24,000
>
> The firm's MVA is:
>
> MVA = $24,000 − $21,000 = $3,000

LOS 32.b: Describe the uses of residual income models.

CFA® Program Curriculum: Volume 4, page 495

There are several commercially available residual income-based valuation models. It is interesting to note that these models, like EVA and MVA, usually apply the concept of residual income to the measurement of managerial effectiveness and executive compensation. However, for the exam we're most interested in the equity valuation applications of residual income models. Residual income models have also been proposed as a method to measure goodwill impairment.

MODULE 32.2: RESIDUAL INCOME COMPUTATION

Video covering this content is available online.

LOS 32.c: Calculate the intrinsic value of a common stock using the residual income model and compare value recognition in residual income and other present value models.

CFA® Program Curriculum: Volume 4, page 497

We can forecast residual income given some basic accounting information and an estimate of future earnings growth using the following formula:

$$RI_t = E_t − (r × B_{t-1}) = (ROE − r) × B_{t-1}$$

where:
RI_t = residual income per share in year t
E_t = expected EPS for year t
r = required return on equity
B_{t-1} = book value per share in year t − 1
ROE = expected return on new investments (expected return on equity)

> **EXAMPLE: Forecasting residual income**
>
> Laura Kraft, CFA, was assigned the task of forecasting the residual income for Delilah Cosmetics, Inc. over the next two years. To accomplish this task, Kraft assembled the information provided in the following figure. Kraft used a required rate of return of 11%. Forecast Delilah's residual income for 2019 and 2020.
>
> **Delilah Data Forecast**
>
> | | |
> |---|---|
> | **Current market price** | **€24.00** |
> | Current book value per share (December 31, 2018) | €18.00 |
> | Consensus annual EPS estimates | |
> | December 31, 2019 | €2.05 |
> | December 31, 2020 | €2.22 |
> | Dividend payout ratio 2019 and 2020 | 65% |
>
> **Answer:**
>
> **Delilah Residual Income Forecast**
>
> | | FY 2019 | FY 2020 |
> |---|---|---|
> | Beginning book value (B_{t-1}) | €18.00 | €18.72 |
> | Earnings per share forecast (E_t) | 2.05 | 2.22 |
> | Dividend forecast ($D_t = E_t \times$ payout ratio) | 1.33 | 1.44 |
> | Forecast book value per share ($B_{t-1} + E_t - D_t$) | 18.72 | 19.50 |
> | Equity charge per share ($r \times B_{t-1}$) | 1.98 | 2.06 |
> | Per share RI_t [$E_t - (r \times B_{t-1})$] | €0.07 | €0.16 |

The residual income valuation model breaks the intrinsic value of a stock into two elements: (1) current book value of equity and (2) present value of expected *future* residual income:

$$V_0 = B_0 + \left\{ \frac{RI_1}{(1+r)^1} + \frac{RI_2}{(1+r)^2} + \frac{RI_3}{(1+r)^3} + \dots \right\}$$

where:
B_0 = current book value of equity
RI_t = $E_t - (r \times B_{t-1})$ = (ROE − r) $\times B_{t-1}$
r = required return on equity
ROE = expected return on new investments (expected return on equity)

Don't let this formula intimidate you! All the above expression really says is that a stock's intrinsic value, V_0, is equal to its current book value per share, B_0, plus the present value of all its expected future residual income, which is the difference between end-of-period earnings and equity charges based on beginning-of-period book value.

The difficulty in implementing this model is that we have to make some assumptions about the pattern of residual income growth in the future because it's difficult to take the present value of an infinite stream of residual incomes without more restrictive assumptions. In the following example, we make it easy by assuming the company ceases operations at the end of three years, so we only have three residual income forecasts to discount back.

EXAMPLE: Computing intrinsic value with a residual income model

Consolidated Pipe Products has a required rate of return of 14%. The current book value is C$6.50. Earnings forecasts for 2019, 2020, and 2021 are C$1.10, C$1.00, and C$0.95, respectively. Dividends in 2019 and 2020 are forecasted to be C$0.50 and C$0.60, respectively. The dividend in 2021 is a liquidating dividend, which means that Consolidated will pay out its entire book value in dividends and cease doing business at the end of 2021. Calculate the value of Consolidated's stock using the residual income model.

Answer:

The residual income forecast is shown in the following table, with calculated values in blue.

Consolidated Pipe Residual Income Forecast

	2019	2020	2021
Beginning book value per share (B_{t-1})	C$6.50	C$7.10	C$7.50
Earnings per share forecast (E_t)	1.10	1.00	0.95
Dividends per share forecast (D_t)	0.50	0.60	8.45
Forecast book value per share ($B_{t-1} + E_t - D_t$)	7.10	7.50	0.00
Equity charge per share ($r \times B_{t-1}$)	0.91	0.99	1.05
Per share RI [$E_t - (r \times B_{t-1})$]	C$0.19	C$0.01	–C$0.10

The intrinsic value of Consolidated Pipe Products is its current book value plus the present value of the future residual income forecasts:

$$V_0 = C\$6.50 + \frac{C\$0.19}{1.14^1} + \frac{C\$0.01}{1.14^2} - \frac{C\$0.10}{1.14^3} = C\$6.61$$

We can also use the cash flow function on our calculators to solve this problem and save ourselves a little time. Here are the keystrokes:

$CF_0 = 6.50$; $C01 = 0.19$; $C02 = 0.01$; $C03 = -0.10$; $I = 14$; $CPT \rightarrow NPV = 6.61$

Value tends to be recognized earlier in the RI approach than in other present value-based approaches. To see this, recall that with a dividend discount model (DDM) or free cash flow to equity (FCFE) model, a large portion of the estimated intrinsic value comes from the present value of the expected terminal value. Yet the uncertainty of the expected terminal value is usually greater than any of the other forecasted cash flows because it occurs several years in the future. Valuation with residual income models, however, is relatively less sensitive to terminal value estimates, which reduces forecast error. This is because intrinsic values estimated with residual income models include the firm's current book value (which is known and doesn't need to be forecasted), and the current book value usually represents a substantial percentage of the estimated intrinsic value.

LOS 32.d: Explain fundamental determinants of residual income.

CFA® Program Curriculum: Volume 4, page 505

The general residual income models make no assumptions regarding the long-term future earnings or dividend growth. However, if we make the simplifying assumption of a constant dividend and earnings growth rate, we can develop a residual income model that highlights the fundamental drivers of residual income. Assuming the stock is correctly priced (i.e., $P_0 = V_0$), value can be expressed in terms of book value:

$$V_0 = B_0 + \left[\frac{(ROE - r) \times B_0}{r - g}\right]$$

This model is actually just another version of the Gordon growth model, so if you can use the same inputs, both models will give you the same value estimates.

This version of the residual income model is referred to as the **single-stage residual income valuation model**. In this formulation (assuming constant earnings and dividend growth) the first term is the current book value, the value of the company's assets net of liabilities. The second term in brackets is the present value of the expected future residual income. We can use this relationship to identify the **fundamental drivers** of residual income:

■ If return on equity (ROE) is equal to the required return on equity, the justified market value of a share of stock is equal to its book value. When ROE is higher than the required return on equity, the firm will have positive residual income and will be valued at more than book value.

■ $\left[\frac{(ROE - r) \times B_0}{r - g}\right]$ is the additional value generated by the firm's ability to produce returns in excess of the cost of equity and, consequently, is the present value of a firm's expected economic profits (i.e., residual income).

Tobin's Q is a related concept:

$$Q = \frac{\text{market value of debt} + \text{market value of equity}}{\text{replacement cost of total assets}}$$

PROFESSOR'S NOTE

The single-stage model assumes constant ROE and constant earnings growth, which implies that residual income will persist indefinitely. Residual income is likely to approach zero over time, however, as competitive forces drive industry profit margins to normal levels. Thus, in practice, the single-stage model is modified to handle declining RI by forecasting continuing residual income.

LOS 32.e: Explain the relation between residual income valuation and the justified price-to-book ratio based on forecasted fundamentals.

CFA® Program Curriculum: Volume 4, page 505

As with the DDM and FCFE models, residual income models can be used to estimate justified price multiples. Among the various market multiples, residual income models are most closely related to the price-to-book value (P/B) ratio because the justified P/B is directly linked to expected future residual income. This can be seen by observing the single-stage model. If ROE is greater than the required return on equity, the second term (the present value of residual income) will be positive, the market value will be greater than book value, and the justified P/B ratio will be greater than one.

MODULE QUIZ 32.1, 32.2

1. The present value of Sporting Shoes (SS) projected residual income for the next five years plus beginning book value is C$75.00 per share. Beyond that time horizon, the firm will sustain a residual income of C$11.25 per share, which is the residual income for Year 6. The cost of equity is 10%. The justified value of SS's common stock is *closest* to:
   A. C$69.85.
   B. C$112.50.
   C. C$144.85.

Use the following information to answer Questions 2 through 4.

Aaron Mechanic, CFA, is responsible for valuing the shares of Duotronics Research Laboratories (DRL). The stock is currently trading at €8.75, and Mechanic gathers the following financial information about the company:
- Expected return on equity (ROE) = 16% annually for each of the next four years.
- Current book value (BV) of equity = €435,000,000.
- Shares outstanding: 60 million.
- Required rate of return on equity = 12%.
- No dividends paid.
- All earnings are reinvested.
- Continuing residual income = 0 after four years.

2. Based on the residual income model, the intrinsic value and the *most likely* recommendation Mechanic would issue for the stock of DRL are:

Intrinsic value	Recommendation
A. €1.10	Sell
B. €8.34	Buy
C. €8.34	Sell

3. Mechanic is considering revising his expectation of the continuing residual income after the 4-year horizon period and believes that it will remain constant at the Year 4 forecast level of residual income for the foreseeable future. Based on the residual income model, the intrinsic value and the *most likely* recommendation Mechanic would issue for the stock of DRL are:

Intrinsic value	Recommendation
A. €8.75	Buy
B. €10.73	Buy
C. €10.73	Sell

4. George Karanopoulos, CFA, is Mechanic's immediate supervisor. He believes that Mechanic's assumption of constant residual income after the initial forecast period is unrealistic. He has suggested that Mechanic re-estimate the value of DRL based on a persistence factor of ω = 0.3 after Year 4. Based on the residual income model, the intrinsic value and the *most likely* recommendation Mechanic would issue for the stock of DRL are:

Intrinsic value	Recommendation
A. €8.95	Sell
B. €8.45	Buy
C. €8.45	Sell

MODULE 32.3: CONSTANT GROWTH MODEL FOR RI

Video covering this content is available online.

LOS 32.f: Calculate and interpret the intrinsic value of a common stock using single-stage (constant-growth) and multistage residual income models.

CFA® Program Curriculum: Volume 4, page 506

EXAMPLE: Calculating value with a single-stage residual income model

Western Atlantic Railroad has a book value of $23.00 per share. The company's return on new investments (ROE) is 14%, and its required return on equity is 12%. The dividend payout ratio is 60%. Calculate the value of the shares using a single-stage residual income model and the present value of expected economic profits.

Answer:

First, calculate the growth rate:

g = retention ratio × ROE = (1 − 0.6) × 0.14 = 0.056 = 5.6%

Then, calculate intrinsic value using the single-stage model:

$$V_0 = \$23.00 + \left[\frac{(0.14 - 0.12) \times \$23.00}{0.12 - 0.056}\right] = \$23.00 + \$7.19 = \$30.19$$

The present value of the firm's expected economic profits is $7.19.

> **EXAMPLE:** Western Atlantic Railroad valuation with Gordon growth model
>
> Use the information in the previous example to calculate the value of Western Atlantic common stock using the Gordon growth model.
>
> **Answer:**
>
> Earnings in Year 1 (E_1) is equal to beginning book value multiplied by ROE: E_1 = $23.00 × 0.14 = $3.22. With a dividend payout ratio of 60%, D_1 = $3.22 (0.6) = $1.932. Then, using the Gordon growth model:
>
> $$V_0 = \frac{\$1.932}{0.12 - 0.056} = \$30.19$$
>
> Notice that this is the same estimate as in the previous example where we used the single-stage residual income model.

 PROFESSOR'S NOTE

Multistage residual income models will be discussed in a later LOS.

LOS 32.g: Calculate the implied growth rate in residual income, given the market price-to-book ratio and an estimate of the required rate of return on equity.

CFA® Program Curriculum: Volume 4, page 507

We can rearrange the single-stage residual income valuation model and solve for the growth rate in terms of the other variables:

$$g = r - \left[\frac{B_0 \times (ROE - r)}{V_0 - B_0}\right]$$

This expression can now be used to directly compute the market's expectations of residual income growth implied by the current market price under the assumption that intrinsic value is equal to market price.

> **EXAMPLE:** Calculating implied growth rate
>
> You are considering the purchase of Tellis Telecommunications, Inc., which has a P/B ratio of 2.50. ROE is expected to be 13%, current book value per share is €8.00, and the cost of equity is 11%. Calculate the growth rate implied by the current P/B ratio.
>
> **Answer:**
>
> The P/B ratio of 2.50 and the current book value per share of €8.00 imply a current market price of €20.00(8 × 2.50). This implies a growth rate of:
>
> $$g = 0.11 - \left[\frac{€8.00 \times (0.13 - 0.11)}{€20.00 - €8.00}\right] = 0.0967 = 9.67\%$$

MODULE QUIZ 32.3

1. An investor is considering the purchase of Capital City Investments, Inc., which has a price-to-book value (P/B ratio) of 5.00. Return on equity (ROE) is expected to be 18%, the market price per share is $25.00, and the growth rate is expected to be 8%. Assume the shares are currently priced at their fair value. The cost of equity implied by the current P/B ratio is *closest* to:
    A. 6%.
    B. 8%.
    C. 10%.

2. Century Scales has a required return on equity of 12% and is expected to grow indefinitely at a rate of 5%. The expected return on equity (ROE) that would justify a price-to-book multiple of 2.14 is *closest* to:
    A. 10%.
    B. 15%.
    C. 20%.

3. Marg Myers, CFA, has determined that Rocky Romano Ice Cream Company can be valued using a single-stage residual income model. Myers estimates Rocky's return on equity (ROE) is greater than the cost of equity capital, which is greater than the sustainable growth rate. Book value per share is greater than zero. What can Myers conclude about Rocky's present value (PV) of future expected residual income (RI) and Rocky's justified price-to-book ratio?

	PV of expected RI	Justified price-to-book ratio
A.	Greater than zero	Greater than one
B.	Less than zero	Greater than one
C.	Greater than zero	Less than one

4. Krackel, Inc., has a book value per share as of FYE 2016 of $4.50. The required return on equity is 10%. Earnings per share in 2017 are forecast to be $0.45. Assume Krackel can be valued using a single-stage residual income model. The justified price-to-book ratio and the present value of expected residual income are *closest* to:

	Justified price-to-book ratio	PV of expected RI
A.	1.0	$0.00
B.	1.45	$0.00
C.	1.45	$4.05

MODULE 32.4: CONTINUING RESIDUAL INCOME

> Video covering this content is available online.

LOS 32.h: Explain continuing residual income and justify an estimate of continuing residual income at the forecast horizon, given company and industry prospects.

CFA® Program Curriculum: Volume 4, page 507

Previously, we mentioned the problem of forecasting residual income indefinitely into the future, which makes it difficult to calculate the present value of residual income and implement the residual income model. However, we can simplify the model by using the same multistage approach we used for DDM and free cash flow models. We'll forecast residual income over a short-term horizon (e.g., five years) and then make some simplifying assumptions about the pattern of residual income growth over the long term after five years. **Continuing residual income** is the residual income that is expected over the long term.

Residual income will continue beyond a specified earnings horizon depending on the fortunes of the industry, as well as on the sustainability of a specific firm's competitive prospects over the longer term. The projected rate at which residual income is expected to fade over the life cycle of the firm is captured by a **persistence factor**, ω, which is between zero and one.

To simplify the model, we typically make one of the following assumptions about continuing residual income at the end of the short-term period:

■ Residual income is expected to persist at its current level forever.

■ Residual income is expected to drop immediately to zero.

■ Residual income is expected to decline over time as ROE falls to the cost of equity (in which case residual income is eventually zero).

■ Residual income is expected to decline to a long-run average level consistent with a mature industry.

An analysis of the firm's position in its industry and the structure of the industry will be necessary to justify one of these assumptions. The third scenario is the most realistic if we assume that over time, industry competition reduces economic profits to the point at which firms begin to leave the industry and ROE stabilizes at a long-run normal level. The strength of the persistence factor will depend partly on the sustainability of the firm's competitive advantage and the structure of the industry. The more sustainable the competitive advantage and the better the industry prospects, the higher the persistence factor.

Higher persistence factors will be associated with the following:

■ Low dividend payouts.

■ Historically high residual income persistence in the industry.

Lower persistence factors will be associated with the following:

■ High return on equity.

■ Significant levels of nonrecurring items.

■ High accounting accruals.

Think of the continuing residual income model as a multistage model similar to the multistage DDM and FCF models from Study Session 10. In the residual income model, intrinsic value is the sum of three components:

$$V_0 = B_0 + (\text{PV of interim high-growth RI}) + (\text{PV of continuing residual income})$$

Step 1: Calculate the current book value per share.

Step 2: Calculate residual income in each year 1 to T − 1 during the interim high-growth period and discount them back to today at the required return on equity.

Step 3: Calculate continuing residual income that begins at the end of the high-growth period starting in year T, and then calculate the present value of continuing residual income as of the end of year T − 1 using the following formula:

$$\text{PV of continuing residual income in year T–1} = \frac{RI_T}{1 + r - \omega}$$

where:
ω = persistence factor, $0 \leq \omega \leq 1$

Assumption #1: Residual Income Persists at the Current Level Forever

If $\omega = 1$, residual income is expected to persist at the current level forever after year T − 1, so residual income in every year after T equals residual income in year T. The present value of continuing residual income at the end of year T − 1 is the present value of a perpetuity:

$$\text{PV of continuing residual income in year T} - 1 = \frac{RI_T}{1 + r - \omega} = \frac{RI_T}{1 + r - 1} = \frac{RI_T}{r}$$

Assumption #2: Residual Income Drops Immediately to Zero

If $\omega = 0$, residual income is expected to drop immediately to zero beginning in year T + 1, and the present value of continuing residual income in year T − 1 is:

$$\text{PV of continuing residual income in year T–1} = \frac{RI_T}{1 + r - \omega} = \frac{RI_T}{1 + r - 0} = \frac{RI_T}{1 + r}$$

Assumption #3: Residual Income Declines Over Time to Zero

If residual income is expected to decline over time after year T as ROE falls to the cost of equity capital, then the persistence factor, ω, is between zero and one, and the present value of continuing residual income in year T − 1 is equal to:

$$\text{PV of continuing residual income in year T} - 1 = \frac{RI_T}{1 + r - \omega}$$

Assumption #4: Residual Income Declines to Long-Run Level in Mature Industry

There is another, simpler approach to calculating the PV of continuing residual income that does not rely on the formula or ω, the persistence factor, if residual income is expected to decline to a normal long-run level consistent with a mature industry after year T.

First, recall from the single-stage residual income model that market value equals book value plus the present value of residual income. Therefore, at any point in time (T), the present value of future residual income is the difference between market value (P_T) and book value (B_T):

PV of continuing residual income in year $T = P_T - B_T$

How do we estimate P_T?

Given a forecasted price-to-book ratio and book value at the end of the year T, the value of the stock is:

$P_T = B_T \times$ (forecasted price-to-book ratio)

To make this approach consistent with the first three that use the persistence factor equation, we can also calculate the present value of continuing residual income at time $T - 1$:

PV of continuing residual income in year $T - 1 = \dfrac{(P_T - B_T) + RI_T}{1 + r}$

EXAMPLE: Calculating value with a multistage residual income model (part 1)

Java Metals is expecting an ROE of 15% over each of the next five years. Its current book value is $5.00 per share, it pays no dividends, and all earnings are reinvested. The required return on equity is 10%. Forecasted earnings in years 1 through 5 are equal to ROE times beginning book value. Calculate the intrinsic value of the company using a residual income model, assuming that after five years, continuing residual income falls to zero.

Answer:

The following table provides an estimate of the present value of residual income.

Java Metals Residual Income Forecast

Year	E_t	Ending Book Value (B_{t-1})	ROE	Equity Charge ($r \times B_{t-1}$)	Residual Income $[E - (r \times B_{t-1})]$
0		$5.00			
1	$0.75	5.75	0.15	$0.50	$0.25
2	0.86	6.61	0.15	0.57	0.29
3	0.99	7.60	0.15	0.66	0.33
4	1.14	8.74	0.15	0.76	0.38
5	1.31	10.05	0.15	0.87	0.44

Under the assumption that residual income after five years is zero (i.e., $\omega = 0$), intrinsic value today is:

$$V_0 = \$5.00 + \left[\frac{\$0.25}{1.10} + \frac{\$0.29}{1.10^2} + \frac{\$0.33}{1.10^3} + \frac{\$0.38}{1.10^4} + \frac{\$0.44}{1.10^5} \right] = \$6.25$$

Remember, you can also use your calculator to solve for the answer: CF0 = 5, C01 = 0.25, C02 = 0.29, C03 = 0.33, C04 = 0.38, C05 = 0.44, I = 10, CPT → NPV = $6.25.

EXAMPLE: Calculating value with a multistage residual income model (part 2)

Suppose we change our assumption regarding Java's residual income after five years to assume instead that it remains constant at $0.44 forever. Calculate the new intrinsic value of Java.

Answer:

The intrinsic value of Java is higher than the first case because we assume the residual income persists at the same level forever, so $RI_5 = RI_6 = \ldots = \$0.44$, and $\omega = 1$. The $0.44 perpetuity beginning in Year 5 is worth $4.40 ($0.44/0.10) in Year 4. The intrinsic value is:

$$V_0 = \$5.00 + \left[\frac{\$0.25}{1.10} + \frac{\$0.29}{1.10^2} + \frac{\$0.33}{1.10^3} + \frac{\$0.38 + \$4.40}{1.10^4} \right] = \$8.98$$

EXAMPLE: Calculating value with a multistage residual income model (part 3)

Now let's make the more realistic assumption that after Year 5, Java's residual income will decay over time to zero with a persistence factor of 0.4. Calculate the new intrinsic value of Java.

Answer:

Residual income begins to decline after Year 5, so the terminal value in Year 4 includes the present value of Year 5 residual income.

$$\text{terminal value in year 4} = \frac{RI_5}{1 + r - \omega} = \frac{\$0.44}{1 + 0.10 - 0.40} = \$0.63$$

The intrinsic value today is book value plus the present value of years 1 through 4 residual income plus the present value of the terminal value in Year 4.

$$V_0 = \$5.00 + \left[\frac{\$0.25}{1.10} + \frac{\$0.29}{1.10^2} + \frac{\$0.33}{1.10^3} + \frac{\$0.38 + \$0.63}{1.10^4} \right] = \$6.40$$

Notice that the more conservative assumption of a lower persistence factor reduces the intrinsic value of the stock because the firm's competitive advantage and economic profits eventually disappear.

EXAMPLE: Calculating value with a multistage residual income model (part 4)

Suppose instead that at the end of Year 5 we assume that Java's ROE falls to a long-run average level and the price-to-book ratio falls to 1.2. Calculate Java's intrinsic value.

Answer:

The book value per share at the end of Year 5 is $10.05, which means the market price is expected to be $10.05 × 1.2 = $12.06. The present value of continuing residual income is:

$$\text{PV of continuing residual income in year 4} =$$
$$= \frac{(P_T - B_T) + RI_T}{1 + r} = \frac{(\$12.06 - \$10.05) + \$0.44}{1.10}$$

$$= \frac{\$2.45}{1.10} = \$2.23$$

Then intrinsic value is:

$$V_0 = \$5.00 + \left[\frac{\$0.25}{1.10} + \frac{\$0.29}{1.10^2} + \frac{\$0.33}{1.10^3} + \frac{\$0.38 + \$2.23}{1.10^4}\right] = \$7.50$$

MODULE QUIZ 32.4

1. Meyer Henderson, CFA, estimates the value of Trammel Medical Supplies to be $68 per share using a residual income model. In his estimate of continuing residual income, he assumes that, after Year 6, residual income will persist at the same level forever. How many of the following assumptions concerning residual income would *most likely* cause his value estimate to fall below $68?

    Assumption #1: Return on equity is expected to fall immediately to Trammel's cost of equity capital.

    Assumption #2: Return on equity is expected to fall over time to Trammel's cost of equity capital with a persistence factor of 0.2.

    Assumption #3: Return on equity is expected to fall over time to the long-run industry average.

    A. One.
    B. Two.
    C. Three.

Use the following information to answer Questions 2 and 3.

Josef Robien, CFA, is valuing the common stock of British Cornucopia Bank (BCB) as of December 31, 2017, when the book value per share is £10.62. In this effort, Robien has made the following assumptions:

■ Earnings per share (EPS) will be 20% of the beginning book value per share for each of the next three years.

■ BCB will pay cash dividends equal to 40% of EPS.

■ At the end of three years, BCB's common stock will trade at four times its book value.

■ Beta for BCB is 0.7, the risk-free rate is 4.5%, and the equity risk premium is 5.0%.

2. The residual income per share in 2020 and the present value of continuing residual income as of the end of 2019 are *closest* to:

	2020 residual income	Continuing residual income
A.	£1.43	£42.89
B.	£1.59	£42.89
C.	£1.59	£59.64

3. The value per share of BCB stock using the residual income model is *closest* to:
    A. £39.17.
    B. £49.80.
    C. £53.20.

MODULE 32.5: STRENGTHS/WEAKNESSES

Video covering this content is available online.

LOS 32.i: Compare residual income models to dividend discount and free cash flow models.

CFA® Program Curriculum: Volume 4, page 512

DDM and FCFE models measure value by discounting a stream of expected cash flows. The residual income model starts with a book value and adds to this the present value of the expected stream of residual income. Theoretically, the intrinsic value derived using expected dividends, expected free cash flow to equity, or book value plus expected residual income should be identical if the underlying assumptions used to make the necessary forecasts are the same. In reality, however, it is rarely possible to forecast all of the common inputs with the same degree of accuracy, and the different models yield different results. It may be helpful though, to use a residual income model alongside a DDM or FCFE model to assess the consistency of results. If the different models provide dramatically different estimates, the inconsistencies may result from the models' underlying assumptions.

LOS 32.j: Explain strengths and weaknesses of residual income models and justify the selection of a residual income model to value a company's common stock.

CFA® Program Curriculum: Volume 4, page 514

Strengths of residual income models include the following:

- Terminal value does *not* dominate the intrinsic value estimate, as is the case with dividend discount and free cash flow valuation models.

- Residual income models use accounting data, which is usually easy to find.

- The models are applicable to firms that do *not* pay dividends or that do not have positive expected free cash flows in the short run.

- The models are applicable even when cash flows are volatile.

- The models focus on economic profitability rather than just on accounting profitability.

Weaknesses of residual income models include the following:

- The models rely on accounting data that can be manipulated by management.

- Reliance on accounting data requires numerous and significant adjustments.

- The models assume that the clean surplus relation holds or that its failure to hold has been properly taken into account.

PROFESSOR'S NOTE

The clean surplus relation can be expressed as $B_t = B_{t-1} + E_t - D_t$, which means that ending book value of equity equals the beginning book value plus earnings less dividends, excluding ownership transactions. This is the relationship that we used in the preceding examples to forecast end-of-period book value. Any accounting charges that are taken directly to the equity accounts (such as currency translation gains and losses) will cause the clean surplus relation not to hold.

Residual income models are *appropriate* under the following circumstances:

■ A firm does not pay dividends, or the stream of payments is too volatile to be sufficiently predictable.

■ Expected free cash flows are negative for the foreseeable future.

■ The terminal value forecast is highly uncertain, which makes dividend discount or free cash flow models less useful.

Residual income models are *not appropriate* under the following circumstances:

■ The clean surplus accounting relation is violated significantly.

■ There is significant uncertainty concerning the estimates of book value and return on equity.

LOS 32.k: Describe accounting issues in applying residual income models.

CFA® Program Curriculum: Volume 4, page 516

PROFESSOR'S NOTE

This section is really just a brief summary of all the financial statement analysis material in Study Sessions 5 and 6. As an analyst, your job is to take financial statements prepared according to GAAP, convert them to something that better reflects economic reality, and use these updated statements to estimate value. Here we discuss the typical adjustments necessary to implement residual income models, but most of these adjustments were also addressed in more detail in the financial statement analysis material.

Conceptually, the residual income model is very straightforward; we just forecast residual income using some easily available accounting numbers and estimate the value of the equity. Unfortunately, in practice it's not quite so simple because we have to make a lot of adjustments to reported net income to arrive at a true measure of comprehensive income, which is an income measure that includes all the firm's valuation changes. Following is a discussion of some common accounting issues that come up when we try to apply residual income models.

Clean Surplus Violations

The clean surplus relationship (i.e., ending book value = beginning book value + net income − dividends) may not hold when items are charged directly to shareholders' equity and do not go through the income statement. Therefore, we have to adjust net income to account for these items if they are not expected to reverse in the future. Items that can bypass the income statement include:

■ Foreign currency translation gains and losses that flow directly to retained earnings under the current rate method.

■ Certain pension adjustments.

■ Gains/losses on certain hedging instruments.

- Changes in revaluation surplus (IFRS only) for long-lived assets.

- Changes in the value of certain liabilities due to changes in the liability's credit risk (IFRS only).

- Changes in the market value of debt and equity securities classified as available-for-sale.

The effect of violations of the clean surplus relationship is that net income is not correct, but book value is still correct. The risk in applying the residual income model when the clean surplus relation doesn't hold is that the ROE forecast will not be accurate if the clean surplus violations are not expected to offset in future years. For example, suppose the analyst determines that the clean surplus relation is violated because of the cumulative translation adjustment (CTA) resulting from the application of the current rate method of currency translation. (See the reading on Multinational Operations if the current rate method doesn't sound familiar!) If the CTA tends to reverse over time and is not consistently positive or negative, the ROE can be forecasted without taking into account the CTA.

Variations from Fair Value

The accrual method of accounting causes many balance sheet items to be reported at book values that are significantly different than their market values. Common adjustments to the balance sheet necessary to reflect fair value include the following:

- *Operating leases* should be capitalized by increasing assets and liabilities by the present value of the expected future operating lease payments.

- *Special purpose entities* (SPEs) whose assets and liabilities are not reflected in the financial statements of the parent company should be consolidated.

- *Reserves and allowances* should be adjusted. For example, the allowance for bad debts, which is an offset to accounts receivable, should reflect the expected loss experience.

- *Inventory* for companies that use LIFO (last in, first out) should be adjusted to FIFO (first in, first out) by adding the LIFO reserve to inventory and equity, assuming no deferred tax impact.

- The *pension asset or liability* should be adjusted to reflect the funded status of the plan, which is equal to the difference between the fair value of the plan assets and the projected benefit obligation (PBO).

- *Deferred tax liabilities* should be eliminated and reported as equity if the liability is not expected to reverse (e.g., if the deferred tax liability results from different depreciation methods for tax and financial statement reporting purposes, and if the company is growing).

Intangible Asset Effects on Book Value

Two intangible assets require special attention: (1) intangibles recognized at acquisition and (2) R&D expenditures.

Recognition of an identifiable intangible asset (such as a license) in the group accounts that was not previously recorded in the investee company balance sheet creates a distortion in valuation under a residual income model. The amortization of such intangible assets reduces the combined ROE, and hence results in lower valuation of the combined entity compared to the sum of the values of individual entities prior to acquisition. To remove this distortion, the amortization of intangibles capitalized during acquisition should be removed prior to computing the ROE used for residual income valuation.

The suggested analytical treatment of **R&D expenditures** is less definitive, but we can make the general statement that the ROE estimate for a mature company should reflect the long-term productivity of the company's R&D expenditures: Productive R&D expenditures increase ROE and residual income, and unproductive expenditures reduce ROE and residual income.

Nonrecurring Items and Other Aggressive Accounting Practices

Nonrecurring items should not be included in residual income forecasts because they represent items that are not expected to continue in the future. Items that may need adjustment in measuring recurring earnings include discontinued operations, accounting changes, unusual items, extraordinary items, and restructuring charges.

Firms may adopt other types of aggressive accounting practices that overstate the book value of assets and earnings by, for example, accelerating revenues to the current period or deferring expenses to a later period.

International Accounting Differences

Residual income models, which are based on accrual accounting information, may not be as useful in valuing foreign firms because of differences in national accounting standards. Some things to consider in applying residual income models in global valuation settings include the following:

- How reliable are earnings forecasts?
- Are there systematic violations of the clean surplus relation?
- Do poor quality accounting rules result in financial statements that bear no resemblance to the economic reality of the business?

LOS 32.1: Evaluate whether a stock is overvalued, fairly valued, or undervalued based on a residual income model.

CFA® Program Curriculum: Volume 4, page 509

If a stock is trading at a price (market price) higher than the price implied by the residual income model (model price), the stock is considered to be **overvalued**. Similarly, if the market price is lower than the model price, the stock is considered to be **undervalued**, and if the model price is equal to the market price, the stock is considered to be **fairly valued**.

MODULE QUIZ 32.5

1. Karuba Manufacturing has a book value of $15 per share and is expected to earn $3.00 per share indefinitely. The company does not reinvest any of its earnings. Karuba's beta is 0.75, the risk-free rate is 4%, and the expected market risk premium is 8%. The value of Karuba stock according to the dividend discount model and the residual income model are *closest* to:

Dividend discount model	Residual income model
A. $42.86	$15.00
B. $42.86	$30.00
C. $30.00	$30.00

2. Kim Dae-Eun, CFA, values Olympic Productions at $78 per share with a residual income model using historical data to estimate return on equity and book value as reported on the balance sheet. Subsequently, he determines that Olympic has, for the past five years, been improperly capitalizing and amortizing expenditures that it should have expensed as they were incurred. What will be the effect on his forecasts of return on equity (ROE), book value, and intrinsic value if he revises his valuation estimate to take these "financial shenanigans" into account?

ROE	Book value	Intrinsic value
A. No effect	No effect	No effect
B. Decrease	No effect	Decrease
C. Decrease	Decrease	Decrease

3. Kim Dae-Eun, CFA, values Zues Printing Company at $46 per share with a residual income model using historical data to estimate return on equity and book value as reported on the balance sheet. Subsequently, he determines that Zues uses the current rate method of foreign currency translation and has, for the past ten years, consistently reported foreign currency translation gains as part of comprehensive income. He expects these foreign currency gains will continue in the future. What will be the effect on his forecasts of return on equity (ROE), book value, and intrinsic value if he revises his valuation estimate to take this new information into account?

ROE	Book value	Intrinsic value
A. Increase	Increase	Increase
B. Increase	No effect	Increase
C. No effect	Increase	Increase

Study Session 11

4. Jill Smart is an analyst with Allenton Partners. Jill is reviewing the valuation of three companies (P, Q, and R) using the residual income model and their corresponding current market prices.

The information below summarizes the findings:

	Stock		
	P	**Q**	**R**
Market price	35	40	38
Residual income model value	40	35	38

Based on the above information, which statement *best* describes the market's valuation of P, Q, and R?

A. P is overvalued, Q is undervalued, and R is fairly valued.
B. P is undervalued, Q is fairly valued, and R is overvalued.
C. P is undervalued, Q is overvalued, and R is fairly valued.

KEY CONCEPTS

LOS 32.a

Residual income is net income less a charge for common stockholders' opportunity cost of capital.

EVA and MVA are alternatives to residual income as measures of economic profit. These models are typically used in the measurement of managerial effectiveness and executive compensation. However, they are gaining acceptance as appropriate models for equity valuation.

$$EVA = NOPAT - (WACC \times total\ capital) = EBIT \times (1 - t) - \$WACC$$

$$MVA = market\ value - total\ capital$$

LOS 32.b

Residual income and related models are used for equity valuation, tests for goodwill impairment, measurement of managerial effectiveness, and calculation of executive compensation.

LOS 32.c

Residual income is calculated from accounting data as:

$$RI_t = E_t - (r \times B_{t-1})$$

where:
E_t = expected EPS for year t
r = required return on equity
B_{t-1} = book value in year $t-1$

The residual income model breaks the intrinsic value of a stock into two elements:

(1) current book value of equity and (2) present value of expected future residual income:

$$V_0 = B_0 + \left\{ \frac{RI_1}{(1+r)^1} + \frac{RI_2}{(1+r)^2} + \frac{RI_3}{(1+r)^3} \cdots \right\}$$

where:
B_0 = current book value
r = required return on equity

Valuation with residual income models is relatively less sensitive to terminal value estimates than dividend discount and free cash flow models. This is because intrinsic values estimated with residual income models include the firm's current book value, which usually represents a substantial percentage of the estimated intrinsic value.

LOS 32.d

The fundamental drivers of residual income are ROE in excess of the cost of equity and the earnings growth rate.

LOS 32.e

If ROE is equal to the required return on equity, the justified market value of a share of stock is equal to its book value. When ROE is higher than the required return on equity, the firm will have positive residual income and will be valued at more than book value. In that case, the P/B ratio will be greater than one.

LOS 32.f

The single-stage residual income model is:

$$V_0 = B_0 + \left[\frac{(ROE-r) \times B_0}{r-g} \right]$$

LOS 32.g

The growth rate implied by the market price in a single-stage residual income model is:

$$g = r - \left[\frac{B_0 \times (ROE - r)}{V_0 - B_0} \right]$$

LOS 32.h

For multistage residual income models, first forecast residual income over a short-term horizon, and then make some simplifying assumptions about the pattern of residual income growth over the long term. Continuing residual income is the residual income that is expected over the long term. The present value of continuing residual income in year $T - 1$ is equal to:

$$\frac{RI_T}{(1 + r - \omega)}$$

- If residual income is expected to persist at the current level forever, $\omega = 1$.
- If residual income is expected to drop immediately to zero, $\omega = 0$.
- If residual income is expected to decline over time after year T as ROE falls to the cost of equity capital, then the persistence factor, ω, is between zero and one.

Another way to estimate continuing residual income without using the persistence factor is to assume residual income is expected to decline to a normal long-run level consistent with a mature industry. Then the premium over book value ($P_T - B_T$) is equal to the present value of continuing residual income in year T, and the present value of continuing residual income in year $T - 1$ is:

$$\frac{(P_T - B_T)+RI_T}{1 + r}$$

In the residual income model, intrinsic value is the sum of three components:

$$V_0 = B_0 + (\text{PV of interim high-growth RI}) + (\text{PV of continuing residual income})$$

LOS 32.i

DDM and FCFE models estimate value as the discounted present value of expected future cash flows. The residual income model estimates value as book value plus the present value of the expected stream of annual residual income.

Residual income models may be used to assess the consistency of other valuation models.

©2018 Kaplan, Inc.

LOS 32.j

The following are strengths of residual income models:

- Terminal value does not dominate the intrinsic estimate.
- Residual income models use accounting data, which is usually easy to find.
- The models are applicable to firms that do not pay dividends or that do not have positive expected free cash flows in the short run.
- The models are applicable even when cash flows are volatile.
- The models focus on economic rather than just on accounting profitability.

The following are weaknesses of the residual income models:

- The models rely on accounting data that can be manipulated by management.
- Reliance on accounting data requires numerous and significant adjustments.
- The models assume that the clean surplus relation holds or that its failure to hold has been properly taken into account.

Residual income models are appropriate under the following circumstances:

- A firm does not pay dividends, or the stream of payments is too volatile to be sufficiently predictable.
- Expected free cash flows are negative for the foreseeable future.
- The terminal value forecast is highly uncertain, which makes dividend discount or free cash flow models less useful.

Residual income models are not appropriate under the following circumstances:

- The clean surplus accounting relation is violated significantly.
- There is significant uncertainty concerning the forecast of book value and return on equity.

LOS 32.k

In applying the residual income valuation approach, analysts often must take into account the following:

- Violations of the clean surplus relationship.
- Balance sheet adjustments for fair value.
- Intangible assets.
- Nonrecurring items.
- Other aggressive accounting practices.
- International accounting differences.

LOS 32.l

If model price is lower than (higher than, equal to) the market price, the stock is considered overvalued (undervalued, fairly valued).

ANSWER KEY FOR MODULE QUIZZES

Module Quiz 32.1, 32.2

1. **C** The stock's terminal value as of Year 5 is:

$$TV_5 = \frac{C\$11.25}{0.10} = C\$112.50$$

The present value of this Year 5 terminal value is:

$$PV = \frac{C\$112.50}{(1.10)^5} = C\$69.85$$

Thus, the justified value of SS is currently C$75.00 + C$69.85 = C$144.85. (Module 32.2, LOS 32.c)

2. **C**

$$B_0 = \frac{\text{book value of equity}}{\text{shares outstanding}} = \frac{€435,000,000}{60,000,000} = €7.25 \text{ per share}$$

Year	E_t	B_t	ROE*	Equity Charge $(r \times B_{t-1})$	Residual Income $E_t - (r \times B_{t-1})$
0		€7.25			
1	€1.16	8.41	0.16	€0.87	€0.29
2	1.35	9.76	0.16	1.01	0.34
3	1.56	11.32	0.16	1.17	0.39
4	1.81	13.13	0.16	1.36	0.45

* Earnings per share (EPS) is equal to beginning book value multiplied by ROE.

In this case, $\omega = 0$. The present value of continuing residual income in Year 3 =

$$\frac{RI_4}{1+r-\omega} = \frac{0.45}{1+0.12-0} = \frac{0.45}{1.12} = \$0.40.$$

$$V_0 = €7.25 + \left[\frac{€0.29}{1.12} + \frac{€0.34}{1.12^2} + \frac{€0.39 + €0.40}{1.12^3}\right] = €8.34$$

Since the shares are valued at €8.34 each and the current market price per share is €8.75, the shares are overpriced, and the analyst should consider issuing a sell recommendation. (Module 32.2, LOS 32.c)

3. **B** We now modify the information in the last problem and assume that residual income remains constant at €0.45 after the initial forecast period, so $\omega = 1$. Continuing residual income in Year 3 is $\frac{0.45}{1+0.12-1} = \frac{0.45}{0.12} = €3.75.$

$$V_0 = €7.25 + \left[\frac{€0.29}{1.12} + \frac{€0.34}{1.12^2} + \frac{€0.39 + €3.75}{1.12^3}\right] = €10.73$$

In this case, the value of the shares exceeds the current price of €8.75 and the analyst should consider issuing a buy recommendation. (Module 32.2, LOS 32.c)

4. **C** Residual income begins to decline after Year 4, ($\omega = 0.3$) so the present value of continuing residual income in Year 3 is:

$$\text{present value of continuing residual income in year } 3 = \frac{€0.45}{1+0.12-0.3} = €0.55$$

The intrinsic value today is book value plus the present value of years 1 through 3 residual income plus the present value of continuing residual income:

$$V_0 = €7.25 + \frac{€0.29}{1.12} + \frac{€0.34}{1.12^2} + \frac{€0.39+€0.55}{1.12^3} = €8.45$$

Since the shares are valued at €8.45 and the current market price is €8.75, the shares are overpriced and the analyst should consider issuing a sell recommendation. (Module 32.2, LOS 32.c)

Module Quiz 32.3

1. **C** We know that: $V_0 = B_0 + \left(\frac{(ROE - r) \times B_0}{r - g}\right)$. Since the shares are fairly priced, $V_0 = P = \$25.00$. It follows that:

$$B_0 = \frac{V_0}{P/B} = \frac{\$25.00}{5.00} = \$5.00$$

Substituting, we get:

$$\$25.00 = \$5.00 + \left(\frac{(0.18-r) \times \$5.00}{r - 0.08}\right)$$

Dividing both sides by $5.00 and rearranging, we get:

$$4.00 = \left(\frac{0.18-r}{r-0.08}\right) \Rightarrow 4r - 0.32 = 0.18 - r$$

$$5r = 0.50 \Rightarrow r = 0.10 = 10\%$$

(LOS 32.f)

2. **C** Use the single-stage residual income model to solve for the justified P/B multiple, then solve for ROE given the other variables:

$$V_0 = B_0 + \left[\frac{(ROE - r) \times B_0}{r - g}\right] \Rightarrow \frac{V_0}{B_0} = 1 + \frac{ROE - r}{r - g}$$

$$2.14 = 1 + \frac{ROE - 0.12}{0.12 - 0.05} \Rightarrow ROE = 0.20 = 20\%$$

or alternatively:

Justified P/B = (ROE − g) / (r − g)

Study Session 11

rearranging …

$$ROE = [(\text{Justified P/B}) \times (r - g)] + g$$

$$ROE = [(2.14) \times (0.12 - 0.05)] + 0.05 = 0.20$$

(LOS 32.f)

3. **A** The single-stage residual income model is:

$$V_0 = B_0 + \left[\frac{(ROE - r) \times B_0}{r - g}\right]$$

The second term in the equation is the present value of future expected residual income. Rocky's ROE is greater than its cost of equity capital, so that second term is positive. That means intrinsic value is greater than book value, and the justified price-to-book ratio is greater than one. (LOS 32.f)

4. **A** ROE is equal to forecasted earnings per share divided by current book value per share:

$$ROE = \frac{\$0.45}{\$4.50} = 0.10 = 10\%$$

The single-stage residual income model is:

$$V_0 = B_0 + \left[\frac{(ROE - r) \times B_0}{r - g}\right]$$

The second term in the equation is the present value of future expected residual income. The ROE is equal to the cost of equity capital (both are 10%), so the second term is zero. That means intrinsic value is equal to book value and the justified price-to-book ratio is equal to one. (LOS 32.f)

Module Quiz 32.4

1. **C** All three alternative assumptions will reduce continuing residual income below the level implied by the assumption that it remains constant forever. A falling ROE will reduce residual income over time because residual income decreases as the spread between ROE and the cost of equity decreases. Therefore, the value estimate will drop below $68 in all three cases. (LOS 32.h)

2. **B** BCB's required rate of return, r, can be computed using the capital asset pricing model (CAPM) as follows:

$$r = 4.5\% + (0.7 \times 5.0\%) = 8.0\%$$

The calculation of $RI = Earnings_t - r \times Book_{t-1}$ for the next three years is shown in the following table.

Expected RI Computations

	2018	2019	2020	2021
Beginning book value per share (B_{t-1})	£10.62	£11.89	£13.32	£14.91
Earnings per share forecast $(E_t = 0.2 \times B_{t-1})$	2.12	2.38	2.66	
Dividends per share forecast $(D_t = 0.4 \times E_t)$	0.85	0.95	1.07	
Forecast book value per share $(B_{t-1} + E_t - D_t)$	11.89	13.32	14.91	
Equity charge per share $(B_{t-1} \times r)$	0.85	0.95	1.07	
Per share RI $[E_t - (B_{t-1} \times r)]$	£1.27	£1.43	£1.59	

The present value in 2017 of 2018 and 2019 residual income is:

$$PV(RI_{2018, 2019}) = \frac{£1.27}{1.08} + \frac{£1.43}{1.08^2}$$

$$= 1.18 + 1.23$$
$$= £2.41$$

As indicated in the preceding table, the book value at the beginning of 2021 (end of 2020) is £14.91. The market price in 2020 for BCB is assumed to be four times B_{2020}, so:

$$P_{2020} = 4 \times 14.91 = £59.64$$

The present value of continuing residual income as of the end of 2019 is:

$$\frac{(P_{2020} - B_{2020}) + RI_{2020}}{1 + r} = \frac{(£59.64 - £14.91) + £1.59}{1.08} = £42.89$$

(LOS 32.h)

3. **B** The present value of residual income in 2017 is:

$$\frac{£42.89}{1.08^2} = £36.77$$

end of 2017 value per share of BCB stock

= current book value + sum of discounted RIs + PV of continuing residual income

$$= £10.62 + £2.41 + £36.77 = £49.80$$

(LOS 32.h)

Module Quiz 32.5

1. **C**   Dividend discount model:

$$r = 4\% + (0.75 \times 8\%) = 10\%$$

$$\text{dividend} = \text{earnings} = \$3.00$$

$$\text{value} = \frac{\$3.00}{0.10} = \$30.00$$

Residual income model:

$$\text{residual income} = \$3.00 - (0.10 \times \$15) = \$1.50$$

$$\text{value} = \$15.00 + \frac{\$1.50}{0.10} = \$30.00$$

(LOS 32.i)

2. **C**   Improperly capitalizing expenditures that should have been expensed will cause return on equity and book value forecasts to be overstated. Correcting the valuation to reflect the overstatement of both of these forecasts would cause the ROE estimate to decrease, the book value per share to decrease, and the intrinsic value from the residual income model to decrease. (LOS 32.k)

3. **B**   The foreign currency translation gains were recorded directly to equity as part of comprehensive income and were not reflected in income, so his ROE forecast was understated. If he expects these gains to continue, he should revise his forecast upward of ROE. Book value was not affected, however, because the gains were recorded to equity. Correcting the valuation to reflect these changes would cause his ROE estimate to increase, the book value per share to stay the same, and the intrinsic value from the residual income model to increase. (LOS 32.k)

4. **C**   Stock P has model price higher than the market price and hence is undervalued. Stock Q has model price lower than the market price and hence is overvalued. Stock R has model price equal to the market price and hence is fairly valued. (LOS 32.l)

The following is a review of the Equity Valuation (3) principles designed to address the learning outcome statements set forth by CFA Institute. Cross-Reference to CFA Institute Assigned Reading #33.

READING
33

Private Company Valuation

EXAM FOCUS

For the exam, be familiar with differences between private and public companies and know the different definitions and approaches for value estimation. Be prepared to normalize earnings, determine an appropriate discount rate, and calculate private firm value using the income, market, and asset-based approaches. Know when and how discounts for control and marketability are applied.

MODULE 33.1: PRIVATE COMPANY BASICS

Video covering this content is available online.

Warm-Up

The valuation of private companies has application in both the private equity and public equity world. Public firms frequently possess or consider buying start-up operations that can be valued using private equity valuation principles. Goodwill from acquisitions and venture capital investments can also be valued using private firm valuation principles and techniques.

LOS 33.a: Compare public and private company valuation.

CFA® Program Curriculum: Volume 4, page 557

Private firms encompass sole proprietorships, privately held corporations, and previously public companies that have been taken private. The characteristics that distinguish private and public companies can be delineated into company-specific and stock-specific factors.

Company-Specific Factors

Company-specific factors include the following.

Stage of lifecycle: Private companies are typically less mature than public firms. Sometimes, however, private firms are mature firms or bankrupt firms near liquidation. The valuation analysis will vary with the lifecycle stage of the firm.

Size: Private firms typically have less capital, fewer assets, and fewer employees than public firms and, as such, can be riskier. Accordingly, private firms are often valued using greater risk premiums and greater required returns compared to public firms. A lack of access to public equity markets can constrain a private firm's growth. However, the regulatory burden associated with issuing public equity may outweigh the benefits of greater access to funds.

Quality and depth of management: Smaller private firms may not be able to attract as many qualified applicants as public firms. This may reduce the depth of management, slow growth, and increase risk at private firms.

Management/shareholder overlap: In most private firms, management has a substantial ownership position. In this case, external shareholders have less influence and the firm may be able to take a longer-term perspective.

Short-term investors: Although manager compensation in public firms often includes incentive compensation such as stock options, shareholders often focus on short-term measures of performance such as the level and consistency of quarterly earnings. In such cases, management may take a shorter-term view compared to private firms where managers are long-term holders of significant equity interests.

Quality of financial and other information: Public firms are required to make timely, in-depth financial disclosures. A potential creditor or equity investor in a private firm will have less information than is available for a public firm. This leads to greater uncertainty, higher risk, and reduces private firm valuations.

Note that in the case of fairness opinions for private firm valuations, the analyst typically has complete access to the firm's financial statements and business records.

Taxes: Private firms may be more concerned with taxes than public firms due to the impact of taxes on private equity owners/managers.

Stock-Specific Factors

The stock-specific differences between private and public firms often include the following:

Liquidity: Private company equity typically has fewer potential owners and is less liquid than publicly traded equity. Thus, a liquidity discount is often applied in valuing privately held shares.

Restrictions on marketability: Private companies often have agreements that prevent shareholders from selling, reducing the marketability of shares.

Concentration of control: The control of private firms is usually concentrated in the hands of a few shareholders, which may lead to greater perquisites and other benefits to owners/managers at the expense of minority shareholders.

Overall, company-specific factors can have positive or negative effects on private company valuations, whereas stock-specific factors are usually a negative. Compared to public companies, private companies have greater heterogeneity so that the appropriate discount rates and methods for valuing them vary widely as well.

LOS 33.b: Describe uses of private business valuation and explain applications of greatest concern to financial analysts.

CFA® Program Curriculum: Volume 4, page 558

There are three reasons for valuing the total capital and/or equity capital of private companies: transactions, compliance, and litigation.

Transaction-Related Valuations

Transaction-related valuations are necessary when selling or financing a firm.

Venture capital financing: Firms in the development stage often need external financing for capital investment and receive private financing from venture capital investors. To reduce risk to the venture capital investor, the capital is often provided in rounds after the achievement of specific benchmarks known as *milestones*. Valuations are usually subject to negotiation and are somewhat informal due to the uncertainty of future cash flows.

Initial public offering (IPO): A public sale of the firm's equity increases its liquidity. Investment banks often perform IPO valuations using the values of similar public firms as a benchmark.

Sale in an acquisition: Development-stage or mature private firms are often sold to generate liquidity for the owners. Valuations are usually performed by both the firm and the buyer and are subject to negotiation.

Bankruptcy proceedings: For firms in bankruptcy, accurate valuation can help determine whether the firm should be liquidated or reorganized. If it is determined that the firm can continue as a going concern, accurate valuation is important in its restructuring.

Performance-based managerial compensation: If a firm compensates employees with stock options, grants of restricted stock, or employee stock ownership plans, accurate valuation is necessary for both accounting and tax purposes.

Compliance-Related Valuations

Compliance-related valuations are performed for legal or regulatory reasons and primarily focus on financial reporting and tax issues.

Study Session 11

Financial reporting: Valuations in this area are often related to goodwill impairment tests in which units of a public firm are valued using private company valuation methods. The reporting of stock-based compensation also requires accurate valuation.

Tax purposes: At the firm level, transfer pricing, property taxes, and corporate restructuring may necessitate valuations. For individual equity owners, estate and gift tax issues may necessitate valuations.

Litigation-Related Valuations

Litigation-related valuations may be required for shareholder suits, damage claims, lost profits claims, or divorce settlements.

Because the valuation methods for transactions, compliance, and litigation are often quite different, most appraisers specialize in a single area. Transaction-related valuations are usually performed by investment bankers, compliance-related valuations by those with accounting or tax knowledge, and litigation-related valuations by those comfortable with a legal setting and specific jurisdictions.

LOS 33.c: Explain various definitions of value and demonstrate how different definitions can lead to different estimates of value.

CFA® Program Curriculum: Volume 4, page 560

Definitions of Value

The appropriate valuation method depends on what the valuation will be used for and whether the firm is a going concern. The following are some common definitions of value:

Fair market value: Most often used for tax purposes in the United States, fair market value is a cash price characterized by:

- A hypothetical willing and able seller sells the asset to a willing and able buyer.
- An arm's length transaction (neither party is compelled to act) in a free market.
- A well-informed buyer and seller.

Fair value for financial reporting: This is similar to fair market value and is used for financial reporting. Using International Financial Reporting Standards (IFRS) and U.S. GAAP, fair value is the current price paid to purchase an asset or to transfer a liability. It is characterized by:

- An arm's length transaction.
- A well-informed buyer and seller.

Fair value for litigation: This is similar to fair value but its definition depends on U.S. state statutes and legal precedent in the jurisdiction of the litigation.

Market value: This is frequently used for appraisals of real estate and other real assets where the purchase will be levered. The International Valuation Standards

Committee defines market value as the value estimated on a particular date characterized by:

- A willing seller and buyer.

- An arm's length transaction.

- An asset that has been marketed.

- A well-informed and prudent buyer and seller.

Investment value: Focuses on the value to a particular buyer and is important in private company valuation. Investment value may be different for different investors, depending on:

- Estimates of future cash flows.

- Perceived firm risk.

- Appropriate discount rates.

- Individual financing costs.

- Perceived synergies with existing buyer assets.

Intrinsic value: This is derived from investment analysis and is described as the market value once other investors arrive at this "true" value. Intrinsic value is independent of any short-term mispricing.

The Effect of Value Definitions on Estimated Value

The definition of value affects the estimated value of an asset. For example, suppose a buyer does not perceive any of the synergies with existing assets that the majority of potential buyers do. If the majority has determined that the asset's *investment value* is $1,000, the *fair market value* could be $1,000. For an investor that does not realize any synergies, however, the *investment value* may only be $800.

A valuation or appraisal should only be used for its intended purpose. A valuation performed on one date according to a specific definition and for a specific purpose may not be relevant for other purposes and dates.

For example, the *fair market value* of equity for a controlling interest will likely be much different than the *investment value* of a minority interest that has little influence over the firm's decisions. The valuation of a minority interest in a private company may incorporate minority and/or marketability discounts not applicable in other situations. Furthermore, valuations prepared for tax purposes will likely require adjustment before they can be used for financial reporting.

LOS 33.d: Explain the income, market, and asset-based approaches to private company valuation and factors relevant to the selection of each approach.

CFA® Program Curriculum: Volume 4, page 562

The three major approaches to private company valuation are the income approach, the market approach, and the asset-based approach.

1. *Income approach:* Values a firm as the present value of its expected future income. Such valuation may be based on a variety of different assumptions and variations.

2. *Market approach:* Values a firm using the price multiples based on recent sales of comparable assets.

3. *Asset-based approach:* Values a firm's assets minus its liabilities.

These methods are similar to those used to value public companies, but they have different names. In the public equity world, the income approach is known as *discounted cash flow* or *present value analysis*. The income approach and the asset-based approach are termed absolute valuation models. That is, the value generated is not relative to recent valuations of other assets, as they are with the market approach.

The selection of an appropriate valuation approach depends on the firm's operations and its lifecycle stage. Early in its life, a firm's future cash flows may be subject to so much uncertainty that an asset-based approach would be most appropriate. As the firm moves to a high growth phase, it might be appropriately valued using an income approach, including a particular form of the income approach known as a *free cash flow valuation model*. A mature firm might be more appropriately valued using the market approach.

Firm size is also a consideration in choosing a valuation methodology. Price multiples from large public firms should not be used to value a small private firm without some assurance that the risk and growth prospects of the firms are similar.

A firm's assets typically consist of both operating and nonoperating assets. Nonoperating assets, those not crucial to the firm's primary operations and focus, are typified by excess cash and investment accounts. However, nonoperating assets constitute a portion of firm value and must be included when valuing a firm.

MODULE QUIZ 33.1

To best evaluate your performance, enter your quiz answers online.

1. Compared to public firms, private firms *most likely* have:
   A. fewer tax concerns.
   B. a longer-term focus.
   C. less managerial ownership.

2. Which of the following *best* describes the process of valuation in venture capital financing?
   A. Valuations are usually based on negotiation.
   B. Discounted cash flow and price multiple analysis are typically used.
   C. The appraiser estimates value using comparable company values and the prices of recent IPOs.

3. An appraiser is working for a large multinational that is considering buying a privately held firm in the southeastern United States. The multinational believes that the acquisition would allow it to realize cost savings in its production process. Which of the following is the *most likely* standard of value the appraiser will use?
   A. Fair value.
   B. Market value.
   C. Investment value.

4. An analyst is valuing the equity of a firm that has been experiencing financial distress for several months. Which of the following is the *most likely* valuation approach the analyst will use?
   A. The market approach.
   B. The income approach.
   C. The asset-based approach.

MODULE 33.2: INCOME-BASED VALUATION

Video covering this content is available online.

LOS 33.e: Explain cash flow estimation issues related to private companies and adjustments required to estimate normalized earnings.

CFA® Program Curriculum: Volume 4, page 563

In valuing a firm, the appropriate earnings definition is **normalized earnings**: "firm earnings *if* the firm were acquired." The adjustments required to arrive at normalized earnings are discussed in the following.

PROFESSOR'S NOTE

In a previous topic review, we calculated normalized earnings as the average earnings over the business cycle. Here, the calculation of normalized earnings requires adjustment for firm-specific characteristics. Normalized earnings in this case is similar to the concept of underlying earnings discussed previously—but with adjustments unique to private companies.

Estimating Normalized Earnings

Normalized earnings should exclude nonrecurring and unusual items. In the case of private firms with a concentrated control, there may be discretionary or tax-motivated expenses that need to be adjusted when calculating normalized earnings. These adjustments can be quite significant when the firm is small.

When a closely controlled firm does business with its owners or other businesses controlled by its owners, firm expenses may be inflated and reported earnings, therefore, may be artificially low. Artificially low earnings may also be the result of excessively high owner compensation or of personal expenses charged to the firm. These expenses will also affect the firm's tax expense. The adjustments are potentially larger when the owners' family members have connections to the firm. Use of company-owned assets (e.g., aircraft, personal residences, company-provided life insurance, loans for managers/owners) potentially require an adjustment to earnings.

On the other hand, if a firm is performing poorly, the owners may be receiving compensation below market levels. In this case, reported earnings would overstate normalized earnings.

Any real estate owned by the firm may merit treatment separate from that of firm operations for the following reasons:

- The real estate may have different risk characteristics than firm operations.
- The real estate may have different growth prospects than firm operations.
- The cost of the real estate owned by the firm will be reported as depreciation expense. However, depreciation is most often based on historical cost and may understate the current cost in the market of the use of the assets.

To address the last issue, some analysts will remove any income and expenses from real estate on the income statement. If it is used in the firm's business, a market-estimated rental expense is used in calculating or estimating earnings. The value of real estate is therefore separated from its operations and treated as a nonoperating asset. If the real estate is leased from a related party, the lease rate should be adjusted to a market rate.

Other adjustments are common to both private and public companies (e.g., adjustments for differences in depreciation and inventory methods). Additionally, some private firm financial statements are *reviewed* rather than audited; some may be only compiled (i.e., no auditor opinion is provided). In any case, the analyst should be prepared to make further adjustments.

EXAMPLE: Normalized earnings

Tim Groh is the principal shareholder, CEO, and founder of Arbutus Generators. Arbutus reports the following:

1. Groh's compensation of $2,500,000 is included in the firm's selling, general, and administrative (SG&A) expenses.

2. Arbutus leases a warehouse for $100,000 a year from one of its largest suppliers.

3. Arbutus owns a vacant office building with reported SG&A expenses of $150,000 and $25,000 of depreciation expense.

4. Arbutus's capital structure has too little leverage.

An analyst determines that a market-based compensation figure for Groh's position is $1,000,000 and that the office building is not needed for core operations. The market lease rate of the warehouse is $130,000.

Based on 1–4 above, what adjustments should the analyst make to Arbutus's reported income to estimate normalized earnings (earnings), assuming the firm will be acquired?

Answer:

1. Because the market rate is $1,500,000 less, SG&A expenses should be reduced by $1,500,000 to reflect a normalized compensation expense.

2. Because the market lease rate is $30,000 higher than reported, SG&A expenses should be increased by $30,000 to reflect a normalized lease rate.

---

3. Because the office building is non-core, SG&A expenses should be reduced by $150,000, and depreciation expense should be reduced by $25,000.

4. Because the capital structure is non-optimal, the analyst will drop interest expense from the calculation of operating income under the assumption that the capital structure will be changed if the firm is acquired. As we will see, interest expense is added back when calculating free cash flow to the firm.

Strategic and Nonstrategic Buyers

A transaction may be either strategic or financial (nonstrategic). In a strategic transaction, valuation of the firm is based in part on the perceived synergies with the acquirer's other assets. A financial transaction assumes no synergies, as when one firm buys another in a dissimilar industry.

When estimating normalized earnings for a strategic transaction, the analyst should incorporate any synergies as an increase in revenues or as a reduction in costs.

EXAMPLE: Incorporating synergies

An analyst is valuing a firm for two different buyers. Buyer A is a firm, in the same industry as the target firm, which expects to reduce costs at the target firm by eliminating redundancies. Buyer B is a firm in another industry.

Calculate the normalized EBITDA for each buyer given the information below.

Reported EBITDA	$4,800,000
Current executive compensation	$900,000
Market-based executive compensation	$600,000
Current SG&A expenses	$8,000,000
SG&A expenses after synergistic savings	$7,600,000

Answer:

Both strategic (Buyer A) and nonstrategic (Buyer B) buyers will attempt to reduce executive compensation to market levels. So the adjustment for both buyers to generate normalized EBITDA is $4,800,000 + ($900,000 − $600,000) = $5,100,000.

However, only Buyer A will be able to realize synergistic savings of $400,000 ($8,000,000 − $7,600,000). So normalized EBITDA for Buyer A is $5,500,000 and for Buyer B it is $5,100,000.

Estimating Cash Flow

Calculating free cash flow to the firm or to equity holders for private firms can be particularly challenging given uncertain future cash flows and figures that are often generated using the current owners' input.

As noted previously, the valuation of equity depends on the definition of value used. Also, controlling and noncontrolling equity interests will have quite different values. These differences should be accounted for in cash flow estimates and assumptions.

Study Session 11

When there is significant uncertainty about a private company's future operations, the analyst should examine several scenarios when estimating future cash flows. For development stage firms, scenarios could include a sale of the firm, an IPO, bankruptcy, or continued private operation. For a mature firm, scenarios might include different ranges of cash flows based on different assumed growth rates.

For each scenario, the analyst must assign a discount rate and probability based on the scenario's risk and probability of occurring. A firm value for each scenario is estimated, and a weighted average of these values is used to estimate firm value. Alternatively, a weighted average scenario cash flow may be discounted using a single discount rate to arrive at an estimate of firm value.

Cash flow estimates often are based on current management estimates or result from analyst consultation with management. The analyst should be aware of the potential bias in management estimates. For example, management may overstate the value of goodwill or understate future capital needs.

Although analysts use FCFF or FCFE depending on the purposes of the valuation, FCFF is usually more appropriate when the significant changes in the firm's capital structure are anticipated. The reasoning is that the discount rate used for FCFF valuation, the weighted average cost of capital (WACC), is less sensitive to leverage changes than the cost of equity, the discount rate used for FCFE valuation. Thus, the FCFF valuation is less sensitive to the degree of financial leverage assumed in the analysis than the FCFE valuation.

 PROFESSOR'S NOTE

The calculations and adjustments here are similar to those in our previous coverage of the estimation of FCFF in that they start at operating income before interest expense. Noncash charges (NCC) are stated as depreciation and amortization here, and fixed capital investment is stated as capital expenditures.

EXAMPLE: Estimation of FCFF

An analyst has normalized the earnings and expenses for a private firm under consideration as an acquisition. Because the capital structure is non-optimal, the analyst assumes that the capital structure will be changed if the firm is acquired and will use the FCFF approach to value the firm.

The following assumptions are used to create a pro forma income statement and to estimate FCFF.

Current revenues	$20,000,000
Revenue growth	4%
Gross profit margin	30%
Depreciation expense as a percentage of sales	2%
Working capital as a percentage of sales	10%
SG&A expenses	$2,200,000
Tax rate	30%

Additionally, capital expenditures will cover depreciation plus 6% of the firm's incremental revenues.

Create a pro forma income statement and estimate FCFF.

Answer:

Pro Forma Income Statement	
Revenues	$20,800,000
Cost of goods sold	$14,560,000
Gross profit	$6,240,000
SG&A expenses	$2,200,000
Pro forma EBITDA	$4,040,000
Depreciation and amortization	$416,000
Pro forma EBIT	$3,624,000
Pro forma taxes on EBIT	$1,087,200
Operating income after tax	$2,536,800
Adjustments to obtain FCFF	
Plus: depreciation and amortization	$416,000
Minus: capital expenditures	$464,000
Minus: increase in working capital	$80,000
FCFF	$2,408,8000

The following provides a line by line explanation for the previous calculations.

Pro Forma Income Statement	Explanation
Revenues	Current revenues times the growth rate: $20,000,000 × 1.04
Cost of goods sold	Revenues times one minus the gross profit margin: $20,800,000 × (1 − 0.30)
Gross profit	Revenues times the gross profit margin: $20,800,000 × 0.30
SG&A expenses	Given in the question
Pro forma EBITDA	Gross profit minus SG&A expenses: $6,240,000 − $2,200,000
Depreciation and amortization	Revenues times the given depreciation expense: $20,800,000 × 0.02
Pro forma EBIT	EBITDA minus depreciation and amortization: $4,040,000 − $416,000
Pro forma taxes on EBIT	EBIT times tax rate: $3,624,000 × 0.30
Operating income after tax	EBIT minus taxes: $3,624,000 − $1,087,200
Adjustments to obtain FCFF	*Explanation*
Plus: depreciation and amortization	Add back noncash charges from above
Minus: capital expenditures	Expenditures cover depreciation and increase with revenues: $416,000 + [0.06 × ($20,800,000 − $20,000,000)]
Minus: increase in working capital	The working capital will increase as revenues increase 0.10 × ($20,800,000 − $20,000,000)
FCFF	Operating income net of the adjustments above

LOS 33.f: Calculate the value of a private company using free cash flow, capitalized cash flow, and/or excess earnings methods.

CFA® Program Curriculum: Volume 4, page 575

The income approach refers to valuation methods based on the idea that the value of an asset is the present value of its future income. Three methods consistent with the income approach are: the free cash flow method (a.k.a. discounted cash flow method), the capitalized cash flow method, and the residual income or excess earnings method.

The Free Cash Flow Method

Once free cash flows have been estimated as we have done previously, they are discounted by a rate that reflects their risk. Typically, there is a series of discrete cash flows and a terminal value that reflects the value of the business as a going concern at some future date. The terminal value is calculated for a point of time in the future, at which the growth rate is expected to level off and remain constant. In practice, most analysts estimate the terminal value five years out.

The terminal value can be calculated using a constant growth model (e.g., dividend discount model). Some analysts use a price multiple approach to estimate a firm's terminal value. Note, however, that if the price multiple is for a firm in a high growth industry, the price multiple applied will often reflect both high growth and normal growth. In this case, the high growth is double counted, once in the price multiple and once in the periodic cash flow forecasts.

PROFESSOR'S NOTE

The free cash flow method here is a two-stage model. The capitalized cash flow method described in the following is a single-stage model.

The Capitalized Cash Flow Method

This method is also known as the capitalized income method or the capitalization of earnings method. Under this method, a single measure of economic benefit is divided by a capitalization rate to arrive at firm value, where the capitalization rate is the required rate of return minus a growth rate. This is a growing perpetuity model that assumes stable growth and is, in effect, a single-stage free cash flow model. It is most often used for small private companies. It may be suitable when no comparables are available, projections are quite uncertain, and stable growth is a reasonable assumption.

If growth is non-constant, the capitalized cash flow method (CCM) should be avoided in favor of the free cash flow method. The CCM could be used to back out the discount rate or growth rate implicit in market data.

Valuing the firm as a whole using the CCM:

$$\text{value of the firm} = \frac{\text{FCFF}_1}{\text{WACC} - g}$$

where:
FCFF_1 = expected free cash flow to the firm over the next year
WACC = weighted average cost of capital (assuming a constant capital structure)
g = sustainable growth rate in free cash flows

To estimate the value of the equity, the market value of the firm's debt is subtracted from firm value. Alternatively, the value of firm equity can be estimated by discounting the free cash flows to equity by the required return on equity (r):

$$\text{value of equity} = \frac{\text{FCFE}_1}{r - g}$$

The denominator in both the FCFF and FCFE equations is the capitalization rate of the CCM.

EXAMPLE: Calculating firm value using the capitalized cash flow method

Given the following figures, calculate the value of the firm and equity using the CCM.

FCFF in one year	$12,100,000
Growth rate of FCFF	4.0%
WACC	15.0%
Market value of debt	$4,000,000

Answer:

Step 1: Calculate the value of the firm.

Using the FCFF formula:

value of firm = ($12,100,000) / (0.15 − 0.04) = $110,000,000

Step 2: Calculate the value of the equity.

Subtract the debt value from firm value:

value of equity = $110,000,000 − $4,000,000 = $106,000,000

Note that the capitalization rate in this example is 11% (15% − 4%). The WACC will be greater when more (relatively expensive) equity and less debt are used, resulting in lower estimates of firm and equity values.

The Excess Earnings Method

Under the excess earnings method, the analyst starts with the earnings that *should* be generated by working capital and fixed assets based on an estimate of the required return. Excess earnings are firm earnings minus the earnings required to provide the required rate of return on working capital and fixed assets. The value of intangible assets can be estimated as the present value of the (growing) stream of excess earnings (using the excess earnings and the growing perpetuity formula from the CCM). This value for the intangible assets is added to the values of working capital and fixed assets to arrive at firm value.

The excess earnings method (EEM) is used infrequently but can be used for small firms when their intangible assets are significant. However, the required return for working capital and fixed assets is subject to estimation error.

EXAMPLE: Calculating firm value using the excess earnings method

Given the following figures, calculate the value of the firm using the EEM.

Working capital	$300,000
Fixed assets	$1,000,000
Normalized earnings (year just ended)	$130,000
Required return for working capital	6%
Required return for fixed assets	10%
Growth rate of residual income	5%
Discount rate for intangible assets	14%

Answer:

Step 1: Calculate the required return for working capital and fixed assets.

Based on the required rates of return for working capital and fixed assets, the required earnings are:

working capital: $300,000 × 6% = $18,000
fixed assets: $1,000,000 × 10% = $100,000

Step 2: Calculate the excess earnings.

excess earnings = $130,000 − $18,000 − $100,000 = $12,000

Step 3: Value the intangible assets.

Using the formula for a growing perpetuity, the discount rate for intangible assets, and the growth rate for excess earnings:

value of intangible assets = ($12,000 × 1.05) / (0.14 − 0.05)
= $140,000

Step 4: Sum the asset values to arrive at the total firm value.

firm value = $300,000 + $1,000,000 + $140,000 = $1,440,000

 PROFESSOR'S NOTE:

In the excess earnings method, the FCFF may be given in place of the normalized earnings. The growth rate in free cash flow may be given in place of the growth rate of residual income. After these substitutions, the calculations are identical to those above.

LOS 33.g: Explain factors that require adjustment when estimating the discount rate for private companies.

CFA® Program Curriculum: Volume 4, page 570

Estimating the discount rate in a private firm valuation can be quite challenging for the following reasons.

Size premiums: Size premiums are often added to the discount rates for small private companies. Estimating this premium using small public firm data may be biased upward by the fact many of the small firms in the sample are experiencing financial distress.

Availability and cost of debt: A private firm may have less access to debt financing than a public firm. Because equity capital is usually more expensive than debt and because the higher operating risk of smaller private companies results in a higher cost of debt as well, WACC will typically be higher for private firms.

Acquirer versus target: When acquiring a private firm, some acquirers will incorrectly use their own (lower) cost of capital, rather than the higher rate appropriate for the target, and arrive at a value for the target company that is too high.

Projection risk: Because of the lower availability of information from private firms and managers who are inexperienced at forecasting, that analyst should increase the discount rate used.

Management may not be experienced with forecasting and may underestimate or overestimate future earnings, requiring adjustment by the analyst. Such adjustments are highly subjective, however.

Lifecycle stage: It is particularly difficult to estimate the discount rate for firms in an early stage of development. If such firms have unusually high levels of unsystematic risk, the use of the CAPM may be inappropriate. Although ranges of discount rates can be specified for the various lifecycle stages, it may difficult to classify the stage a firm is in.

LOS 33.h: Compare models used to estimate the required rate of return to private company equity (for example, the CAPM, the expanded CAPM, and the build-up approach).

CFA® Program Curriculum: Volume 4, page 570

Using the CAPM, the expanded CAPM, and build-up methods to estimate discount rates for private firms may not be as straightforward as that for public firms.

CAPM: Typically, beta is estimated from public firm data, and this may not be appropriate for private firms that have little chance of going public or being acquired by a public firm. Due to the differences between large public firms and small private firms, some U.S. tax courts have rejected the use of the CAPM for private firms.

Expanded CAPM: This version of the CAPM includes additional premiums for size and firm-specific (unsystematic) risk.

Build-up method: When it is not possible to find comparable public firms for beta estimation, the build-up method can be used. Beginning with the expected return on the market (beta is implicitly assumed to be one), premiums are added for small size, industry factors, and company specific factors.

EXAMPLE: Private equity valuation methods

An analyst is examining a private firm under consideration as an acquisition and determines the following:

- The current capital structure is non-optimal because the owner avoids the use of debt.

- A small stock premium and company-specific risk premium are determined because the private firm is much smaller and much less diversified than the public firms that beta is estimated from.

- The industry risk premium reflects the additional risk in this industry compared to the broad market.

The relevant figures are listed below.

Risk-free rate	3.6%
Equity risk premium	6.0%
Beta	1.3
Small stock premium	3.0%
Company-specific risk premium	2.0%
Industry risk-premium	1.0%
Pretax cost of debt	9.0%
Debt/total cap for public firms in industry	30%
Optimal debt/total cap	12%
Current debt/total	3%
Tax rate	30%

a. Calculate the required return on equity using the CAPM, the expanded CAPM, and the build-up method.

b. Calculate the WACC using the current capital structure and the optimal capital structure, assuming a cost of equity of 16%.

c. Comment on the appropriate capital structure weights.

Answer:

a. The required return on equity using the CAPM is: $3.6\% + 1.3(6\%) = 11.4\%$.

   Using the expanded CAPM, a small stock premium and company-specific risk premium are added: $11.4\% + 3\% + 2\% = 16.4\%$.

   Using the build-up method, beta is omitted, but an industry risk premium is added to the risk-free rate, the equity risk premium, the small stock premium, and a company-specific risk premium: $3.6\% + 6\% + 3\% + 2\% + 1\% = 15.6\%$.

b. The WACC, using the current capital structure, factors in the debt to total capitalization, the cost of debt, the tax rate, and the given cost of equity:

$$\text{WACC} = (w_e \times r_e) + [w_d \times r_d \times (1 - \text{tax rate})]$$
$$= (0.97 \times 16\%) + [0.03 \times 9\% \times (1 - 30\%)]$$
$$= 15.7\%$$

The WACC, using the optimal capital structure, is:

$$WACC = (w_e \times r_e) + [w_d \times r_d \times (1 - tax\ rate)]$$
$$= (0.88 \times 16\%) + [0.12 \times 9\% \times (1 - 30\%)]$$
$$= 14.8\%$$

c. The current capital structure reflects the current owner's conservative use of debt. The optimal capital structure can be determined through discussions with financiers. The optimal capital structure should be used to calculate the (lower) WACC for the acquisition, given that the firm can support this level of debt.

The current capital structure reflects the current owner's conservative use of debt. The optimal capital structure can be determined through discussions with financiers. The optimal capital structure should be used to calculate the (lower) WACC for the acquisition, given that the firm can support this level of debt. The capital structure for public firms in the same industry should not be used because public firms are likely to have better access to debt financing. A public firm could likely take on more (less expensive compared to equity) debt than a private company. For this reason, a private firm will likely have a greater WACC than a public firm in the same industry would have.

MODULE QUIZ 33.2

To best evaluate your performance, enter your quiz answers online.

1. Given the following figures, calculate the normalized EBITDA for a financial and strategic buyer.

Reported EBITDA	$6,700,000
Current executive compensation	$800,000
Market-based executive compensation	$650,000
Current SG&A expenses	$8,100,000
SG&A expenses after synergistic savings	$7,300,000
Current lease rate	$200,000
Market-based lease rate	$250,000

The normalized EBITDA for each type of buyer is:

	Financial buyer	Strategic buyer
A.	$6,800,000	$7,600,000
B.	$6,900,000	$6,800,000
C.	$6,900,000	$7,700,000

2. Given the following figures, calculate the FCFF for the next year. Assume the earnings and expenses are normalized and that capital expenditures will equal depreciation plus 4% of the firm's incremental revenues.

Current revenues	$10,000,000
Revenue growth	5%
Gross profit margin	20%
Depreciation expense as a percentage of sales	1%
Working capital as a percentage of sales	12%
SG&A expenses	$1,600,000
Tax rate	40%

The FCFF is:
A. $157,000.
B. $277,000.
C. $407,000.

3. Using the following figures, calculate the value of the equity using the CCM, assuming the firm will be acquired.

Normalized FCFE in current year	$2,200,000
Reported FCFE in current year	$1,800,000
Growth rate of FCFE	6.0%
Equity discount rate	18.0%
WACC	14.5%
Risk-free rate	4.2%
Cost of debt	11.0%
Market value of debt	$3,000,000

The value of the equity is:
A. $15,900,000.
B. $19,433,333.
C. $27,435,294.

4. Using the following figures, calculate the value of the firm using the EEM.

Working capital	$400,000
Fixed assets	$1,800,000
Normalized earnings	$235,000
Required return for working capital	4%
Required return for fixed assets	12%
Growth rate of residual income	3%
Discount rate for intangible assets	16%

The value of the firm is:
A. $2,223,077.
B. $2,223,769.
C. $4,061,923.

5. Which of the following *best* describes the appropriate approach to estimating the WACC for a private company acquisition? The WACC should be:
   A. the target's WACC.
   B. the acquirer's WACC.
   C. a weighted average of the target's and acquirer's WACC that factors in financing arrangements.

6. Which of the following models is recommended for estimating the discount rate for a private company if there are no comparable public equity firms?
   A. The CAPM.
   B. The build-up method.
   C. The expanded CAPM.

Use the following information to answer Questions 7 and 8.

Income return on bonds	5.7%
Capital return on bonds	1.1%
Long-term Treasury yield	4.8%
Beta	1.5
Equity risk premium	5.5%
Small stock premium	3.8%
Company-specific risk premium	2.5%
Industry risk-premium	2.0%
Pretax cost of debt	10.0%
Optimal debt/total cap	15.0%
Current debt/total	4.0%
Debt/total cap for public firms in industry	40.0%
Tax rate	35.0%

7. Calculate the cost of equity for a mature private firm of similar size and firm-specific risk as its public comparable. The cost of equity is:
   A. 13.1%.
   B. 15.1%.
   C. 19.4%.

8. Calculate the WACC for the acquisition of a small private firm with a high degree of firm-specific risk. The firm is dissimilar to public firms. The WACC is:
   A. 12.1%.
   B. 16.8%.
   C. 17.4%.

MODULE 33.3: MARKET-BASED VALUATION

LOS 33.i: Calculate the value of a private company based on market approach methods and describe advantages and disadvantages of each method.

Video covering this content is available online.

CFA® Program Curriculum: Volume 4, page 579

Market approaches to valuing private firms use price multiples and data from previous public and private transactions. The three methods discussed in the following are the guideline public company method (GPCM), the guideline transactions method (GTM), and the prior transaction method (PTM).

Many practitioners prefer market approaches to valuation over income and asset approaches because actual sales data are used. Although U.S. tax courts accept both market and income approaches, they usually prefer market approaches.

As discussed previously, private firms may have risks not common to public firms, such as greater company risk and illiquidity. Therefore, it is important that the public comparables be chosen carefully. Furthermore, price multiples reflect both risk and growth. Each of these should be extracted from the price multiple and compared to the subject private firm to decide what adjustments might be made. When choosing the comparables, commonalities in industry, operations, size, and lifecycle are desired.

Although public firms are often valued on the basis of price-earnings ratios, large private firm valuation is usually based on EBIT or EBITDA multiples. The numerator would be the market value of invested capital (MVIC), from which the market value of debt could be subtracted when examining equity value. Because the market value of debt is often hard to ascertain, the book value can be used if the firm has low financial leverage and is stable. If the firm has high debt levels or volatility, an analyst could use matrix pricing, where the prices of similar debt are used to infer a value for the subject's debt.

For small private companies with limited assets, net income multiples might be used instead of EBITDA multiples. A revenue multiple might be used for extremely small firms, given the greater likelihood and impact of discretionary expenses such as owner compensation.

Nonfinancial measures may be appropriate in some industries. For example, a hospital's price per bed could be used. These measures should be accepted in its industry and accompanied by financial measures.

In the following discussion, we will see that the advantage of each of these methods is that the comparable data are usually available. The disadvantage, however, is that the comparable transactions may not be similar to the subject transaction. The issues of comparability are discussed for each of these methods in the following sections.

Guideline Public Company Method

The guideline public company method (GPCM) uses price multiples from trade data for public companies, with adjustments to the multiples to account for differences between the subject firm and the comparables. Although there are usually numerous public company transactions available, the data should be checked to see that they are comparable.

When evaluating a controlling equity interest in a private firm, the control premium (i.e., the value of control) should be estimated. The control premium equals the difference between the pro rata value of a controlling interest and the pro rata value of a noncontrolling interest. Most public share trades are for small, noncontrolling interests; therefore, the price multiple does not reflect a control premium.

To estimate a control premium, a public transaction should be used where a firm was acquired. When estimating a control premium, the following issues should be considered:

Transaction type: Recall that a transaction may be either strategic or financial (nonstrategic). A strategic buyer is one who will have synergies with the target, and a financial buyer is one who is buying the firm for its stand-alone value. A financial transaction typically has a smaller price premium.

Industry conditions: Periodically, there is a flurry in industry acquisition activity, driving up acquisition prices. In such markets, share prices of public companies may already reflect some premium for control, and adding a standard control premium to such share prices may overstate the appropriate premium for control.

Type of consideration: Some historical acquisitions involve the acquirer's stock rather than cash. Estimates of the control premium when acquisitions are made with shares that are at higher temporary or "bubble" values will be overstated.

Reasonableness: The use of control premiums and price multiples can quickly result in significant differences in valuations from historical pricing. For example, suppose a 20% historical control premium is estimated on top of a 6 price multiple for public comparables (i.e., a multiple of 6 × 1.2 = 7.2). Later on, if the price multiple from public comparables at the valuation date is 10, a price multiple of 10 × 1.2 = 12 would be then applied to the private firm. The price multiple of 12 is substantially different than the 7.2 estimated earlier. The 12 multiple should be investigated for reasonableness.

> **EXAMPLE:** Valuation using the guideline public company method
>
> An analyst, Natalie Hoskins, is valuing a private firm, Rensselaer Components, using the GPCM and MVIC to EBITDA multiples. Hoskins has gathered data for comparable public firms; however they are larger in size than Rensselaer. Hoskins decided to deflate the average public company multiple by 20% to account for the higher risk of Rensselaer.
>
> A premium of 30% was paid for a firm by an acquiring firm in the same industry. The acquirer exchanged stock for the target.

Other data are as follows:

Market value of debt	$1,100,00
Normalized EBITDA	$12,800,000
Average MVIC/EBITDA mutliple	8.0

a. Comment on the relevance of the information above for the valuation of Rensselaer.
b. Calculate the equity value of Rensselaer using the GPCM.

Answer:

a. The application of control premiums is difficult and requires subjective judgment. The control premium of 30% is probably not relevant for the valuation of Rensselaer. The premium for the prior acquisition likely contained some value for synergies since it was a strategic transaction, and because stock was used for the purchase, there is also the possibility that the stock value at the time was inflated, adding to the estimated premium.

The adjustment to the public company multiple of 20% is appropriate because growth and risk may differ between public comparables and private firms.

b. The adjustment to the MVIC/EBITDA multiple for the higher risk of Rensselaer is:

$$8.0 \times (1 - 0.20) = 6.4$$

No control premium is applied, for the reasons mentioned above.

The adjusted multiple is applied against the normalized EBITDA:

$$6.4 \times \$12,800,000 = \$81,920,000$$

Subtracting out the debt results in the equity value:

$$\$81,920,000 - \$1,100,000 = \$80,820,000$$

Control premium adjustments are made only to the equity portion of the firm's value. There are two ways to incorporate control premium under a guideline public company method:

1. Use the raw multiple to estimate firm value (without control premium) and estimate the equity portion (by subtracting debt). Apply the control premium to the equity portion as estimated.

2. Beginning with an equity control premium, we adjust this control premium for valuation using an MVIC multiple:

adjusted control premium (applicable for MVIC multiple)
= (control premium on equity) × (1 − DR)

where:

DR = debt-to-asset ratio of the private company

This adjusted control premium is then applied to a MVIC-multiple-based value.

Guideline Transactions Method

When using the guideline transactions method (GTM), prior acquisition values for entire (public and private) companies that already reflect any control premiums are used, so no additional adjustment for a controlling interest is necessary.

Although data on the sale of public companies are readily available, the data on the sale of private firms are more limited and not always accurate. When using multiples from historical transactions, several issues should be considered.

Transaction type: As mentioned previously for the GPCM, a prior transaction may be a strategic transaction where firm value was based, in part, on perceived synergies. If the subject transaction is nonstrategic, the analyst may need to adjust the historical multiple.

Contingent consideration: Contingent consideration refers to that part of the acquisition price that is contingent on the achievement of specific company performance targets, such as receiving FDA approval for a drug. As contingent consideration increases the risk to the seller, transactions with contingent consideration should be scrutinized before they are compared to transactions without such contingencies.

Type of consideration: As noted previously, some transactions are for stock rather than cash. Comparing transactions of different consideration type may not be relevant.

Availability of data: The historical data for comparables that are relevant and accurate may be limited.

Date of data: If the sales of the comparable companies were very long ago, the prices and estimated premiums may not be relevant to the extent that macroeconomic and industry conditions have changed.

EXAMPLE: Valuation with the guideline transactions method

Natalie Hoskins is valuing a private firm, Lafayette Furniture, for acquisition using the Guideline Transactions Method and MVIC to EBITDA multiples. Hoskins deflates the average public company multiple by 30% to account for the higher risk of Lafayette.

Other data are as follows:

Market value of debt	$1,400,000
Normalized EBITDA	$18,200,000
Average MVIC/EBITDA multiple	7.2

 PROFESSOR'S NOTE:

Recall that in the Guideline Transactions Method, historical transactions are not adjusted for control premiums because the transactions are for the acquisition of entire companies.

Calculate the equity value of Lafayette Furniture using the Guideline Transactions Method.

> **Answer:**
>
> The adjustment to the MVIC/EBITDA multiple for the higher risk of Lafayette Furniture is:
>
> $7.2 \times (1 - 0.30) = 5.0$
>
> The adjusted multiple is applied against the normalized EBITDA:
>
> $5.0 \times \$18,200,000 = \$91,000,000$
>
> Subtracting out the debt results in the equity value:
>
> $\$91,000,000 - \$1,400,000 = \$89,600,000$

Prior Transaction Method

The prior transaction method (PTM) uses transactions data from the stock of the actual subject company and is most appropriate when valuing minority (noncontrolling) interests. The valuation under this method can be based on the actual transaction price or multiples derived from such transactions.

Ideally, the previous transactions would be arm's-length, of the same motivation (strategic or financial) as the subject transaction, and fairly recent.

LOS 33.j: Describe the asset-based approach to private company valuation.

CFA® Program Curriculum: Volume 4, page 586

The asset-based approach estimates the value of firm equity as the fair value of its assets minus the fair value of its liabilities. It is generally not used for going concerns. Because it is easier to find comparable data at the firm level compared to the asset level, the income and market approaches would be preferred when valuing going concerns. Additionally, it is difficult to find data for individual intangible assets and specialized assets.

Of the three approaches, the asset-based approach generally results in the lowest valuation because the use of a firm's assets in combination usually results in greater value creation than each of its parts individually.

The asset-based approach might be appropriate in the following circumstances:

- Firms with minimal profits and little hope for better prospects. In this situation, the firm might be valued more highly for its liquidation value rather than as a going concern by a firm that can put the assets to better use.

- Finance firms such as banks, where their asset and liability values (loan and security values) can be based on market prices and factors.

- Investment companies such as real estate investment trusts (REITs) and closed-end investment companies (CEICs) where the underlying assets values are determined using the market or income approaches. Management fees and the value of management expertise may result in values different from net asset value.

- Small companies or early stage companies with few intangible assets.
- Natural resource firms where assets can be valued using comparables sales.

MODULE QUIZ 33.3

To best evaluate your performance, enter your quiz answers online.

1. An analyst is valuing a private firm on the behalf of a strategic buyer and deflates the average public company multiple by 30% to account for the higher risk of the private firm. The analyst plans to calculate the value of firm equity using the Guideline Public Company Method (GPCM).

Market value of debt	$2,600,000
Normalized EBITDA	$27,100,000
Average public company MVIC/EBITDA multiple	9.0
Control premium from past transaction	25%

The value of the firm's equity is *closest* to:
   A. $168,130,000.
   B. $210,162,500.
   C. $214,090,000.

2. Which of the following would *least likely* be valued by the asset-based approach?
   A. A natural resource firm.
   B. A financial firm such as a bank.
   C. A firm with significant intangible assets.

Video covering this content is available online.

MODULE 33.4: VALUATION DISCOUNTS

LOS 33.k: Explain and evaluate the effects on private company valuations of discounts and premiums based on control and marketability.

CFA® Program Curriculum: Volume 4, page 588

In general, adjustments are required when the liquidity or control position of an acquisition differs from that of the comparable companies. If, for example, the comparable firm values are for the purchase of an entire public company and we wish to value a minority stake in a private firm, we would need to apply discounts for both a lack of control and a lack of marketability (liquidity).

The variability of estimated discounts varies with the following:

- The data used to estimate them and the analyst's interpretation of them.
- The perceived importance of the invested position.
- The allocation of shares and the resulting effect on control.
- The relationships between various parties.
- The protection provided to minority shareholders by state laws.
- The likelihood of an IPO or sale.
- The payment of dividends.

The Discount for Lack of Control

Minority shareholders are at a disadvantage relative to controlling shareholders because they have less power to select the directors and management. Without a voice, they cannot determine the investment and payout policies that affect the value of the firm and the distribution of earnings.

Controlling shareholders can also enjoy excessive compensation and other perquisites to the detriment of minority shareholders. However, firms that will experience an IPO or sale are less likely to pursue actions that damage minority shareholders.

The factors for determining a discount for lack of control (DLOC) are the same as those for the control premium discussed earlier. Because it is difficult to measure the disadvantage from a lack of control, the discount is usually backed out of the control premium.

$$DLOC = 1 - \left[\frac{1}{1 + \text{control premium}} \right]$$

For example, if the control premium is 25%, the DLOC is 20%: example, if the control premium is 25%, the DLOC is 20%:

$$DLOC = 1 - \left[\frac{1}{1 + 0.25} \right] = 20\%$$

To calculate control premiums, data from the acquisitions of public companies are typically used.

The table below summarizes when control premiums or discounts are appropriate.

Figure 33.1: Premiums (Discounts) for Controlling Interest

Scenario	Comparable Data	Subject Valuation	Adjustment to Comparable Data for Control
1	Controlling interest	Controlling interest	None
2	Controlling interest	Noncontrolling interest	DLOC
3	Noncontrolling interest	Controlling interest	Control premium
4	Noncontrolling interest	Noncontrolling interest	None

An example of Scenario 2 would be when the Guideline Transactions Method is used for valuing a noncontrolling interest. Recall that in the GTM, the comparable price multiple data is for the sale of entire firms where control is acquired.

An example of Scenario 3 would be when the GPCM is used for valuing a controlling interest. Recall that in the GPCM, the comparable price multiple data is from noncontrolling interests.

The use of discounted cash flow methods such as the FCF and CCM could also require adjustments, depending on whether the estimated and subject cash flows were on a controlling or noncontrolling interest basis.

The Discount for Lack of Marketability

If an interest in a firm cannot be easily sold, discounts for lack of marketability (DLOM) would be applied (sometimes termed a discount for lack of liquidity). It is often the case that if a DLOC is applied, a DLOM will also be applied. For example, if a controlling shareholder believes that a private firm should not be sold, minority shareholders both lack control and lack the ability to sell their position.

The DLOM varies with the following:

- An impending IPO or firm sale would decrease the DLOM.
- The payment of dividends would decrease the DLOM.
- Earlier, higher payments (i.e., shorter duration) would decrease the DLOM.
- Contractual restrictions on selling stock would increase the DLOM.
- A greater pool of buyers would decrease the DLOM.
- Greater risk and value uncertainty would increase the DLOM.

To estimate the DLOM, an analyst can use one of three methods. In the first method, the price of restricted shares is used. As an example, SEC Rule 144 may restrict the sale of shares acquired in a firm prior to its IPO. In this case, the price of the restricted shares is compared to the price of the publicly traded shares.

In the second method, the price of pre-IPO shares is compared to that of post-IPO shares. One complicating factor is that post-IPO firms are generally thought to have more certain cash flows and lower risk, so the estimated DLOM may not purely reflect changes in marketability.

A third method would estimate the DLOM as the price of a put option divided by the stock price, where the put used is at-the-money. The time to maturity of the valued option could be the time to the IPO. The volatility used could be based on the historical volatility of publicly traded stock or the implied volatility of publicly traded options. The advantage of this approach over the other two DLOM estimation methods is that the estimated risk of the firm can be factored into the option price. The drawback of this approach is that a put provides a certain selling price, not actual liquidity.

Although these methods provide a basis for calculating the DLOM, it is often challenging to implement them. The data may be limited, the interpretation of the data will vary, and the magnitude of the DLOM applied to a company will vary by analyst. In addition to the DLOC and DLOM, other discounts could be applied, such as key person discount.

Because they are applied in a sequential process, the DLOC and DLOM are multiplicative, not additive. So if the DLOC is 20%, and the DLOM is 13%, the total discount is:

$$\text{total discount} = 1 - [(1 - \text{DLOC})(1 - \text{DLOM})]$$
$$\text{total discount} = 1 - [(1 - 0.20)(1 - 0.13)] = 30.4\%$$

This is not the 33% found when using an additive calculation.

PROFESSOR'S NOTE
This point seems very testable.

EXAMPLE: Calculating the value of a minority interest

Suppose that a minority shareholder holds 15% of a private firm's equity and that the CEO holds the other 85%. There are two possible scenarios.

In Scenario 1, the CEO will likely sell the firm very soon. In this case, valuation discounts will be very small. A DLOM of 5% will be applied and a DLOC will not be applied under the assumption that all selling shareholders will receive the same price. The value of the firm's equity is estimated at $10 million.

In Scenario 2, the CEO has no plans to sell the firm, and the minority shareholder cannot sell its interest easily. A DLOM of 20% will be applied. A DLOC will be estimated by using reported earnings instead of normalized earnings to provide an estimated firm equity value of $9 million.

Given these figures, calculate the value of the minority shareholder's equity interest under both scenarios.

Answer:

The following provides the calculations under each scenario.

Scenario 1: Assuming sale is likely

Firm's equity value	$10,000,000
Minority interest	15%
Value of minority interest without discounts	$1,500,000
minus DLOC of 0%	0
Value of interest if marketable	$1,500,000
minus DLOM of 5%	$75,000
Value of minority interest	$1,425,000

Scenario 2: Assuming sale is unlikely

Firm's equity value	$9,000,000
Minority interest	15%
Value of minority interest without discounts	$1,350,000
minus DLOC of 0%	0
Value of interest if marketable	$1,350,000
minus DLOM of 20%	$270,000
Value of minority interest	$1,080,000

The smaller value of the minority interest in Scenario 2 is due to the higher DLOM and the DLOC (as reflected in the lower firm equity value of $9,000,000). The $9,000,000 value assumes that certain firm inefficiencies (e.g., above-market compensation for the owner) cannot be corrected without a sale of the firm.

LOS 33.1: Describe the role of valuation standards in valuing private companies.

CFA® Program Curriculum: Volume 4, page 595

There has been an increased focus on the valuation of private companies, in part due to the use of fair value estimates for financial reporting. As a result, a number of valuation standards have been developed, which specify the formation and dissemination of the valuation. There is no single valuation standard.

In response to the U.S. savings and loan crisis in the late 1980s and early 1990s, the Uniform Standards of Professional Appraisal Practice (USPAP) were created by the Appraisal Foundation. These standards cover real estate, fixed income, and private business valuations. Although the Appraisal Foundation is a congressionally authorized provider of standards, business appraisers are not required to adhere to the standards.

The International Valuation Standards Committee (IVSC) has created the International Valuation Standards, covering businesses, business interests, real estate, and tangible as well as intangible assets. These standards also include a separate application standard covering valuations for financial reporting.

There are many challenges involved with the implementation of appraisal standards:

- The compliance with these standards is usually at the discretion of the appraiser because most buyers are still unaware of them.

- Because most valuation reports are private, it is very difficult for the organizations to ensure compliance to the standards.

- Although the organizations provide technical guidance on the use of their standards, it is necessarily limited due to the heterogeneity of valuations.

MODULE QUIZ 33.4

To best evaluate your performance, enter your quiz answers online.

1. Which of the following would result in a larger DLOM, other things equal?
   A. An IPO.
   B. Lower asset risk.
   C. A longer asset duration.

2. An analyst determines that a control premium of 18% is included in the acquisition prices of the comparable firms used for valuing a minority interest in a private company. If she also determines that a discount for lack of marketability of 22% is appropriate for the private company interest, what is the total adjustment she will make to the value of the comparables when valuing the private company interest?
   A. 33.9%.
   B. 36.0%.
   C. 40.6%.

3. Which of the following *best* describes the implementation of valuation standards?
    A. Technical guidance is limited.
    B. Appraisal organizations periodically review valuations for compliance.
    C. The U.S. government mandates the use of AICPA standards for appraisals.

KEY CONCEPTS

LOS 33.a

Both company-specific and stock-specific factors distinguish private and public companies. Company-specific factors for private firms may include the degree to which they:

- Are less mature.

- Have less capital.

- Have fewer assets.

- Have fewer employees with less depth of management.

- Are riskier.

- Have higher managerial ownership.

- Have a longer-term focus.

- Provide less disclosure of information about the firm.

- Have greater tax concerns.

Stock-specific factors for private firms may include the degree to which they:

- Have less liquidity in the equity interests.

- Often have restrictions on liquidity.

- Have concentration of control to the possible detriment of noncontrolling shareholders.

Company-specific factors can have positive or negative effects on private company valuations while stock-specific factors are usually negative. There is more heterogeneity in private firm risk, discount rates, and valuation methods.

LOS 33.b

Private company valuations are used for transactions, compliance, and litigation. Transaction-related valuations are performed when there is venture capital financing, an IPO, a sale of the firm, bankruptcy, or performance-based managerial compensation. Compliance-related valuations are performed for financial reporting and tax purposes. Litigation-related valuations may be required for shareholder suits, damage claims, lost profits, or divorces.

LOS 33.c

The definition of value will affect estimated asset value, and a valuation should only be used for the purpose it was generated. The main definitions of value are:

- Fair market value: used for tax purposes in the United States and based on an arm's length transaction.

- Fair value for financial reporting or litigation: similar to fair market value and used for financial reporting or legal purposes.

- Market value: used in real asset appraisals for a particular date characterized by well-informed parties.

- Investment value: in contrast to the previous definitions that were market based, this is the value to a particular buyer.

- Intrinsic value: the "true" value derived from investment analysis.

LOS 33.d

The three major approaches to private company valuation are the income approach, the market approach, and the asset-based approach. The valuation should consider the firm's operations, lifecycle stage, size, risk, and growth.

LOS 33.e

Normalized earnings are calculated by adjusting for:

- Nonrecurring and unusual items.

- Discretionary expenses.

- Non-market levels of compensation.

- Personal expenses charged to the firm.

- Real estate expenses based on historical cost.

- Non-market lease rates.

The normalized earnings for a strategic buyer incorporate acquisition synergies, whereas a financial (nonstrategic) transaction does not.

When estimating free cash flow to value the firm or equity, the following issues should be considered:

- Estimates may vary for controlling and noncontrolling equity interests.

- Several scenarios of future cash flows should be examined.

- The scenarios should consider the lifecycle stage of the firm.

- Management biases should be anticipated.

- FCFF would be used when there will be capital structure changes.

LOS 33.f

The three methods of valuation using the income approach:

- Free cash flow method: discounts a series of discrete cash flows plus a terminal value. It is a 2-stage model.

- Capitalized cash flow method: discounts a single cash flow by the capitalization rate. It is a single-stage model.

- Excess earnings method: values tangible and intangible assets separately and is useful for small firms and when there are intangible assets to value.

LOS 33.g

Estimating the discount rate in a private firm valuation should factor in the following elements:

- Size premiums: the appraiser may use data from small cap public firms, but these may include a distress premium not applicable to the private firm.

■ Availability and cost of debt: compared to a public firm, a private firm may not be able to obtain as much debt financing or at as cheap a rate.

■ Acquirer vs. target: the WACC used should be that for the target, not the acquirer.

■ Projection risk: projecting cash flows for private firms is riskier given the lower availability of information and reliance on management for projections.

■ Lifecycle stage: it is difficult to estimate the discount rate for early stage firms.

LOS 33.h

Using discount rate models for private firms includes the following:

■ CAPM: may not be appropriate for private firms because beta is usually estimated from public firm returns.

■ Expanded CAPM: adds premiums for size and firm-specific risk.

■ Build-up method: adds an industry risk and other risk premiums to market rate of return and is used when betas for comparable public firms are not available.

LOS 33.i

The three market approach methods are as follows:

1. The *guideline public company method* (GPCM) uses price multiples from traded public companies with adjustments for risk differences. The advantage is that there are usually numerous public company transactions available, but the public firms may not be comparable. When estimating a control premium for a controlling interest, the transaction type, industry conditions, type of consideration, and reasonableness should be considered.

2. The *guideline transactions method* (GTM) uses the price multiples from the sale of whole public and private companies with adjustments for risk differences. The following issues regarding the comparable data should be considered: transaction type, contingent consideration, type of consideration, availability of data, and date of data.

3. The *prior transaction method* (PTM) uses historical stock sales of the subject company and is best when using recent, arm's-length data of the same motivation.

LOS 33.j

The asset-based approach is usually not used for going concerns but is used for troubled firms, finance firms, investment companies, firms with few intangible assets, and natural resource firms. It values equity as the asset value minus the debt value of a firm.

LOS 33.k

The application of discounts and premiums to comparable company values depends on differences between the characteristics of the interest in the comparable company (companies) that serves as the benchmark value and the characteristics of the interest in the target company to be valued. A discount for lack of control (DLOC) is applied when the comparable values are for the sale of an entire company (public or private), and the valuation is being done for a minority interest in the target company. A control premium is added when the comparable company values are for public shares or other minority interests, and the target company valuation is for a controlling interest.

A DLOC can be estimated using valuations based on reported earnings rather than normalized earnings or as:

$$\text{DLOC} = 1 - \left[\frac{1}{1 + \text{control premium}} \right]$$

Discounts for lack of marketability (DLOM) are applied when the comparables are based on highly marketable securities, such as public shares, and the interest in the target company is less marketable, as in the case of a minority interest in a private firm. The DLOM can be estimated using restricted share versus publicly traded share prices, pre-IPO versus post-IPO prices, and put prices. It can be challenging to implement these methods.

The DLOC and DLOM are applied multiplicatively using:

$$\text{total discount} = 1 - [(1 - \text{DLOC})(1 - \text{DLOM})]$$

LOS 33.1

The challenges involved with valuation standards are:

- There are many different valuation standards.
- Compliance is at the appraiser's discretion.
- It is difficult to ensure compliance to the standards.
- Technical guidance on the use of standards is limited.
- Valuation will depend on the definition of value used.

ANSWER KEY FOR MODULE QUIZZES

Module Quiz 33.1

1. **B** Private firms can take a longer-term view because their managers/owners do not have to focus on the short-term needs of external shareholders. Private firms, however, are more concerned with taxes because of the impact of firm policies on the taxation of the firm's owners. In most private firms, management has substantial ownership. (LOS 33.a)

2. **A** In venture capital financing, the private company valuations are usually subject to negotiation and are informal due to the uncertainty of future cash flows. (LOS 33.b)

3. **C** The appraiser will most likely use investment value. This valuation provides value to a particular buyer. In this case, the multinational may place a higher value on the private firm due to the perceived synergies. (LOS 33.c)

4. **C** The analyst will most likely use the asset-based approach which values a firm as its assets minus liabilities. The firm's future cash flows are uncertain, and it may have to be liquidated given its distress. Therefore, the income approach should not be used, and the firm should not be compared to other firms that are going concerns, as in the market approach. The amount that equity holders could reasonably expect is their claim after liabilities have been satisfied. (LOS 33.d)

Module Quiz 33.2

1. **A** Both strategic and financial buyers will attempt to reduce executive compensation to market levels by $150,000 ($800,000 − $650,000). They will also have to pay a higher lease rate of $50,000 ($250,000 − $200,000). So the initial adjustment for both buyers to generate normalized EBITDA is $6,700,000 + $150,000 − $50,000 = $6,800,000.

    However, only a strategic buyer will be able to realize additional synergistic savings of $800,000 ($8,100,000 − $7,300,000). So normalized EBITDA for a strategic buyer is $7,600,000 and for a financial buyer it is $6,800,000. (LOS 33.e)

2. **A** The answer is calculated as follows.

Pro Forma Income Statement

Revenues	$10,500,000
Cost of goods sold	$8,400,000
Gross profit	$2,100,000
SG&A expenses	$1,600,000
Pro forma EBITDA	$500,000
Depreciation and amortization	$105,000
Pro forma EBIT	$395,000
Pro forma taxes on EBIT	$158,000
Operating income after tax	$237,000

Adjustments to obtain FCFF	
Plus: depreciation and amortization	$105,000
Minus: capital expenditures	$125,000
Minus: increase in working capital	$60,000
FCFF	$157,000

The following provides a line by line explanation for the previous calculations.

Pro Forma Income Statement	Explanation
Revenues	Current revenues multiplied by the growth rate: $10,000,000 × (1.05)
Cost of goods sold	Revenues multiplied by one minus the gross profit margin: $10,500,000 × (1 − 0.20)
Gross profit	Revenues multiplied by the gross profit margin: $10,500,000 × 0.20
SG&A expenses	Given in the question
Pro forma EBITDA	Gross profit minus SG&A expenses: $2,100,000 − $1,600,000
Depreciation and amortization	Revenues multiplied by the given depreciation expense: $10,500,000 × 0.01
Pro forma EBIT	EBITDA minus depreciation and amortization: $500,000 − $105,000
Pro forma taxes on EBIT	EBIT multiplied by tax rate: $395,000 × 0.40
Operating income after tax	EBIT minus taxes: $395,000 − $158,000
Adjustments to obtain FCFF	*Explanation*
Plus: depreciation and amortization	Add back noncash charges from above
Minus: capital expenditures	Capital expenditures equal depreciation plus 4% of the firm's incremental revenues:
	($10,500,000 × 1%) + [4% × ($10,000,000 × 5%)] = $105,000 + $20,000 = $125,000

(continued)

Pro Forma Income Statement	Explanation
Minus: increase in working capital	The working capital will increase as revenues increase $0.12 \times (\$10,500,000 - \$10,000,000)$
FCFF	Operating income net of the adjustments above

(LOS 33.e)

3. **B** To arrive at the value of the equity using the CCM, it can be estimated using the free cash flows to equity and the required return on equity (r):

$$\text{value of equity} = \frac{\text{FCFE}_1}{r-g}$$

$$\text{value of equity} = \frac{\$2,200,000 \times (1.06)}{0.18 - 0.06} = \$19,433,333$$

Note that we grow the FCFE at the growth rate because the *current* year FCFE is provided in the problem (not next year). We use normalized earnings, not reported earnings, given that normalized earnings are most relevant for the acquirers of the firm. The relevant required return for FCFE is the equity discount rate, not the WACC.

An alternative approach to calculate the value of the equity would be to subtract the market value of the firm's debt from total firm value. However, the FCFF are not provided, so a total firm value cannot be calculated. (LOS 33.f)

4. **B** The answer is calculated using the following steps.

Step 1: Calculate the required return for working capital and fixed assets.

Given the required returns in percent, the monetary returns are:

working capital: $\$400,000 \times 4\% = \$16,000$

fixed assets: $\$1,800,000 \times 12\% = \$216,000$

Step 2: Calculate the residual income.

After the monetary returns to assets are calculated, the residual income is that which is left over in the normalized earnings:

residual income = $\$235,000 - \$16,000 - \$216,000 = \$3,000$

Step 3: Value the intangible assets.

Using the formula for a growing perpetuity, the discount rate for intangible assets, and the growth rate for residual income:

value of intangible assets = $(\$3,000 \times 1.03) / (0.16 - 0.03) = \$23,769$

Step 4: Sum the asset values to arrive at the total firm value.

firm value = $\$400,000 + \$1,800,000 + \$23,769 = \$2,223,769$

(LOS 33.f)

5. **A** The private target's WACC should be used. It may be much different than the acquirer's, given that acquirers are usually larger and more mature than targets. (LOS 33.g)

6. **B** If there are no comparable public firms with which to estimate beta by, then the build-up method can be used where various risk premiums are added to the risk-free rate. (LOS 33.h)

7. **A** The CAPM will be used because the private firm is mature and of similar size and firm-specific risk as the public comparable. The expanded CAPM is not used because premiums for size and firm-specific risk are not needed. The build-up method is not needed because the private firm has a public comparable.

   The CAPM calculation uses the risk-free rate, the beta, and the equity risk premium: $4.8\% + 1.50(5.5\%) = 13.1\%$.

   The risk-free rate is the Treasury yield, not the returns for bonds in general. (LOS 33.h)

8. **B** The build-up method is used when there are no comparable public firms with which to estimate beta. Because the firm is small with a high degree of firm-specific risk, risk premiums will be used for these. An industry risk premium is used in the build-up method but not beta.

   Because the firm is being acquired, we assume the new owners will utilize an optimal capital structure and weights in the WACC calculation. The capital structure for public firms should not be used because public firms have better access to debt financing.

   The resulting calculations are as follows.

   Using the build-up method: the risk-free rate, the equity risk premium, the small stock premium, a company-specific risk premium, and an industry risk premium are added together:

   $$4.8\% + 5.5\% + 3.8\% + 2.5\% + 2.0\% = 18.6\%$$

   The WACC using the optimal capital structure factors in the debt to total cap, the cost of debt, the tax rate, and the given cost of equity:

   $$\begin{aligned} \text{WACC} &= (w_e \times r_e) + [w_d \times r_d \times (1 - \text{tax rate})] \\ &= (0.85 \times 18.6\%) + [0.15 \times 10\% \times (1 - 35\%)] = 16.8\% \end{aligned}$$

   (LOS 33.h)

Module Quiz 33.3

1. **B**   The adjustment to the MVIC/EBITDA multiple for the higher risk of the private firm is: $9.0 \times (1 - 0.30) = 6.3$.

    The adjusted multiple is applied against the normalized EBITDA:

    $6.3 \times \$27,100,000 = \$170,730,000$

    Subtracting out the debt results in the equity value:

    $\$170,730,000 - \$2,600,000 = \$168,130,000$

    Since the buyer is a strategic buyer, a control premium of 25% is added:

    $168,130,000(1.25) = \$210,162,500$

    (LOS 33.i)

2. **C**   It is difficult to find comparable data for individual intangible assets, so the asset-based approach would not be used. Natural resource firms and finance firms where their asset values can be determined by examining market prices would be easier to value using the asset-based approach. (LOS 33.j)

Module Quiz 33.4

1. **C**   An IPO would increase liquidity and decrease the DLOM. Lower asset risk would result in less value uncertainty and a lower DLOM. A longer asset duration (later, lower payments) would result in reduced liquidity and a higher DLOM. (LOS 33.k)

2. **A**   The discount for lack of control (DLOC) can be backed out of the control premium:

    $$DLOC = 1 - \left[\frac{1}{1 + \text{control premium}} \right]$$

    $$DLOC = 1 - \left[\frac{1}{1 + 0.18} \right] = 15.25\%$$

    The total discount also uses the discount for lack of marketability (DLOM):

    total discount $= 1 - [(1 - DLOC)(1 - DLOM)]$

    total discount $= 1 - [(1 - 0.1525)(1 - 0.22)] = 33.9\%$

    (LOS 33.k)

3. **A**   Although various organizations provide technical guidance on the use of their valuation standards, it is limited due to the heterogeneity of valuations. It is very difficult for the organizations to ensure compliance to the standards because most valuations are confidential. There is no single mandated valuation standard. (LOS 33.l)

TOPIC ASSESSMENT: EQUITY VALUATION

You have now finished the Equity topic section. The following topic assessment will provide immediate feedback on how effective your study of this material has been. The test is best taken timed; allow three minutes per subquestion (18 minutes per item set). This topic assessment is more exam-like than typical Module Quizzes or QBank questions. A score less than 70% suggests that additional review of this topic is needed.

Use the following information to answer Questions 1 through 6.

Bjarni Gunnarsdottir, an equity analyst at Boasson Partners in Reykjavik, is reviewing a report that he is scheduled to present to the firm's principals. The first stock discussed in the report is for Gulmor Industries. Selected latest financial data for Gulmor is shown in Exhibit 1.

Exhibit 1: Gulmor Industries, Selected Financial Data
(in millions of Icelandic króna, except per share data)

Price per share	kr 200
Shares outstanding	10 million
Market value of debt	kr 1,400 million
Book value of debt	kr 1,200 million
Net income	kr 178 million
Net income from continuing operations	kr 166 million
Cash and investments	kr 120 million
Interest expense	kr 66 million
Depreciation and amortization	kr 78 million
Taxes	kr 44 million

Gunnarsdottir is also evaluating the common stocks of Arctic Home Builders (AHB) and Advani Specialty Components (ASC). AHB is in the highly cyclical residential construction industry that has experienced significant recovery in earnings following large losses incurred during the recent recession. ASC is a manufacturer of specialty components for the global telecommunications industry. ASC was recently awarded a patent that turned out to be an immediate game changer for a particular class of optoelectronic components. Gunnarsdottir is uncertain of the price multiple that would be appropriate to use in performing a relative valuation on AHB and on ASC.

In his report, Gunnarsdottir plans to include the analysis of Sigurdur Halldorsson, a colleague. Halldorsson has used a residual income model to value Lagerback Breweries (LB). Lagerback does not pay any dividends and is not expected to in the near future. Exhibit 2 shows relevant data used in Halldorsson's analysis.

Finally, Gunnarsdottir needs to revise his projections for Havlett hf, a firm in the passenger transportation industry. In his previous analysis of Havlett, Gunnarsdottir had underestimated the interest cost for next year by kr 78,000 and overestimated cash operating expenses by kr 12,000. Havlett's marginal tax rate is 20%.

Exhibit 2: Lagerback Breweries

Market price per share	kr 132
Shares outstanding	12 million
Book value per share	kr 120
Book value of debt	kr 1,500 million

1. Based on information in Exhibit 1, the enterprise value-to-EBITDA multiple for Gulmor Industries is *closest* to:
   A. 9.27.
   B. 9.60.
   C. 10.19.

2. For the purpose of performing a relative valuation of Arctic Home Builders, the *most* appropriate price multiple is:
   A. price-to-book value.
   B. price-to-earnings using trailing earnings.
   C. price-to-earnings using normalized earnings.

3. For the purpose of performing a relative valuation of Advani Specialty Components, the *most* appropriate price multiple is:
   A. price-to-book value.
   B. price-to-sales.
   C. price-to-earnings using leading earnings.

4. If Halldorsson calculates the intrinsic value of Lagerback as kr 132, then it is *most likely* that Halldorsson has estimated Lagerback's cost of equity to be:
   A. equal to its ROE.
   B. greater than its ROE.
   C. lower than its ROE.

5. For this question only, assume that Lagerback's ROE is 12% and that its cost of equity is 9.6%. Furthermore, assume that after three years, Lagerback's residual income will decline towards its cost of equity with a persistence factor of 0.6. The intrinsic value of a share of Lagerback's stock is *closest* to:
   A. kr 125.
   B. kr 128.
   C. kr 131.

6. What would be the impact on Havlett's estimated free cash flow to equity and free cash flow to the firm due to the adjustments made by Gunnarsdottir?
   A. FCFE would decrease by kr 66,000 while FCFF would increase by kr 12,000.
   B. FCFE would decrease by kr 52,800 while FCFF would increase by kr 9,600.
   C. FCFE would increase by kr 9,600 while FCFF would increase by kr 12,000.

Use the following information to answer Questions 7 through 12.

Charles Porter, a Level II CFA candidate, is a junior analyst for ValueSegment, an independent provider of equity analysis and valuations. Porter has been tasked with valuing four different firms and has questions regarding the valuation models and techniques to apply to each. The firms that he has been assigned to value are described in the following:

■ Firm 1 is a publicly traded retail fashion store that has been in operation for more than 70 years. The firm has a consistent dividend policy with a target dividend growth rate of 3.5% per year. Additionally, its earnings are projected to steadily increase in the near future. A ValueSegment customer who is looking to become the majority shareholder of the firm requested the independent valuation of this firm.

■ Firm 2, a software manufacturer, has a consistent track record of paying dividends that is related to its earnings. The firm is projected to have a growth rate of 25% for the next five years and has an estimated required rate of return of 14%. The valuation of Firm 2 will be included in a ValueSegment research report targeted toward common investors.

■ Firm 3 is a steel manufacturer that has been in business for more than 50 years. The firm has a stable dividend history with a historical growth rate of 7.5% over the last 10 years. The most recent dividend per share was $2.25. Porter has estimated that the required rate of return (r) for Firm 3 is 12%.

■ Firm 4 is an upstart internet retailer that is growing at an extremely fast rate. The firm's guidance suggests that the dividend growth rate will gradually decline over the next five years to a lower, more sustainable rate. The most recent earnings per share (EPS) was $3.25, and Porter estimates that EPS next year will be $3.90. The estimated required rate of return is 10.25%.

After collecting information on his assigned firms, Porter believes that he will need to use the Gordon growth model (GGM) to value at least one of the firms. Since he is concerned about using the model, he decides to consult a coworker, Albert Huang, about the strengths and weaknesses of the GGM. Huang makes the following statements to Porter regarding the GGM:

■ **Statement 1:** The Gordon growth model is simple to use and discuss and can be applied to stable, dividend-paying firms.

■ **Statement 2:** The Gordon growth model is sensitive to estimates of the required rate of return but is insensitive to estimates of the dividend growth rate.

7. The type of valuation model that is *most appropriate* for Porter to use to value Firm 1 is a:
    A. dividend discount model.
    B. free-cash flow model.
    C. residual income model.

8. Would it be appropriate for Porter to use a dividend discount model (DDM) to value Firm 2?
    A. Yes.
    B. No, the DDM should only be used when an investor takes the perspective of a majority shareholder.
    C. No, the dividend growth rate is higher than the required rate of return.

9. If the current stock price of Firm 3 is $34.50, the growth rate implied by the Gordon growth model would be:
    A. 5.86%.
    B. 5.14%.
    C. 7.50%.

10. The valuation model that would be *most appropriate* to value Firm 4 would be the:
    A. two-stage DDM.
    B. general three-stage DDM.
    C. H-model.

11. If Firm 4's shares trade at $45, then the present value of growth opportunities (PVGO) for Firm 4 is *closest* to:
    A. $13.29.
    B. $31.71.
    C. $6.95.

12. Are Huang's statements to Porter regarding the Gordon growth model accurate?
    A. No, one of the statements is inaccurate.
    B. No, both statements are inaccurate.
    C. Yes, both statements are accurate.

TOPIC ASSESSMENT ANSWERS: EQUITY VALUATION

1. **A** Enterprise value = MV of equity + MV of debt − cash and investments

   = 2,000 + 1,400 − 120 = kr 3,280 million

   EBITDA = net income from continuing operations + interest cost + depreciation and amortization + taxes

   = 166 + 66 + 78 + 44 = kr 354 million

   EV/EBITDA = 3,280/ 354 = 9.27

   (Study Session 11, Module 31.4, LOS 31.n)

2. **C** AHB is in a cyclical industry, and hence, normalized earnings would be the best metric to use in relative valuation. (Study Session 11, Module 33.2, LOS 33.e)

3. **C** Due to a major event (i.e., the granting of a patent), forward-looking metrics (such as leading earnings) would be the most appropriate to use for valuing ASC. (Study Session 11, Module 31.1, LOS 31.c)

4. **C** Lagerback's book value is given as kr 120. The higher intrinsic value (of kr 132) implies positive residual income and hence an ROE greater than the cost of equity. (Study Session 11, Module 32.2, LOS 32.d)

5. **C** $B_0 = 120$ (given). $E_1 = ROE \times B_0 = 0.12 \times 120 = 14.40$

   Cost of equity $COE_1 = r \times B_0 = 0.096 \times 120 = 11.52$

   $RI_1 = 14.40 − 11.52 = kr\ 2.88$

   $B_1 = B_0 + E_1 − D_1 = 120 + 14.40 − 0 = 134.40$

   $E_2 = ROE \times B_1 = 0.12 \times 134.40 = 16.13$

   Cost of equity $COE_2 = r \times B_1 = 0.096 \times 134.40 = 12.90$

   $RI_2 = 16.13 − 12.90 = kr\ 3.23$

   $B_2 = B_1 + E_2 − D_2 = 134.40 + 16.13 − 0 = 150.53$

   $E_3 = ROE \times B_2 = 0.12 \times 150.53 = 18.06$

   Cost of equity $COE_3 = r \times B_2 = 0.096 \times 150.53 = 14.45$

   $RI_3 = 18.06 − 14.45 = kr\ 3.61$

   $$\text{intrinsic value} = 120 + \frac{2.88}{(1.096)} + \frac{3.23}{(1.096)^2} + \frac{3.61}{(1 + 0.096 − 0.6)(1.096)^2} = kr\ 131.38$$

   (Study Session 11, Module 32.2, LOS 32.c)

6. B

Adjustment	Impact on	
	FCFE	FCFF
Increase in interest expense	–78,000(1-0.20)	0
Decrease in cash operating expense	+12,000(1-0.20)	+12,000(1–0.20)
Net	–52,800	9,600

(Study Session 11, Module 30.3, LOS 30.c)

7. B Because the valuation is being done on the customer's behalf, Porter will need to use a model that accounts for the perspective of a majority shareholder. The free cash flow model is the best choice because it can be used to value a firm when the perspective is that of a controlling shareholder. (Study Session 11, Module 30.1, LOS 30.b)

8. A The dividend discount model (DDM) is an appropriate valuation methodology to use when:

- The company has a history of dividend payments.
- The dividend policy is clear and related to the earnings of the firm.
- The perspective is that of a minority shareholder.

Based on the information provided, the firm meets the requirements of a dividend discount model. The fact that the current growth rate is higher than the required rate of return means that the single-stage Gordon growth model could not be applied, but a multiple stage dividend discount model may be appropriate. (Study Session 10, Module 29.1, LOS 29.a)

9. B We start with the standard Gordon growth model (GGM) and input the known variables:

$$P_0 = \frac{D_0(1+g)}{r-g} = \frac{\$2.25(1+g)}{0.12-g} = \$34.50$$

Then, we rearrange the terms and solve for g as follows:

$2.25 + \$2.25g = \$34.50 \times 0.12 - \$34.50g$

$1.89 = \$36.75g$

$g = 0.0514 = 5.14\%$

(Study Session 10, Module 29.2, LOS 29.d)

10. C The dividends for Firm 4 start out high and then linearly decrease over time to a constant future rate. The two-stage and three-stage DDM models are inappropriate because they assume that dividend growth remains constant during a phase and then immediately changes at the start of the next phase. The H-model, on the other hand, assumes that dividends start out at a high rate and then gradually decline to a lower, constant rate. (Study Session 10, Module 29.3, LOS 29.i)

11. **C** The present value of growth opportunities can be calculated as follows:

$$V_0 = \frac{E_1}{r} + \text{PVGO} \longrightarrow \text{PVGO} = V_0 - \frac{E_1}{r}$$

$$\text{PVGO} = \$45 - \frac{\$3.90}{10.25\%} = \$6.95$$

(Study Session 10, Module 29.2, LOS 29.e)

12. **A** Statement 1 is correct. The Gordon growth model is easily communicated and explained, and it is applicable to stable, mature, dividend-paying firms.

Statement 2 is inaccurate. The Gordon growth model is sensitive to estimates of both the growth rate and the required rate of return.
(Study Session 10, Module 29.2, LOS 29.h)

FORMULAS

Holding period return: $r = \dfrac{P_1 - P_0 + CF_1}{P_0} = \dfrac{P_1 + CF_1}{P_0} - 1$

Gordon growth model equity risk premium:

$$\begin{pmatrix} \text{GGM equity} \\ \text{risk premium} \\ \text{estimate} \end{pmatrix} = \begin{pmatrix} \text{1-year forecasted} \\ \text{dividend yield on} \\ \text{market index} \end{pmatrix} + \begin{pmatrix} \text{consensus long-term} \\ \text{earnings} \\ \text{growth rate} \end{pmatrix} - \begin{pmatrix} \text{long-term} \\ \text{government} \\ \text{bond yield} \end{pmatrix}$$

Blume adjusted beta = (2/3 × regression beta) + (1/3 × 1.0)

Weighted-average cost of capital:

$$WACC = \frac{\text{market value of debt}}{\text{market value of debt \& equity}} \times r_d \times (1 - \text{tax rate}) + \frac{\text{market value of equity}}{\text{market value of debt \& equity}} \times r_e$$

Gordon growth stock valuation model: $V_0 = \dfrac{D_0 \times (1+g)}{r-g} = \dfrac{D_1}{r-g}$

Two-stage stock valuation model:

$$V_0 = \left[\sum_{t=1}^{n} \frac{D_0 (1+g_S)^t}{(1+r)^t} \right] + \left[\frac{D_0 \times (1+g_S)^n \times (1+g_L)}{(1+r)^n \times (r-g_L)} \right]$$

Value of perpetual preferred shares: $V_p = \dfrac{D_p}{r_p}$

Present value of growth opportunities: $V_0 = \dfrac{E_1}{r} + PVGO$

H-model: $V_0 = \dfrac{D_0 \times (1+g_L)}{r-g_L} + \dfrac{D_0 \times H \times (g_S - g_L)}{r-g_L}$

Sustainable growth rate:

$$g = \left(\frac{\text{net income} - \text{dividends}}{\text{net income}}\right) \times \left(\frac{\text{net income}}{\text{sales}}\right) \times \left(\frac{\text{sales}}{\text{total assets}}\right) \times \left(\frac{\text{total assets}}{\text{stockholders' equity}}\right)$$

Value with free cash flow models:

firm value = FCFF discounted at the WACC

equity value = FCFE discounted at the required return on equity

Free cash flow to the firm and free cash flow to equity:

FCFF = NI + NCC + [Int × (1 – tax rate)] – FCInv – WCInv

FCFF = [EBIT × (1 – tax rate)] + Dep – FCInv – WCInv

FCFF = [EBITDA × (1 – tax rate)] + (Dep × tax rate) – FCInv – WCInv

FCFF = CFO + [Int × (1 – tax rate)] – FCInv

FCFE = FCFF – [Int × (1 – tax rate)] + net borrowing

FCFE = NI + NCC – FCInv –WCInv + net borrowing

FCFE = CFO – FCInv + net borrowing

Forecast FCFE = NI – [(1 – DR) × (FCInv – Dep)] – [(1 – DR) × WCInv]

Weighted average cost of capital: $\text{WACC} = (w_e \times r) + [w_d \times r_d \times (1 - \text{tax rate})]$

Single-stage FCFF model: $\text{value of the firm} = \dfrac{\text{FCFF}_1}{\text{WACC} - g} = \dfrac{\text{FCFF}_0 \times (1 + g)}{\text{WACC} - g}$

Single-stage FCFE model: $\text{value of equity} = \dfrac{\text{FCFE}_1}{r - g} = \dfrac{\text{FCFE}_0 \times (1 + g)}{r - g}$

Price multiples:

$$\text{trailing P/E} = \frac{\text{market price per share}}{\text{EPS over previous 12 months}}$$

$$\text{leading P/E} = \frac{\text{market price per share}}{\text{forecasted EPS over next 12 months}}$$

$$\text{P/B ratio} = \frac{\text{market value of equity}}{\text{book value of equity}} = \frac{\text{market price per share}}{\text{book value per share}}$$

$$\text{P/S ratio} = \frac{\text{market value of equity}}{\text{total sales}} = \frac{\text{market price per share}}{\text{sales per share}}$$

$$\text{P / CF ratio} = \frac{\text{market value of equity}}{\text{cash flow}} = \frac{\text{market price per share}}{\text{cash flow per share}}$$

where:
cash flow = CF, adjusted CFO, FCFE, or EBITDA

$$\text{EV/EBITDA ratio} = \frac{\text{enterprise value}}{\text{EBITDA}}$$

$$\text{trailing D/P} = \frac{4 \times \text{most recent quarterly dividend}}{\text{market price per share}}$$

$$\text{leading D/P} = \frac{\text{forecasted dividends over next four quarters}}{\text{market price per share}}$$

Justified P/E multiples:

$$\text{justified trailing P/E} = \frac{P_0}{E_0} = \frac{D_0 \times (1+g)/E_0}{r-g} = \frac{(1-b) \times (1+g)}{r-g}$$

$$\text{justified leading P/E} = \frac{P_0}{E_1} = \frac{D_1/E_1}{r-g} = \frac{1-b}{r-g}$$

Justified P/B multiple:

$$\text{justified P/B ratio} = \frac{\text{ROE}-g}{r-g}$$

Justified P/S multiple:

$$\text{justified } \frac{P_0}{S_0} = \frac{(E_0/S_0) \times (1-b) \times (1+g)}{r-g}$$

Justified P/CF multiple:

$$V_0 = \frac{\text{FCFE}_0 \times (1+g)}{r-g}$$

Justified dividend yield:

$$\frac{D_0}{P_0} = \frac{r-g}{1+g}$$

PEG ratio:

$$PEG\ ratio = \frac{P/E\ ratio}{g}$$

Weighted harmonic mean:

$$weighted\ harmonic\ mean = \frac{1}{\displaystyle\sum_{i=1}^{n}\frac{w_i}{X_i}}$$

Residual income:

$$RI_t = E_t - (r \times B_{t-1}) = (ROE - r) \times B_{t-1}$$

$$V_0 = B_0 + \left[\frac{(ROE-r)\times B_0}{r-g}\right]$$

$$g = r - \left[\frac{B_0 \times (ROE-r)}{V_0 - B_0}\right]$$

Economic value added:

$$EVA = NOPAT - \$WACC$$

$$NOPAT = EBIT \times (1-t) = (sales - COGS - SGA - dep) \times (1-t)$$

$$\$WACC = WACC \times total\ capital$$

total capital = net working capital + net property, plant, and equipment

= long-term debt + stockholders' equity

INDEX

©2018 Kaplan, Inc.

Notes

Notes

Notes